LIFE AMONG THE POWERS

LIFE AMONG THE POWERS

A Political Spirituality of Resistance

RICK ELGENDY

CASCADE *Books* • Eugene, Oregon

LIFE AMONG THE POWERS
A Political Spirituality of Resistance

Copyright © 2024 Rick Elgendy. All rights reserved. Except for brief quotations in critical publications or reviews, no part of this book may be reproduced in any manner without prior written permission from the publisher. Write: Permissions, Wipf and Stock Publishers, 199 W. 8th Ave., Suite 3, Eugene, OR 97401.

Cascade Books
An Imprint of Wipf and Stock Publishers
199 W. 8th Ave., Suite 3
Eugene, OR 97401

www.wipfandstock.com

PAPERBACK ISBN: 979-8-3852-1324-5
HARDCOVER ISBN: 979-8-3852-1325-2
EBOOK ISBN: 979-8-3852-1326-9

Cataloguing-in-Publication data:

Names: Elgendy, Rick, author.

Title: Life among the powers : a political spirituality of resistance / Rick Elgendy.

Description: Eugene, OR : Cascade Books, 2024 | Includes bibliographical references and index.

Identifiers: ISBN 979-8-3852-1324-5 (paperback) | ISBN 979-8-3852-1325-2 (hardcover) | ISBN 979-8-3852-1326-9 (ebook)

Subjects: LCSH: Christian life. | Spirituality—Christianity.

Classification: BV4501.3 .E47 2024 (paperback) | BV4501.3 .E47 (ebook)

VERSION NUMBER 11/12/24

Contents

Preface | vii

Acknowledgments | xi

Chapter 1   The Powers That Be | 1

Chapter 2   Power and the Powers: Against Exteriority | 34

Chapter 3   Vulnerability and the Visible Church | 69

Chapter 4   Healing Vision | 99

Chapter 5   Where There Are Powers | 137

Chapter 6   A Spirituality of Resistance | 166

Bibliography | 207

Index | 219

Preface

Many books have been written about the principalities and powers, and many more about the figures—particularly Karl Barth and Michel Foucault—discussed in detail here. There is every reason to wonder, then, what purpose yet another can serve.

This book aims to serve three such purposes. First, it is an argument laying out one understanding of how each person's participation in modern society, however differentiated by the particular shape of their circumstances and identity, shares in a set of common dynamics and the range of thoughtful responses that are made possible by this understanding. Like all arguments, this one exists from and within traditions of thought that both enable and constrain its effective power. It is a theological argument, though I intend many of its conceptual structures to be available, through some labor of translation, to those who find themselves elsewhere than in the orbit of its Christian convictions. It is an argument focused on the social and political life of the post-industrial "West" as a focal point of a global network of relations, but its applicability may stretch beyond those boundaries of place and time. In this regard and others, it reflects the situation and resulting preoccupations of its author, though it attempts to express these in a self-aware and self-critical way.

Second, this book joins a conversation that shares its concerns. As such, it is both an expression of gratitude for the literature that makes up this conversation as well as a suggestion that some of its own founding insights be more rigorously embraced. I hope that what I perceive to be persistent tensions and problems besetting the exemplars of this tradition conceal potential within it: that by pushing for a more radical (in the sense of its Latin origin, *radix*, "from the roots") application of its own positions, the argument here can help set the literature on which it depends free from certain besetting distortions. Following the advice of a great teacher, I have found that where profound thinkers offer insight mixed with persistent ambivalence, or ambiguity, or tension, it is a sign that there is likely some contradiction hidden within their thought that remains to be uncovered, awaiting recognition. The driving argument below may not depend directly on the strength of its interpretive choices, since I intend to draw inspiration, and not authority, from the figures I engage. To the extent that my constructive argument arises as a response to persistent misreadings of the figures under discussion, it is also a recommendation to read these figures differently. But I am less interested in offering a new way to read Barth, or Foucault, or even the "principalities and powers" literature that I find so helpful, than I am in calling for a revised, critical approach to discourse about power, complicity, and resistance within Christian social thought broadly.

Finally, this book outlines and recommends a spiritual discipline of repentance in social and political life. For reasons discussed below, it steadfastly refuses to draw any hard, theoretical distinction between the personal and the political, the private and the public. Accordingly, its vision for a political spirituality is shaped not only by aspirations for increasingly just social orders, but also by a belief in the value of social and political life as a form of *askēsis* for the human person. It is especially concerned with the political and spiritual effects of cynical disaffection from collective life. Though such cynicism is surely overdetermined in this moment, this book only addresses one of its roots directly: the disappointment resulting from the deep ambiguity and checkered past of our traditions and communities. Rather than deny the power of criticisms incarnating such disappointment, I attempt here to harness and reorient their force toward a self-conscious form of activism. That is to say, in a way of understanding oneself that anticipates cynicism by properly accounting for its very real causes, what could spawn disengagement becomes instead an opportunity for repentant self-criticism, opening toward a realm of helpful social and political practices. As far as I can see, the limits to this realm of practices pale in comparison to its space for the creative and imaginative possibilities of free people.

All three of these purposes organize various responses to a question that has long haunted me: must resistance merely reorganize the power that it seeks to oppose? This is not the only guiding question that structures what follows, but it has been its original and motivating impulse. The trajectory of the project is largely shaped by my dissatisfaction with simple answers to this question, as well as the instinct that its form conceals certain assumptions that ought to be interrogated. Somewhere in the contact between these assumptions and stated answers exists, I believe, a convincing account of power and resistance that can inspire and inform thoughtful practice. What I offer here ought to be evaluated with these three purposes in mind, counting equally as evidence for (or against) its conclusions, its plausibility as an account of contemporary life, its faithfulness—of a particular kind—to the forms of literature that precede it, and its usefulness as a prescription for political spirituality.

First, a confession.

This book argues that there is no "outside" relative to the structures that make up our world as such, but there very much is an outside (indeed, a conceptual realm far more extensive than the "inside") to the experiences, categories, and social location of its author.

Because so many of those structures—race, gender, class, ability, sexuality, and many more—work by default and systematically to the benefit of people like me and the detriment of others, a significant number of theologians and ethicists take their departure from the stubborn categories by which modern societies differentiate their populations. To those sharing in this sensibility, what is most urgent is to name and resist the structures that relegate the oppressed to abjection and empower others to be their oppressors. This is a crucial impulse of conscience and reorientation of intellectual work. Many instances of this inclination will be cited in the pages that follow, and it is hard to overstate the influence of such liberation-oriented work on the conversation in which this book participates, and my own thinking.

In what I offer here, I understand myself to be allied with such projects, though I proceed from a different angle. This book represents a wager that part of the story has to be a certain kind of human solidarity in our vulnerability to these structures: the oppressed and the oppressor, the marginalized and the celebrated, are formed differentially by the same systems of social organization. When I describe the difficulty in escaping techniques of social power, I take myself to be charting some of their insidious power, which often takes the form of horrors. In a meaningful way, we share a common subjection to these powers, though that should never blur our vision of the real harm and real benefits that are distributed unjustly as a result, an obligation I have attempted to honor in what follows.

Writing this book has been a part of the work I am summoned to do to understand and reimagine my own implication in systems not strictly of my own making but that conscript my agency and determine a great deal of my social existence. It has been, for me, a way and a moment of reckoning. I offer these thoughts in the hope that they can be useful in the larger conversation about justice, particularly for those who sense, as I do, that the complexity of the world and our responsibility for its distortions cannot paralyze our attempts to change.

Acknowledgments

This is a book largely about what we receive and transform from others, and I have much to be grateful for on precisely that score.

So many teachers have patiently and skillfully shared their own reflections in ways that have empowered my own. The previous occasion for a version of this book's argument was a dissertation at the University of Chicago Divinity School, and I cannot imagine its construction without the conversation and guidance of Arnold Davidson, Franklin I. Gamwell, Dwight Hopkins, Willemien Otten, Susan Schreiner, William Schweiker, and Charles Mathewes (from afar), each of whom offered something distinct to my education. I also came to know many unofficial classrooms in which gifts were shared with me by friends and colleagues, including Joseph Blosser, Olivia Bustion, Julius Crump, Joshua Daniel, Mary Emily Duba, Tim Hiller, Russell Johnson, Kyle Rader, Larisa Reznik, Bryce Rich, Rebekah Stackhouse, Sally Stamper, Willa Swenson-Lengyel, and many others. This project was also supported by a fellowship from the Martin Marty Center, for which I am enduringly grateful.

Kathryn Tanner's work persuaded me of the creative power of contemporary theological scholarship, and her patient kindness made it possible for me to pursue my own. Kevin Hector called forth the very best version of everything I did in our work together, allowing me to find my own voice in an enduring conversation. "Advisor" would be too narrow a descriptor for either of them.

I have been supported by the Louisville Institute in two deeply transformative ways: first, through a dissertation fellowship, and then through a cohort-based postdoctoral fellowship. I am deeply grateful for this support, and for guidance and mentorship provided by Terry Muck, Edwin Aponte, Susan Briehl, Don Richter, and Bill Cahoy. The Louisville Institute also provided the venue in which I met Derek Woodard-Lehman, whose encouragement and keen insight have helped me immeasurably, beyond the pages of this work. Rev. John Graham has also been an engaged and wise conversation partner in this project, in addition to a mentor and pastor in every sense.

My colleagues at Wesley Theological Seminary have helped me to become a better, more humane thinker, and I cannot express enough gratitude for everything that this community has held for me. Each of my faculty colleagues has said things that have stayed with me as I thought through this project, and often encouraged me in my slow progress; Sondra Wheeler, Robert Martin, Sathi Clarke, Phil Wingeier-Rayo, Bruce Birch, and Carla Works, in particular, have offered indispensable institutional support and mentorship. Veronice Miles recommended Cascade Books as a venue for my work and encouraged me at the eleventh hour, which was a meaningful vote of confidence in them and in me.

But I cannot imagine this book without the conversations I get to have with students at Wesley. As I have substantially rewritten and added to its first versions, I have had in mind the structures of the world and the possibilities for life within it that we talk about, day in and day out. There are more I should name than I can here, but Alyssa Densham, Jo Schonewolf, Ethan Shearer, and Corey Simon have made indispensable contributions to my sense of what the task of the moment is. Katie Beth Miksa and Will Newton made significant investments of their time and attention to earlier drafts in ways that helped me better understand what I was saying, and I'm glad to count them and many others as friends and colleagues in the work.

David Newheiser, Alda Balthrop-Lewis, Mandy Burton, and Kristel Clayville have been sincere companions and in many respects among my greatest teachers. I can feel my voice moving among theirs constantly, and there is just no adequate way to cite their influences on this book, and on me.

I simply would not have completed this manuscript without countless afternoons reading and writing alongside Lucila Crena, as generous a reader and interlocutor as one could hope for in a colleague, at probably most coffee shops in metropolitan DC. Her friendship is itself a practice of spiritual presence and a unique gift.

Finally, my loved ones—Mom, Dad, Suzanne, Nick, Abe, and Jo, among wider networks of kith and kin—have been great sources of hope, and unfailingly supportive for years. And to Liz: partner, friend, coadventurer, and bringer of joy, who reads a lot, including a lot of my words. Those words are vastly better for it. In everything I do, I carry you all with me.

CHAPTER 1

The Powers That Be

SUBJECT AND STRUCTURE

In the summer of 2023, the temperature of the North Atlantic reached 1.1 degrees Celsius higher than what is historically typical. One reading from a buoy off the coast of the Florida Keys read 101.1 degrees Fahrenheit.[1] On the other side of the globe, residents of Fiji and other nations in Oceania wrestle with the rising sea claiming long-standing graveyards and coastal communities.[2] Nor are the symptoms of a planet in distress limited to the seas: diffuse smoke from larger, hotter wildfires, more intense storms, and dangerous heat waves seem more and more frequent. One prominent criticism of the twentieth-century developed world asserted that "the fully-enlightened earth radiates triumphant calamity";[3] in the twenty-first century, that radiation, trapped in a thickening cocoon of carbon, seems more literal than ever. Many people are moved to grief and anxiety in the face of looming devastation and dislocation; some people are moved to act in response to climate crisis.

One such person is "Carrie," one of several people living in Portland, Oregon, who spoke with Kirstin Munro for her book, *The Production of Everyday Life in Eco-Conscious Households*.[4] Carrie describes the means her household employs to forge a sustainable lifestyle: thinking critically about plastic packaging brought into their house, using natural cleaning products,

---

1. Shao, "What This Year's 'Astonishing' Ocean Heat."
2. "Graves Sink."
3. Horkheimer and Adorno, *Dialectic of Enlightenment*, 1.
4. Munro, *Production of Everyday Life*. Munro has changed the names of all her interview subjects.

managing interior temperature and comfort without energy use. Her husband, "Chris," talks about directing their children away from hobbies (like collecting Pokémon cards) that involve consumption and avoiding the use of their natural gas fireplace. Others documented by Munro report the lengths they go to in child-rearing, minimizing household waste, taking a critical eye toward informational and consumer culture, and many more fronts on which they wage a battle against overconsumption on behalf of the planet. These people of conscience know that the choices they make will not themselves suffice to transform society, but they aim at least to live a less "eco-hostile" existence than they might otherwise.[5]

Nevertheless, they struggle: Carrie describes the guilt that arises from her airplane travel, particularly, she knows, as a well-informed, conscientious consumer, that such travel's impacts outweigh the collective effects of their household discipline. Chris observes the various costs in taking non-curbside recyclables to the local for-profit recycling center.[6] Others have to make choices about how to allocate resources of money, time, and energy toward labor-intensive disciplines, occasionally "giving things up for sanity" or compromising, for instance, with children who are picky eaters.[7] Munro concludes that, though these choices express important convictions and practices on the part of her interview subjects, those choices are subject to prior constraints that lead to "impossible situations" on the terms of the norms the interview subjects hold. "Balancing regular life with sustainability priorities," she writes, "means that my informants are frequently faced with difficult decisions, and the compromises involved make them feel guilty and upset about their inability to live in a way that is fully compatible with their ideals."[8] They are trying to do their best in a world on fire. Their efforts matter, and they also cannot help but to fan the flames occasionally.

They are not alone. It is not difficult to conjure images of political subjects like these in the developed world—indeed, perhaps this describes you, in some measure. Such a person may have more or less access to the lifestyles, consumption habits, and range of choices possessed by Munro's interview subjects. They may be more or less cognizant of the forms of social identity assigned to them by prevalent forms of classification, and how that shapes, enables, and constrains their agency in the world. They may have a more or less informed sense of how their choices resound in consequences felt globally. They are likely awash in media representations.

---

5. Munro, *Production of Everyday Life*, 158.
6. Munro, *Production of Everyday Life*, 87.
7. Munro, *Production of Everyday Life*, 162–63.
8. Munro, *Production of Everyday Life*, 159.

They probably, though not necessarily, know if and how they tend to vote (when obstacles do not prevent them from doing so), and which sorts of issues give them an orientation and stake in the political world. They may have cast their identity partly around a political party, or a movement, or a thematization of their social experience. Whoever this person is, whatever their coordinates within the political world, I venture that they have a sense of coming up against forces that are far larger than their own agency: maybe their political opposition ("they"), maybe apparently mute but intransigent economic drives, maybe histories of race, colonialism, and gender that seem to have built a world around all of us. Maybe our political subject feels specifically *subjected* to forces that they would describe using that old standby, "the powers that be."

Many of our longest traditions and prevalent habits of thought take the individual—this social and political subject, decontextualized—as the paradigmatic actor. Perhaps the individual enters into a social contract; perhaps the individual possesses one or another set of social obligations. We can imagine a collection of prosocial or antisocial individuals in a "state of nature" or having come together to build a society. But that individual is too often seen as the locus of action and focus of theory, causing a one-sidedness that tends to obscure rather than illuminate social issues.

Anyone familiar with conversations in public theology, political theology, or social ethics—as well as anyone who occupies spaces dedicated to working toward social justice—has heard this critique of individualism: the pursuit of better social arrangements in societies structured by Eurocentric political traditions is always working off a deficit spent on the primacy of the sovereign individual. Of course, their familiarity makes such critiques no less urgent or trenchant. The problem lurking within them lies in the intuitive implication of collectivity as a solution to the problem of individualism: that a community or a movement, by virtue of wielding the power of constitutive, inescapable relationship, will loosen the hold of the figure of the individual on our political imagination. One crucial argument of this book is that the "community," no less than the "individual," is subjected to the patterning and forming influence of structural power,[9] and therefore neither in itself is a sign under which one can feel assured of faithful agency and life in the political world.

Public conversations about race in the US, for instance, suffer from confusions rooted in misunderstanding social structures. Many Americans, including the United States Supreme Court as recently as the April 2014 decision in *Schuette v. Coalition to Defend Affirmative Action*, favor

---

9. On this, see especially Joseph, *Against the Romance of Community*.

a "colorblind" approach in which institutional neutrality, combined with personal disavowals of racism, suffice to establish a racially just social order. Yet, for all the avowed "colorblindness" of public life, there remains a system of racial structures that systematically distributes privileges and marginalization on the basis of race: to use Eduardo Bonilla-Silva's terminology, denials of prejudice leave in place "the totality of the social relations and practices that reinforce white privilege."[10] For example, Bonilla-Silva details a subtle white *habitus*, composed of social psychological dispositions as well as patterns of association and proximity, that fosters racial solidarity even among those who are quite concerned not to sound racist.[11] The existence of this habitus, borne out by study after study of white attitudes on race, strongly suggests that the reform of our personal beliefs and practices only goes so deep without accompanying reflection and action on the social patterns that shape us. There is no retreat to community available here either, since whiteness in part just is a matrix of affiliation and association.[12] To subscribe to and enforce an ethos wherein avowed racists lose social capital will not accomplish racial equity alone, and without an understanding of personal *and* collective interaction with social structures, public conversation will only remain beset by confusion.

This type of story about social structures is now sufficiently familiar, at least to the audiences of this book, which can make it easy to miss the elusiveness and complexity of the "structure." Given that these conversations are often occasioned by how we[13] relate (or fail to relate) to official institutions, one might be tempted to overidentify structural power with public policy or sovereign authority. We might think primarily of the pattern of structural powers' effects in terms of disparity or double standards. We might prove far more adept at identifying how our ideological opponents are in the grip of such structures, with a gauzier sense of our own participation in them. So, too, do we inherit a variety of literatures on deeply

---

10. Bonilla-Silva, *Racism without Racists*, 9.
11. Bonilla-Silva, *Racism without Racists*, 123–24.
12. I owe this phrasing to Winant, "Social Question."
13. When I use the often-problematized ecumenical "we" here, I have in mind what Linn Tonstad describes as a "non-substantial, non-ontological 'we' that precedes its own creation," one in which "people whose social identifications and economic resources are very different are nevertheless subjected to similar economic forces," for example ("Debt Time," 435). Much of the burden of the work that follows in this book is to establish that there is a meaningful "we" to be found in our common, if differentiated, subjection to social structures and the possibility of solidarity provided thereby. Criticisms of an undifferentiated "we" that inappropriately levels forms of social identity are necessary, in my view, but there are also reasons that a form of "we" is so commonly reached for, reasons beyond political naivete.

relevant subjects—long debates about structure and agency, or between a "structuralism" or "poststructuralism." This book argues that there are significant stakes in how we understand the mutual implication of the subject, her community, and the structure, which dynamic interrelation is the basis for the spirituality contained here.

If Christians intend to speak publicly today—as we must—then we will have to employ some means of understanding such structures. What we need, this book argues, is a grammar and vocabulary for representing our participation in modern society that can set upon a new foundation the self-understanding we mobilize in public engagement. The retrieval of the traditional forms of such speech—which hearkens back to the prophets' conception of social sin, repentance, and deliverance—as well as their extension and application to contemporary life, has long been underway in social ethics, liberation theology, and other strands of thought, even if their influence has yet to filter out to many corners of church, academy, and society. This book intervenes in these recent traditions of thought, primarily with the intent of arguing for their applicability and value, though it claims that some of their implications lead to theoretical distortions and practical dead-ends. By refining this vocabulary, I hope that this book contributes to the resources possessed by public theology to speak clearly to and about its context.

In what follows, I make an argument about participation in contemporary life that attempts to get some handle on the theological import of structures of power. To do this, I will draw on the twentieth-century reemergence of discourse about the "principalities and powers" in political theology and social ethics. I argue that this tradition of thought helps us incorporate such structures into a systematic theology that takes social and political phenomena with appropriate seriousness. However, and using resources from Karl Barth and Michel Foucault, I will argue that the grammar for a theology of structures that this tradition represents ought to be revised in certain important ways. Namely, while most versions of "powers-discourse"[14] offer what I will call an "exteriority account" of the powers, there are good reasons to prefer a "total complicity" account. Though much more will be said about this distinction below, an "exteriority" here refers to a social position, granted either by identity or action, from which one or one's community can claim not to be complicit with a particular instance of structural power or a form of its working. "Complicity," which I mean to use differently from "responsibility," entails one's implication in the working of the powers: that

---

14. Sometimes this discourse also goes by the name "exousiology," a reference to the word *exousia* (typically "power" or "authority") occasionally used by the New Testament authors.

a structure of power works on, in, and through one or one's community, whatever the balance of harm and benefit it works in doing so. As I will show, this tradition has been biased toward exteriority accounts because of the assumption that complicity with and resistance to the powers are annihilating opposites: that, insofar as one is complicit with the powers, one cannot meaningfully resist their operations. By way of addressing this assumption, motivating a total complicity account, and describing the ethical disposition that this project recommends, I will conclude by describing an ethics of the self—one that I will call "self-attentive asceticism"—that shows how resistance can become a part of everyday life amidst the powers.

Along the way, I intend for this account to imply and to refer back to a systematic account of Christian faith. Thus, I will make this argument, in turn, by referring not just to theological anthropology and social theory but also to soteriology, ecclesiology, revelation, ethics, and Christology. While this is not an exhaustive list of crucial Christian concerns, I hope that my inclusion of these topics allows the reader to perceive the theological sensibilities that undergird this argument, sensibilities that depend on the insistence that writing theology is itself a practice implicated in a world of principalities and powers that awaits a yet deeper catastrophe of grace—that there are conditions for the possibility of this book and the conversations in which it participates that themselves ought to be resisted in light of a hope of transformation.[15]

This chapter sets up the problem by means of considering an example—racial caste and mass incarceration, as described by Michelle Alexander—and how it eludes the political imagination underwritten by many prevalent theological anthropologies. It then considers how theological discourse that employs the powers as a historical subject—both topic and agent—offers a remedy by using the example of William Stringfellow. Stringfellow's solution, however, introduces its own problem that motivates the further argument of this book: it assumes some form of moral escape, some position of exteriority from which unambiguous resistance is possible. This tangle—structural awareness, thematized theologically, but represented moralistically[16]—is the point of departure for the chapters that follow.

---

15. More will be said about the implication of theological knowledges themselves in the world of the powers below, in chapter 4.

16. Here I am working with an understanding of "moralism" similar to Wendy Brown's in *Politics Outside of History*: "The identity of the moralist is . . . staked against intellectual questioning that might dismantle the foundations of its own premises" (30). The moralist, therefore, "having lost . . . faith in history, reif[ies] and prosecute[s] its *effects* in one another, even as [they] reduce [their] own complexity and agency to those misnamed effects" (Brown, *Politics*, 30).

MASS INCARCERATION, RACIAL CASTE, AND STRUCTURAL POWER

Michelle Alexander's landmark work, *The New Jim Crow: Mass Incarceration in the Age of Colorblindness*, frames the racialized regime of policing and prisons as a particular problem for an era of colorblind racism. Along the way, however, the book illustrates how structural power exhibits a kind of patterning, world-building agency that cannot be identified with any single actor, and that displays a devious tactical sense for self-preservation.[17] Before the analytical work to come in chapter 2, then, it will be useful to have this example on board.

Alexander's thesis is as momentous as it is sweeping: that mass incarceration is the third large-scale iteration of racial caste in America, following on the heels of its previous forms as chattel slavery and institutions of legal segregation. She opens her work with the story of Jarvious Cotton, who, like his male ancestors stretching back five generations, cannot vote.[18] Cotton's great-great grandfather was a slave; his great-grandfather was beaten to death by the Klan for attempting to vote. His grandfather was subject to Klan intimidation, and his father subject to poll taxes and literacy tests that prevented him from voting. Because Cotton himself is labeled as a felon, he now cannot vote in his home state of Mississippi, since voting is one of many rights lost upon felony conviction.[19] Cotton's story retells, on the personal level, the changing face of institutional racism in the United States: "in each generation, new tactics have been used for achieving the same goals."[20] That goal has been to create and preserve a system of racial caste, which Alexander uses to describe "a stigmatized racial group locked into an inferior position by law and custom."[21] The loss of voting rights is just one effect of the system of mass incarceration, which not only imprisons

---

17. Adam Kotsko uses *The New Jim Crow* to document parallel processes of "demonization" in relation to the moral regime of the neoliberal drug war in *Neoliberalism's Demons*, 90–93. I am grateful for and agree with this analysis; the section here presented traverses a similar territory, but to slightly distinct ends.

18. Alexander, *New Jim Crow*, 1.

19. Alexander, *New Jim Crow*, 1.

20. Alexander, *New Jim Crow*, 1.

21. Alexander, *New Jim Crow*, 12. Chapter 2 will argue that "law and custom" will need to be specified with much more detail truly to get a handle on structures of power, and that the concept of the "group" might redirect us away from how racial caste is a network of relationships that include those not stigmatized, or stigmatized differently. But as a way of focusing attention on those most directly harmed by racial caste, this definition serves Alexander's purposes well.

persons at an astonishing rate, but also creates a widespread class of those under correctional control.

The features of this system are strikingly wide-reaching. Its legal initiatives expanded rapidly during the "War on Drugs" declared by the Reagan administration in October of 1982, but they have found extension and support from every corner of the criminal justice and political systems. Local police forces deploy a volume approach to drug enforcement, in which they actively attempt to uncover small-scale drug offenders.[22] They do this not only at the behest of federal policymakers, but in order to obtain huge cash grants, to perform and benefit from civil forfeiture, and to receive federal assistance in the formation of the paramilitary units we have come to know as SWAT teams.[23] Simultaneously, the US Supreme Court has dramatically reduced the scope of the protections guaranteed by the Fourth Amendment, permitting nearly all police tactics, ranging from pretext stops to consent searches.[24] As the court has considered other cases relating to drug enforcement, it has constantly protected and expanded the scope of police and prosecutorial "discretion," making it impossible to base legal defenses on claims of racial bias against the criminal justice system in the absence of explicit racial statements.[25] Meanwhile, public perceptions and media portrayals fuel certain images of the "drug offender" as a violent, menacing threat, despite the fact that most people processed by the system are charged with nonviolent crimes—in fact, incarceration rates have soared while national levels of violent crime have largely decreased.[26]

All of this pertains merely to the apparatus in its workings *before* imprisonment. Afterwards, the criminalized class can expect to be denied employment, housing and other government benefits, and voting rights, among other social prerogatives, as well as to be subject to correctional control in the form of probationary officers, fees and fines incurred from imprisonment and continued correctional control, and social stigma. Every aspect of the system, not least the financial incentives for both police and the emerging for-profit prison industry, is set up actively to recruit persons for incarceration and correctional control. As of 2008, that system had succeeded in populating prisons and jails with 2.3 million people, with an

---

22. Alexander, *New Jim Crow*, 71.

23. Alexander, *New Jim Crow*, 73–74.

24. Alexander, *New Jim Crow*, 62–67.

25. Alexander, *New Jim Crow*, 103. See *McCleskey v. Kemp*, *Armstrong v. United States*, and *Purkett v. Elm*, among others.

26. Alexander, *New Jim Crow*, 101.

additional 5.1 million on probation or parole, all of whom will be trapped, to use Loïc Wacquant's phrase, in a "closed circuit of perpetual marginality."[27]

In the context of this chapter's argument, the salient feature of this set of phenomena is its series of adaptations to shifting racial and social attitudes, as well as attempts to intervene through social policy. Despite the fact that rates of drug crimes are fairly constant across racial lines—in fact, studies suggest that white youth are more likely to engage in illegal drug dealing than people of color—the rate of incarceration for people of color, especially African Americans, dramatically outstrips that of whites. Three-fourths of those imprisoned for drug offenses have been black or Latine, and in at least fifteen states, black persons are imprisoned at a rate of twenty to fifty-seven times greater than that of white men.[28] Enforcement activity occurs largely in (and in fact, seizes upon the past effects of power dynamics to create) segregated urban neighborhoods predominantly occupied by people of color. In these ways, racial and economic privilege and marginality conspire to lead certain populations to become the target of drug enforcement—indeed, to make those populations as objects of control precisely in and through that enforcement. In the words of one former prosecutor, "It's a lot easier to go out to the 'hood, so to speak, and pick somebody than to put your resources in an undercover [operation in a] community where there are potentially politically powerful people."[29] Yet, since explicit racial targeting (with the exception of considering race along with other factors in the profile of a certain type of criminal) is neither legally or socially acceptable among many constituencies, the structures of mass incarceration have to make use of "colorblind" rhetoric. As a result, those enforcing mass incarceration have had to discipline their explanations carefully to exclude overt reference to race, differentiating the discourse of mass incarceration as a form of racial caste from its previous instantiations in slavery and Jim Crow. This is enforced institutionally by court rulings, which will protect any agent of the criminal justice system from scrutiny as long as they avoid explicit mention of race, and sustained by the cognitive biases of law enforcement and the general public, most of whom will make explicit disavowals of racial discrimination while demonstrably showing biases.[30] Mass incarceration is the instance of racial caste appropriate to the colorblind regime of attachment to formal equality wielded against historical, material accounts of inequity. It is as if this set of dynamics, despite depending on a host of different

---

27. Alexander, *New Jim Crow*, 94–95.
28. Alexander, *New Jim Crow*, 98–99.
29. Alexander, *New Jim Crow*, 124.
30. Alexander, *New Jim Crow*, 106–8.

actors in different social positions, maneuvers so as to avoid being exposed and opposed according to the measure of its effects.

This apparent intention-imitating character of the system of mass incarceration is the product of a longer history of what we can call the powers of racism and class division in America. To an extent, the shape taken by these powers is attributable to the interests of those with authority. After Bacon's Rebellion in 1675, for example, in which black slaves and poor and indentured whites attempted to overthrow the planter elite, that elite began to use a "racial bribe" to prevent class interests from organizing across racial lines. Increasing numbers of Africans were enslaved and imported, while white settlers were given increased access to Native American lands, competitive protections against slave labor, and the ability to police slaves through patrols and militias.[31] Over the following decades, what had been a hodgepodge of forms of labor developed into a much more strictly organized system of racial caste in which chattel slavery, based on race, was not just a tactic used in the labor market but the determining structure of the division of labor itself. After the demise of legal slavery in the US and following Reconstruction, a new racial order emerged, again designed especially to prevent coalitions among poor whites and freed blacks.[32] White supremacists, threatened by radicals and populists who sought to challenge the racial and economic elite, applied constant pressure to the possibility of that organizing by pushing for the laws that would set up institutionalized discrimination and segregation.[33] "Following the collapse of each system of control," Alexander summarizes, "there has been a period of confusion—transition—in which those who are most committed to racial hierarchy search for new means to achieve their goals within the rules of the game as currently defined."[34] At key junctures, then, collective interests, usually the interests of those in a ruling class, guided the development of structures of racial caste in America.

At the same time, these powers shift and reconfigure themselves in unpredictable ways. Some adventitious moments, such as the mass production of the automobile and the later development of the interstate system,

---

31. Alexander, *New Jim Crow*, 24–25.

32. Bryan Stevenson argues for a distinct "institution" characteristic of this era in the "reign of terror" represented by white supremacist lynching, which shaped a generation of expectations and habits before the full institutionalization of Jim and Jane Crow. The "racial terrorism of lynching," Stevenson writes, "in many ways created the modern death penalty," which, as Alexander does, connects mass incarceration to historically antecedent forms of white supremacy (Stevenson, *Just Mercy*, 299–300).

33. Alexander, *New Jim Crow*, 33–35.

34. Alexander, *New Jim Crow*, 21.

could be appropriated to divide space along racial lines: mostly white suburbs could retain access to city centers while urban neighborhoods could be cordoned off from each other by the clever construction of new roadways.[35] At other times, the exigencies of electoral politics have served to accelerate and deepen the effects of mass incarceration. As Alexander notes, though much of the War on Drugs was implemented during Republican administrations from 1982–93, Bill Clinton, true to his vows as a "New Democrat," proclaimed that "he would never permit any Republican to be perceived as tougher on crime than he."[36] Clinton escalated the drug war, through a federal "three strikes" law and budget authorizations for new prisons and police efforts, thus appropriating the "tough on crime" label for his party as well as its opposition and foreclosing the possibility of drug policy reform entering into electoral calculation. Though a particular person in authority is associated with and bears responsibility for these policies, it is not difficult to hear in these developments what we will encounter in Stringfellow's warning that those called "leaders" are often constrained by the situational logic of the powers.

Perhaps most saliently: though clearly visible only on a large scale, the powers involved reorganize in response to opposition. As the Civil War amendments took effect, the new legal institutions formed could offer nominal observance of newly established protections by using the institutions of slavery as a foil. Where slavery required intimate contact between racial groups so that slave owners could supervise and discipline slaves, segregation spawned racial caste by creating apparent distance between racialized groups, purportedly negating the power imbalance to those for whom "separate but equal" was a plausible outcome of social policy.[37] Once the civil rights movement enshrined policies meant to stigmatize explicit racism (with ambiguous success, we have to observe), a new colorblind ethos appears that creates space for discrimination in the careful silences characteristic of public and personal conversation on race. At every turn, the powers of racism and social division reorient themselves in an attempt to appropriate the moral energy and credibility of past efforts at reform. Crucially, these strategic developments exceed the capacities of narration and the actual intention of each individual or collective actor: the judge who is constrained by mandatory minimums and the cases brought before her court, the police officer whose department financially depends on

---

35. See, e.g., the story of the construction of the Dan Ryan Expressway in Chicago, which used a less direct route to create "a classic racial barrier between the black and white South Sides" of the city, detailed in Cohen and Taylor, *American Pharaoh*, 188–89.

36. Alexander, *New Jim Crow*, 56.

37. Alexander, *New Jim Crow*, 27.

triangulating federal funding priorities and public relations, the media outlets that decide which murders and court cases are newsworthy and which are not, as well as the giant cast of social characters, not one of which can act on the scale of the powers or likely identify their interests with the survival of those powers. Alexander concludes that, in arriving at mass incarceration:

> The system functioned relatively automatically, and the prevailing system of racial meanings, identities, and ideologies [needed to sustain it] already seemed natural. Ninety percent of those admitted to prison for drug offenses in many states were black or Latino, yet the mass incarceration of communities of color was explained in race-neutral terms, an adaptation to the needs and demands of the current political climate. The New Jim Crow was born.[38]

In Alexander's observation of the apparently "automatic" workings of structures of racial caste, and in relation to the huge scale of these structures and the social atmosphere whose air they breathe, it is clear that these dynamics are not reducible without remainder to the interests or preferences of a particular group, however correlated they may be. Without the flexibility and creativity that comes with their own brand of vitality, these structures would fall under the weight of changing attitudes and movements that seek reform.

The historical and social forces that Alexander lays bare lend themselves handily to a narration in terms of powers discourse. The structures that mediate and form social life, once alienated from their original goods, seek their own survival and subject humanity to injustice and confusion, small and large. They do this in imitative performance of living subjectivity: they change over time in response to conditions, they appear to have goals, they deceive and make false promises. Alexander cites a legal scholar who calls this "preservation through transformation" amid changes in rules and rhetoric; that preservation is a manifestation of a deep attachment of the powers to their own survival.[39] Individuals and communities cannot help but to have some relation to these powers—even if that relation is defined by opposition, even if that relation is death-dealing. There are some who deliver themselves to the animus of racism; others who accept the comforting discourse of "colorblindness" and its permission to remain silent; others who attempt to expose and reform the conditions that mass incarceration both creates and conceals from plain view. We might recognize these latter actors as those who imitate and embody Christ's rejection of racial and

38. Alexander, *New Jim Crow*, 58.
39. Alexander, *New Jim Crow*, 21.

ethnic divisions and extension of human community and care across such lines. Even so, one seeking to resist the powers must remain ever vigilant, since they will make countermotions in response to resistance, often attempting to appropriate that resistance for their own ends.

THE TRANSFORMATION OF A DISCOURSE

Alexander's account of the emergence of mass incarceration and the shifting dynamics of racial caste establishes the descriptive challenge for accurate public witness and, more urgently, names the class of phenomena that calls for investigation and mapping that opens to meaningful resistance. It can and should be a part of Christian witness to argue for personal transformation that includes an ever-deeper awareness of our own biases, attachments, and affiliations as occasions for faithfulness to a new way of living. Christians likewise ought to argue for and support changes to public policy and common practices that, for instance, better embody a community of equals living together in peace. But a vital element is missing from public witness—and its absence distorts the deliverances of the other elements—if it does not incorporate into its analysis and prescriptions some sense of how power is structural. In short, Christian public witness needs a discourse of the powers to talk more honestly about power.

The use of the New Testament's language of principalities and powers to meet this need itself has a history. This book's principal aims are to reflect on the possibilities for political subjectivity faithful to an integrated vision of the reign of God, and not to document in detail the intellectual histories that precede its sources and discourse. However, some accounting of these histories will help us make explicit the preconditions and the limits of talk about the powers today, precisely as an aid to the task of living a faithful political life. Reading and stewarding forms of literature, too, are political acts caught up in structures of power that themselves bear a potent excess with respect to those structures' current configuration, as the contemporary resurgence in censorship in the Anglophone world strongly suggests.

There are deep roots to this literature, both from within and without the theological "disciplines." The biblical language of principalities and powers as a discourse for resistance has held potency for those subjected to the disciplining, dominating power of racial capitalism and chattel slavery. Thus, David Walker, in his *Appeal to the Coloured Citizens of the World*, without detour into the Eurocentric soteriological discourse, can spontaneously figure Bishop Richard Allen as one who "had to wrestle against principalities and the powers of darkness to diffuse that gospel" entrusted to him, and whose success entailed "having overcome the combined powers of devils and wicked men" to establish the African Methodist Episcopal Church in the US.⁴⁰ Another strand of influence on discourse about the powers—one that gets the official and officializing attention of scholars—comes from a particular set of European theologians in the late-nineteenth and early-twentieth centuries. These figures wanted to think Christology and soteriology in relation to but also beyond the disputes among Protestants that characterized Reformation traditions. Johann and Christophe Blumhardt, for instance, argued for a reorientation of Protestant norms around the motto "Jesus is Victor," employed in (father) Johann's notable practice of exorcism and then in (son) Christophe's engagement with the German Social Democratic Party. In the handing down of the conviction that "Jesus is Victor" from one Blumhardt to another, what had been figured as healing of the body accomplished through the defeat of evil spirits by a champion, Christ, became extended to a struggle with the social structures that oppress humanity.⁴¹ This shift in the Blumhardts' practice is reiterated in the argument of Swedish theologian Gustaf Aulén's *Christus Victor: An Historical Study of the Three Main Types of the Idea of Atonement*. Aulén's study, first published in 1930, argues for the retrieval of a "classical" type of atonement theory, Christus Victor, that would govern soteriological statements differently than popular Lutheran accounts (themselves not fully faithful to Luther, Aulén thinks) using penal substitution. On Aulén's rendering of Christus Victor, God and the world are reconciled through Christ's exposure and defeat, in his life, death, and resurrection, of the powers that alienate created life from God. Sin is thus seen as an objective power interposing itself between creation, especially humanity, and God, allowing one to cast salvation as "a deliverance both from sin and from death, and an entrance into life, [preventing] the degradation either of the idea of sin to a moralistic level, or of the idea of the forgiveness of sin to the level of a mere remission of punishment."⁴² Whatever the status of Aulén's historical judgments or systematic contributions, the full-throated rearticulation of this theory meaningfully intervenes in European theology to suggest new retrievals of ancient ways to understand the gospel in relation to modern life.

Hendrikus Berkhof's *Christus en de Machten* (1953) is among the first to receive these traditions of European theology and rework them into a political theology that speaks directly to the social life of his contemporaries.

---

40. Walker, "Walker's Appeal," 65.
41. See Collins Winn, *"Jesus is Victor!,"* xv.
42. Aulén, *Christus Victor*, 48.

Berkhof credits the two world wars with the creation of new eyes through which to read Pauline texts discussing principalities and powers, in which theologians found a resonance with their social experience.[43] God intends the powers to hold human life together, "not as barriers but as bonds" mediating God's intentions for creation.[44] But in the era of fallen creation, the powers do not form a cosmos that mediates loving intention, but rather distort and destroy, especially in their pretensions to divinity and demands to be worshipped. Berkhof believes that these "powers of the air" are detectable almost empirically, as an ambient, palpable ethos and spirit of a time and place, as he experienced while studying in Berlin in 1937.[45] And nevertheless, Berkhof maintains that the powers will, ultimately, be redeemed: their domination broken, their agency reformed by Christ, and their work of mediation restored to what God intends.[46] The existence of the church itself, Berkhof thinks, indicates the instability of the reign of the powers—their waning credibility, the tenuous grasp on humanity—and prefigures a new order.[47]

In the second half of the twentieth century, a range of New Testament scholars attempt to document and contextualize powers discourse as well. Some early instances—such as George Bradford Caird's 1954 lecture series compiled in *Principalities and Powers: A Study in Pauline Theology*—leave much of the political import of the discourse implicit; Caird himself removes sin and death from among the powers, leaving a choice before the Christian person to "contract out" of involvement with the worldly powers.[48] Others push for something closer to a maximal interpretation. Oscar Cullman describes the powers as the invisible backdrop for visible authorities, such as the state.[49] In Heinrich Schlier's 1961 study, *Principalities and Powers in the New Testament*, the powers "do not merely possess power and the other attributes, they are power. . . . They exist as power."[50] This seems to mark the first time that the powers are cast as potentially internal features to human agency, rather than external phenomena in which people

---

43. Berkhof, *Christ and the Powers*, 15.

44. Berkhof, *Christ and the Powers*, 29. Berkhof is here reading Colossians 1 and, it appears, casting the powers as the means by which "all things have their being" in Christ.

45. Berkhof, *Christ and the Powers*, 32.

46. Berkhof, *Christ and the Powers*, 36–41.

47. Berkhof, *Christ and the Powers*, 51. Much more on these robust ecclesiological claims below.

48. Caird, *Principalities and Powers*, 46, 30.

49. Cullmann, *Christ and Time*, 99–111, for instance.

50. Schlier, *Principalities and Powers*, 19.

participate. Indeed, Schlier's extensive reading of the powers leads him to posit that "there is nothing on earth which is absolutely immune from their power," even "Christian revelation."[51] He does, however (and more on this below), privilege the church as a site of escape from their influence, much like Berkhof and Caird.

Ernst Käsemann elaborates a more expansive view of the powers within his biblical theology. God's love demands a free obedience, especially in the recognition that one belongs to God and no one else. The powers resist this recognition, "and we are . . . constantly meeting the gods of this world, namely whatever the world has nearest to its heart."[52] True freedom occurs when one "can meet those gods defiantly and without embarrassment, since at bottom they no longer concern [one]."[53] Yet, we ought to see those powers not as simply given existents, but as the objective manifestations of our desires and fears, born from ourselves. As one's life is determined in part by the anonymous powers that compose the world, the human person is not simply the agent of history but also its object and the scene on which it plays out.[54] The liberation of Christ therefore comes from a victory that "begins in our hearts," and the church is consequently "the band of people in which the love of God has broken the spell of demons and strange gods and is now pushing its way into the world."[55] Käsemann draws out a theology of the powers in which they play a significant role as the antagonists to Christ's reign in the world. Subsequent biblical scholars—such as J. Christiaan Beker and J. Louis Martyn—find plenty to dispute in Käsemann, for instance, disputes that concern how to read Reformation theology's hermeneutics, how to structure a Christian apocalyptic imagination, and how to live in a world that includes the powers.

Those debates are important on their own terms, but for this book's purposes, their conclusions form a loose consensus about the range of apostolic understandings of the powers.[56] The powers were created by God in

---

51. Schlier, *Principalities and Powers*, 28.
52. Käsemann, *Jesus Means Freedom*, 77.
53. Käsemann, *Jesus Means Freedom*, 77.
54. Käsemann, *Jesus Means Freedom*, 133.
55. Käsemann, *Jesus Means Freedom*, 77.
56. To be clear, I do not intend to vouch for the status of this consensus either within the field of biblical studies or vis-à-vis the New Testament texts themselves, though it seems to me to enable a well-reasoned and fruitful gloss on the relevant passages. I only mean to illustrate the type of discourse about the powers (as well as many of the material concerns of that discourse) that they made available to second-generation thinkers. For a sense of the range of recent interpretations of these passages, see, e.g., Forbes, "Paul's Principalities and Powers"; Forbes, "Pauline Demonology"; Betz, "Dynamis"; Wendland, "Contextualising the Potentates."

order to give structure and coherence to God's world, especially the human world. The powers participate in the fallenness of that world, though, and are alienated from their created role: though God patiently endures their pretensions to preserve order among creation, the powers attempt to usurp the unconditional loyalty and freedom proper only to God. The powers are particularly visible in the life, death, and resurrection of Christ as Christ's true antagonists: behind the nameable actors—Pilate, Judas, Peter, the Sanhedrin—lie the felt demands of structural and social logics. In their overreach to crucify Christ, the powers are visible as violently self-preserving; in the resurrection, the powers are shown insufficient to destroy Christ's opposition to them. The church, however and wherever it is truly found, is called to appropriate to itself, through grace, just this opposition through resistance to the powers and their effects, recalling to the world and to the powers the destiny that they, along with all creation, await in the eschaton.

However one figures the relationships between these strands of use for and reflection on the language of principalities and powers, I argue that they can be roughly periodized as a first generation of powers discourse. The object of this grouping is to name how these early uses, whatever their (significant!) differences, invoked the imagery of principalities and powers to understand social problems as cosmically significant, world-making phenomena, but usually do not systematize this analysis to give a detailed accounting of structural power. This book gratefully receives but significantly revises this story. To examine in some detail the problematic that animates such a revision, I turn to William Stringfellow's long arc of witness—in word and deed—in relation to the powers.

ON THE WORKS OF POWERFUL OTHERS

A Harlem-based activist and attorney himself, Stringfellow writes in order to call the American church back to its prophetic vocation, defined by witnessing to and celebrating the Word over and against the powers that distort life. In surveying the daily life of cities in the 1960s, Stringfellow finds cause for Christian concern. The poor are confined to contained areas, while more space is zoned for luxury housing and the middle-classes flee to the suburbs.[57] Urban policies and trends that encourage these developments

---

57. Though the dynamics that Stringfellow evidently has in mind here—"white flight" and urban decay—may have changed shape in the last fifty years, his sense that communal life is governed by structural dynamics and powerful interests would seem no less plausible on its face today. It is also worth noting that Stringfellow has principled reasons for focusing on urban life generally—he argues that "the city is the frontier today for the Church in American society" since cities concentrate and bring into "acute

are "an accommodation to the interests of the utilities, builders, insurance companies, banks, some unions and universities, and other heavy investors in real estate."[58] Stringfellow seamlessly continues to discuss these actors under a new label: "For principalities such as these," he claims, "it is more advantageous to redevelop the city for the rich than to rehabilitate it for the poor," though many more than simply the poor are governed by the principalities that rule the city.[59] Stringfellow's concern for the integrity of life, understood in light of the Word, takes him into the daily struggles of modern existence, which draws him into the zone of the regular (and regularizing) activities of the powers.

For Stringfellow, the life and death of Christ render the powers visible: the handing over of Christ to the religious and political authorities of his day reveals the relationship between Christ and all principalities and powers.[60] In *Free in Obedience*, Stringfellow ventures his earliest direct treatment of the principalities.[61] Originally subjected to human dominion (though, importantly, neither made nor instituted by human activity), in the fallen order they are alienated from their original "integrity . . . and wholeness of life in the worship of God."[62] These realities, to which the biblical terms refer and which are distinguishable from human and other types of organic life, can be categorized into ideologies, institutions, and images.[63] In the form of "images," they accompany every person as their self-presentation and, eventually, the symbolic or characteristic understanding others hold of them. The person Marilyn Monroe, accordingly, is dead, but "the image called 'Marilyn Monroe' did not die but went on to a new and, some would say, more vigorous life. In point of fact, then, Marilyn Monroe is not dead because there were two lives that claimed and used that name: one a principality, the other a person."[64] That is, the symbolic power of her image takes on

---

juxtaposition" the realities present throughout American society (Stringfellow, *Free in Obedience*, 18–19). Because that difference is one of degree, however, one ought not to suppose that nonurban areas are exempt from similar dynamics of power.

58. Stringfellow, *Free in Obedience*, 24.

59. Stringfellow, *Free in Obedience*, 24.

60. Stringfellow, *Free in Obedience*, 49. Notice that Stringfellow takes *these* powers, especially against the backdrop of the coming crucifixion, to be paradigmatic; I will argue below how this informs his understanding of their character.

61. *A Private and Public Faith* makes use of the discourse but does not treat it as a separate topic.

62. Stringfellow, *Free in Obedience*, 53.

63. Stringfellow, *Free in Obedience*, 52.

64. Stringfellow, *Free in Obedience*, 53. It is interesting to consider—as a kind of performance of his own point—that Stringfellow does not seem to know that he could identify her as Norma Jeane Mortenson. It is also the case that Stringfellow reads as

a life of its own, becoming an idol with "an existence, character, and power quite distinguishable from the person who bore the name."[65] The same is true of all public lives, though the idolization and influence that comes from the image of the celebrity result from an extreme degree of visibility. As an instance of the powers' relative autonomy from and influence over human life, Stringfellow cites Adolf Hitler, whose image became such a point of focal intensity and influence that it continues to register beyond his bodily life on the scale of institutions and ideologies. The symbol of the personality of Hitler itself became so resiliently powerful that "it may well be that long before his actual suicide the person named Hitler had been wholly obliterated by the principality named Hitler, that the person had indeed been possessed by a demon of that name; and that the devastation and massacre wrought in the name of Hitler [resulted from] the awesome demonic power that possessed him."[66] It is unclear to what extent Stringfellow intends to include literal, rather than metaphorical, supernatural power in his description of this phenomenon. Nevertheless, the activity of the powers as images cannot be reduced to conscious human intention. They are caught up into a milieu that uses them to tap into symbolic power far beyond the limitations of the individual person.

As institutions, the powers demand commitment to their primary purpose: survival. The logic of institutions demands that all else "must finally be sacrificed to the cause of preserving the institution, and it is demanded of everyone who lives within its sphere of influence—officers, executives, employees, members, customers, and students—that they commit themselves to the service of that end."[67] The claims that institutions make about the goods they are meant to protect or achieve on behalf of persons obscure their self-serving function. Much of his later exposition of institutions as powers will be explored below, but it is important to register that even early in his writing career, Stringfellow believes this to be the temptation to which the church is most subject. He asserts that Christian conviction, symbolized and sealed in baptism, is meant to set one free from the basic human captivity to the competitive struggle to preserve one's own existence.[68] Within that freedom lies the call to engagement with the world and the daily travails of everyday people: no longer in the clutches of the power of death, the

---

someone who has not been prompted to think about his participation in a genre of gazing, almost paradigmatically at Monroe herself. See Wollen, "Looking at Pictures."

65. Stringfellow, *Free in Obedience*, 54.
66. Stringfellow, *Free in Obedience*, 54–55.
67. Stringfellow, *Free in Obedience*, 56.
68. Stringfellow, *Private and Public Faith*, 66.

church is meant to live outside its own walls in self-sacrifice for the common good. Indeed, Stringfellow claims that "the Christian must live in this world, where Christ lives: he must live in this world *in* Christ."[69] When they fail to do this and instead become preoccupied with self-perpetuation, then do the churches "most resemble the worldly principalities and powers."[70] Ecclesial communities are prone to the same institutional momentum that many of the powers exemplify, and in those ecclesial cases a specific calling at the heart of Christian life is ignored.

Finally, the powers are frequently manifest as ideologies. Stringfellow names, as among the most self-evident powers of his day, "Communism, fascism, racism, [and] nationalism," but also includes the purportedly benevolent powers of "humanism, capitalism, democracy, [and] rationalism."[71] These powers assail persons with the message that the moral worth of their lives depends on identification with causes or political communities, like the United States.[72] In this light, the challenge issued in John F. Kennedy's inaugural address—"Ask not what your country can do for you; ask what you can do for your country"—appears not as an inspirational call to service but as the rare explicit surfacing of the implicit demand, made by the state, for constant personal sacrifice, a demand enforced profoundly unequally.[73] Stringfellow thinks this dynamic is intensified in more systematic and theoretical ideologies in how those ideologies claim for themselves more power to narrate personal and communal life and to endow them with significance, authorizing those ideologies to demand a rigid obedience.[74] Notwithstanding either this difference in degree or their shifting prominence throughout history, though, ideologies share characteristic features that differentiate them from images and institutions. Of course, the three, though distinguishable, are often inseparable: "every nation is a principality, but it would be ridiculous to identify a nation as just an institutional power."[75] The configurations of power that we name first as nations draw strength from and embody ideological powers, while also occasionally becoming personified in the image of a particular sovereign. These three forms of the powers constantly interact—now cooperating to amplify their effects, now

---

69. Stringfellow, *Private and Public Faith*, 74.

70. Stringfellow, *Private and Public Faith*, 74–75. It is interesting, and will be explored below, that Stringfellow here only claims that the churches (not the "Church") *resemble* the powers in their self-concern.

71. Stringfellow, *Free in Obedience*, 57.

72. Stringfellow, *Free in Obedience*, 58.

73. John F. Kennedy, quoted in Stringfellow, *Free in Obedience*, 58.

74. Stringfellow, *Free in Obedience*, 57.

75. Stringfellow, *Free in Obedience*, 59.

in competition for allegiance and service.[76] Within the economy of grace, however, the dominion given to human persons "is lost to them in the fall and, as it were, reversed, so that now the principalities exercise dominion over men and claim in their own names and for themselves idolatrous worship of men."[77] Humanity is now subject to the maelstrom of forces that guide history, those forces claiming for themselves a quasi-divine status and the corresponding regard from created persons.

As Stringfellow develops and extends his account of the powers, he increasingly insists on their dependence on the power of death, which is fundamentally situated within the sphere of the Word of God. In *Free in Obedience*, Stringfellow claims not merely that death is greater than any of the other powers, but that death is "the imminent truth about every and any event in this world."[78] *An Ethic for Christians and Other Aliens in a Strange Land* picks up and elaborates on the basic opposition between God and death. The ethical dialectic of Christian life is characterized by negating the power of death, but in the same breath enacting the authority of life freed from captivity to death.[79] This negation involves setting oneself in opposition to the powers while perceiving that death acts as their god.[80] "The truth," as Stringfellow sees it, "is that human beings are concerned with nothing else but death, though that be seldom realized."[81]

Death, in this broad sense, is a moral power and a social purpose: it has psychological, anthropological, economic, political, and social guises. It makes threats, demanding that humans deploy their power in cooperation with it. It is a constant companion—or, better, constant tyrant—over fallen human life as such. In this vein, Stringfellow thinks the ongoing Vietnam War "expresses, grotesquely, the moral presence of death which has *always* been in America . . . and the end of the war promises no end, no diminishment even, to *that* presence."[82] The war is elementally symptomatic of death, rather than vice versa: as many deaths as were caused by military action, the war as a wider phenomenon emerges from the prior influence death has

---

76. Stringfellow, *Free in Obedience*, 60.

77. Stringfellow, *Free in Obedience*, 63.

78. Stringfellow, *Free in Obedience*, 64, 69. It is interesting to think about whether or not he meant "immanent."

79. Stringfellow, *Ethic for Christians*, 63.

80. Stringfellow, *Ethic for Christians*, 67. By this time in the text Stringfellow had already claimed that "the Christian is always committed permanently to radical protest in society. He is always dissatisfied with the existing state of affairs" (22). Below, I raise some issues with how these claims are performed in relation to the one who protests.

81. Stringfellow, *Ethic for Christians*, 69.

82. Stringfellow, *Ethic for Christians*, 70.

over the collective imagination and ethos of the nation.[83] That entanglement with death also generates racial segregation, wasteful consumerism, the increasing control of emerging technology over policy, and the militarization of police power, among other phenomena.[84] In this milieu, Stringfellow calls for a certain type of ethics: "ethics concerns human action in relation to the principalities and powers in the Fall, where both human beings and principalities, as well as the rest of Creation, exist under the claim that death is morally sovereign in history."[85] An attempt at ethics that neglects this category of phenomenon and obscures the power of death simply fails to address the lived reality of modern humanity, delivering it into ideological anti-ethics.[86]

With this understanding of the power behind the powers, the evangelical core of Stringfellow's ethics is clear. God and death are the two powers that ultimately lie behind every claim for allegiance and service on humanity. In God, reality finds its truest and most powerful source, but in this world, many more ethical roads terminate in service to death. By treating "survival" as the unsurpassable good for human persons and communities, the power of death surreptitiously encourages its own idolization: in sacrificing all to hold death at bay, we deliver ourselves ever deeper into its clutches, desperately visiting its power on others, hypnotically obsessed with eluding it, as the phenomena of mass incarceration show. The freed person is the one who, as no longer subject to the moral power of death, is able to refuse the survival ethic and expend life for the good of others without fear. Thus, every ethical decision enacts a part of the larger theological drama of history, becoming either a fall through surrender to the power of death or a self-sacrificial gift in the hope of resurrection. Though the freed person may have several options for living in light of the Word, Stringfellow rejects certain approaches that reflect hope for the reformation of the powers. "Americans" in particular, he thinks, "persevere in belaboring the illusion that at least some institutions are benign and viable and within human direction or can be rendered so by discipline or reform or revolution or displacement."[87] Against these persistent hopes, Stringfellow marshals a theological claim—that they underestimate the effects of fallenness and overestimate human control over history—and an empirical one—that reformist attempts to tame the powers dismiss the enormity of the suffering

---

83. Stringfellow, *Ethic for Christians*, 70.
84. Stringfellow, *Ethic for Christians*, 71.
85. Stringfellow, *Ethic for Christians*, 77.
86. Stringfellow, *Ethic for Christians*, 77.
87. Stringfellow, *Ethic for Christians*, 83.

they inflict structurally and beyond mastery.[88] Stringfellow's theological and ethical portrait of human life before the powers, then, is characterized by a stark and radical opposition between trust in the redemptive promise of God and misbegotten attempts to rearrange the powers in service of one's own false hopes. Sainthood—true and simply human life that shows uncalculating concern for others—requires that one perceive and refuse the game of death that the powers play.[89]

Though the character of the fundamental ethical decision is sharply binary, the possible shapes of agency in relation to the powers vary widely. Humans can easily misrecognize how they live and act in relation to these categorically differently powerful others. And because human persons do not readily recognize the complete extent of their subjection (Stringfellow refers to this as their "victim status") to the principalities, human actors can come to occupy certain positions of service to the powers under the misconception that they themselves wield power. These become "acolytes," eager servants of the powers who "actually define their humanity as nonhuman or subhuman loyalty and diligence to [their] interests and appetites," becoming automatons through which the powers wreak havoc: Stringfellow here names Emperor Domitian, King George III, Hitler, and Stalin.[90] Beyond this class of the "possessed," there are "leaders," about whom the "conspicuous moral fact . . . is that they are the most obvious and pathetic prisoners in American society":

> There is unleashed among the principalities in this society a ruthless, self-proliferating, all-consuming institutional process which assaults, dispirits, and destroys human life even among, and *primarily* among, those persons in positions of institutional leadership. They are left with titles but without effectual authority; with the trappings of power, but without control over the institutions they head; in nominal command, but bereft of dominion. These same principalities, as has been mentioned, threaten and defy and enslave human beings of other status in diverse ways, but the most poignant victim of the demonic in America today is the so-called leader.[91]

The common error of everyday political thinking is this misidentification of the powerful others whose acts suppress and condition our own: attributing the state of the world to a "they" that includes nameable humans rather than

88. Stringfellow, *Ethic for Christians*, 84.
89. Stringfellow, *Ethic for Christians*, 93.
90. Stringfellow, *Ethic for Christians*, 87–88.
91. Stringfellow, *Ethic for Christians*, 88–89.

deep-seated powers that flow across the agency of human persons. Leaders are constrained by their position as executors of the powers' intentions: the exigencies of institutions or ideologies militate against the ability of leaders to exercise anything like control over history. Whatever their intentions, these leaders are caught within patterns that, Stringfellow thinks, dictate (or at least severely delimit) their responses to new situations of power. Their apparent benevolence or malevolence comes from their attempts or refusals to put a kindly human face on the harsh necessities imposed by the powers' survival ethic.

Though Stringfellow believes in the possibility of wicked leaders, then, his biggest concern—and, in some ways, sharpest polemic—is reserved for those "who have become captive and immobilized as human beings by their habitual obeisance to institutions or other principalities as idols."[92] No matter how many truly evil people hold positions of leadership, "they are far outnumbered . . . by those bereft of conscience . . . [in whom] the American institutional and ideological ethos incubates a profound apathy toward human life as such."[93] The "silent majority," so prominently mentioned in the 1970s, is the class of those whose moral impoverishment leads to the apathetic despair of the paralyzed conscience. Stringfellow identifies this as hardness of heart in its unwillingness to perceive mass immiseration. In that hardness of heart, bourgeois Americans are beaten down into "a strange and terrible quitting as human beings," leading to their acquiescence to the regime of the powers.[94] Rather than political engagement, the ranks of those so dehumanized seek respite by fleeing into the embrace of other powers: commercial sports and diversions, indulgence in various intoxicants, nostalgia for an idealized past, and occasionally acts of political expulsion and expurgation of those who refuse conformity.[95] Failure of conscience is carefully cultivated by the powers in order to render the middle classes compliant, encouraging despair in the face of massive injustices and self-concern through the various pressures on the preservation of individual life. Though the powers particularly work through those who misrecognize their evil as good, those powers need the cooperation, or at least the indifference, of the larger social body.

The last among these roles, the "saints," are those who refuse this way of life by aspiring to maturity, conscience, and true freedom. Such qualities are only apparent "among those who are in conflict with the established

---

92. Stringfellow, *Ethic for Christians*, 29–30.
93. Stringfellow, *Ethic for Christians*, 30.
94. Stringfellow, *Ethic for Christians*, 31.
95. Stringfellow, *Ethic for Christians*, 31.

order—those who are opponents of the status quo, those in rebellion against the system, those who are prisoners, resisters, fugitives, and victims."[96] These are not social and political heroes, but merely those who respond to the call to live humanely under inhuman conditions. A saint is "just an exemplary human being, a mature and free person, a humanized human being."[97] In many cases, as it was for those living under National Socialism, resistance becomes the only stance worthy of a human being, the only alternative to submission to the moral power of death. Though that case of resistance is extreme for its occurrence under conditions in which familiar senses of hope could not pertain, it exemplifies the oppositional character of Christian—indeed, human—concern for the neighbor under the regime of the powers.[98] The saint is fully involved in the course of the world, but utterly at odds with its constitution: she refuses the ethic of survival in favor of solidarity with and care for fellow humanity. The saint has a conscience fully alive, sensitive to the true cost of bargains with the powers and agitated to constant witness of another way of life. Never fearing the cost to herself, the saint is truly free from the demands of the powers to dispose of her own life in response to the Word.

Stringfellow believes the church is called to this kind of sainthood: human involvement in the world that is simultaneously based on opposition to the moral power at its center. "The Church exists," Stringfellow writes, "as the company of participants in God's witness to Himself in the world. The church exists for the sake of the world into which God enters and in which He acts and for which He expends His own life."[99] The character of this "participation" in God's self-witness is less clear, especially with respect to whether the church as such ought to be named among the powers. In Stringfellow's writings of the 1960s, it appears that only communities who have failed to embody the church but retain ecclesiastical trappings constitute a principality; this is, after all, when the churches "resemble" them.[100] In *Free in Obedience*, Stringfellow claims that "religion, *as distinguished from the Christian faith*, is a principality."[101] The church is continually assaulted (as if from outside?) by the workings of the powers, and may even defer to them through, for example, denominationalism.[102] When churches condone or

---

96. Stringfellow, *Ethic for Christians*, 31.
97. Stringfellow, *Ethic for Christians*, 87.
98. Stringfellow, *Ethic for Christians*, 118–19.
99. Stringfellow, *Private and Public Faith*, 77–78.
100. Stringfellow, *Private and Public Faith*, 74–75.
101. Stringfellow, *Free in Obedience*, 60; emphasis added.
102. Stringfellow, *Free in Obedience*, 77.

practice segregation in their own midst, they surrender to the principality of racism.[103] In the extreme case, the church becomes so preoccupied with the maintenance and preservation of its own institutional life that it too becomes a principality.[104] Though Stringfellow thinks this situation endemic to the American churches, it seems clear that in his early writings he assumed that the church is called and able to be a social phenomenon sui generis, in opposition to and therefore not to be counted among the powers.

As Stringfellow continues to develop these themes in *An Ethic for Christians and Other Aliens in a Strange Land*, he becomes more focused on the character of the church as event. Rather than an ideology or dogma, the Word itself has an empirical vitality, speaking to persons directly and concerning their whole lives.[105] The church is called to enact a "holy nation, standing apart from but ministering to the secular powers."[106] Though the responses to this calling created by confessing movements may be "secreted within the established churches or detached from them," this embodiment of the "Jerusalem Vocation" cannot be relegated to an invisible, eschatological church. This new Jerusalem cannot exist as "some nebulous, ethereal, idealistic, otherworldly, or disembodied Church," but rather must arrive in "a visible, historic community and institution . . . incarnating and sacramentalizing human life in society freed from bondage to the power of death."[107] As he exegetes Revelation, Stringfellow casts ecclesiology within the opposition between Jerusalem and Babylon: "while Babylon represents the principality in bondage to death in time—and time is actually a form of *that* bondage—Jerusalem means the emancipation of human life in society from the rule of death that breaks through time, transcends time, anticipates within time the abolition of time."[108] The hope for the church, then, is to live on the strength of the vitality as the Word, which will liberate it not only from the hypnotic power of death, but from time itself, becoming an event of grace that places it in opposition to the world.

In many of these argumentative moves, Stringfellow is unique, and his animating concerns reflect his preoccupation with the state of the church

---

103. Stringfellow, *Free in Obedience*, 78. I observe that this implies that some core of the church is "other" to the power of racism.

104. Stringfellow, *Free in Obedience*, 95.

105. Stringfellow, *Ethic for Christians*, 50.

106. Stringfellow, *Ethic for Christians*, 54.

107. Stringfellow, *Ethic for Christians*, 58. I am worried about the potentially supersessionist implications of this identification of the church with Jerusalem, which might be a crack in Stringfellow's form of Christianity that itself allows the powers to reinscribe themselves through his best efforts.

108. Stringfellow, *Ethic for Christians*, 60.

in post-war America. Yet, the larger structure of his theological and ethical account of the powers is fairly typical of what I am designating the second generation of powers discourse. Though the chapters that follow will continue to investigate this discourse, a certain overarching narrative predominates within this conversation. The fallen condition of the world has not only alienated humanity from God, but both humanity and God from the powers meant to structure and facilitate human life.[109] As a result, the powers have, in Stringfellow's words, "their own existence, personality, and mode of life"[110] both ontologically and morally, apart from humanity and God: their activity can neither be reduced to nor identified with human intention, conscious or otherwise. In this condition, humans are newly subjected to the dynamics of the powers, which make up the fabric of social and political life. Christ's life, death, and resurrection provide an occasion for the powers to reveal what they truly are: in overstepping their ordained role as creatures and claiming unchecked loyalty, they become imbued with the spirit of violent control, ultimately answering to death alone. Yet, Christ defeats these powers, and that defeat means that, in one way or another, the powers do not have the last word about human life and hope. The church represents those who, in light of this salvific event, gather to live in the power of the Spirit by recalling this defeat and bearing witness to, perhaps even instantiating, a life beyond the world of the powers.

The work of second-generation theorists, such as Stringfellow, has unique virtues as a theological and ethical discourse. First, it draws together core Christian convictions and the operations of social structures in a way that makes those structures theologically legible. In comparison to most theology, then, it both attributes more significance to and gives a more convincing account of the social structures that make up a significant part of human lives made possible by the modern West. In relation to social theory, it offers some of the insights into human life and thought characteristic of Christian theology: for example, the theological valences of the human encounter with death. Second, it allows a theological reading of the New Testament that can, in appropriating the idiom of "principalities and powers," make sense of the traditional idea of mediating phenomena between God and humanity. As such, it is useful in constructing a theology that resists,

---

109. In the thought of some, such as Barth (as will be seen in chapter 2), the powers are originally human capacities that, once fallen, take on a life of their own. In others, such as Stringfellow, the powers are a separate genus of creation altogether, resulting from God's activity, not human activity (Stringfellow, *Ethic for Christians*, 80). Though this has implications for complicity that I will discuss in chapter 2, it does not dramatically change the narrative on this large scale.

110. Stringfellow, *Ethic for Christians*, 79.

especially by deploying specifically theological value to such mediators, frequent errors (perhaps particularly in popular Christian discourse) such as a reductive individualism. Finally, this work occupies a rare space in its shuttling between the academy and the church. While marginal in some corners of theological academe, this discourse resounds in many churches because it is unusually relatable and informative for Christian praxis. It marginalizes the practice of theologizing through interpreting literature (like this book does!) in favor of offering Christians a practice of describing and intervening in their actual political lives. These are genuine achievements.

THE AMBIGUITY OF CHRISTIAN RESISTANCE

There is, nevertheless, a besetting problem in much of this second generation of discourse about the powers, which is the point of departure for the argument of this book.

The call to resistance[111] often marks the ethic that accompanies discourse about the powers: given this theological and social description of the human situation, the vocation of the ethical person generally (and, more often, the Christian specifically) is to name, refuse, inhibit, and deter the activities of the powers. In those accounts wherein the powers are cast more ambiguously than as simply "demonic," calls are issued at the very least for thoughtful participation with them.[112] Indeed, as suggested above, one of the notable strengths of the discourse appropriating the language of the powers is to cast this resistance as internal to Christian discipleship by placing the powers within the evangelical core. Resistance, then, is the social ethic for the interim between the exposure and defeat of the powers in the

---

111. Though later chapters will have more to say about how to define "resistance," suffice it to say here that it refers to conscious, willed opposition to the powers or their effects (whether understood theologically or otherwise), enacted through ethical and political practices.

112. It is possible (and likely) that there are instances that do not call for outright resistance to the powers, or at least to a particular operation of one of the powers at a given time. I take it that, given the picture of human agency in relation to the powers that will emerge in the next chapter, acquiescence or approval—even in morally permissible conditions—do not stand in need of theoretical explanation, whereas it is much more difficult to account for resistance. Scott Prather includes a discussion of how Barth reads the powers in eschatological determination, referring to the "angelic service" they perform when following God's creative intentions, in *Christ, Power, and Mammon*, 22–25. This includes a helpful theological reminder that the "demonization" of the powers is not, logically speaking, inevitable, even if we do not have access to this condition, historically.

Paschal Mystery and the arrival of the eschaton, the ethic appropriate to a life set free from the powers, most of all death.

Stringfellow reserves harsh judgment for the critic who doubts the efficacy of his brand of resistance. While acknowledging the challenges in understanding the manifestations of the event of the church and its witness, he casts such criticism in these terms:

> The stereotypical response to an act of conscience is an accusation of arrogance by which someone who has done nothing denounces the conscientious for claiming moral superiority. That may be an appropriate construction of the nature and operation of conscience so far as the world is concerned, but it is not the biblical comprehension of conscience.... It is not only not idiosyncratic, but rather the opposite, since the conscientious stand does not separate from but instead identifies with the common interest of human life. And the act of conscience is not inherently arrogant, as the conformed or the lazy or the fearful assert, because it strives not to approximate divine judgment but to represent mature human will.[113]

Two concerns typical of Stringfellow's thought are evident in this passage. First, Stringfellow seeks to clarify and defend the moral direction of Christian ethical practices against the charge of idiosyncrasy, which since his time has also often been leveled against those seen as "sectarian." As is clear in his persistent assertions that the church is called to intimate involvement in the daily life of the world with a commitment to the common good, this charge would seem not to do justice at least to his account. Second, Stringfellow deflects criticisms of claims to moral superiority on behalf of the conscientious. Human actions cannot be identified with divine judgment (something acutely visible in, for instance, Stringfellow's critique of pacifism as an ideology),[114] but conscientious human action is, relatively, morally superior to inaction. Attempts at moral leveling through criticism of the conscientious, in his view, tend to serve as defenses for conformed participation with the powers.

Yet, Stringfellow's stridency bespeaks, perhaps, a sense of vulnerability regarding a larger, subterranean tension within his use of the discourse of the powers. For the purpose of exploring this tension, one could grant these two of Stringfellow's conclusions: the issue in this case is neither idiosyncratic sectarianism as such nor the relative moral distinctions among responses to the powers. However, these two points both signal, even if they do not

113. Stringfellow, *Ethic for Christians*, 62.
114. Stringfellow, *Ethic for Christians*, 132–33.

fully diagnose, a pervasive ambiguity within Stringfellow's work: the status of the church, particularly the thoughtful Christian resistance in which the church is instantiated as event, in relation to the powers. This ambiguity allows Stringfellow to subject individual churches (even large swaths of them, as his estimation of the American churches is fairly sweeping) to intense criticism, while apparently setting at least some Christians apart from the criticism properly aimed at the powers and their collaborating churches. The chronic discomfort Stringfellow exhibits with the possibility of naming the church among the powers—claiming that at times it "resembles" them, that religion "as distinct from" Christian faith as a principality, and others mentioned above and elsewhere, including the exemption of ecclesial bodies from his many long lists calling out the powers—seems to place the church not only in opposition to the fallenness of the powers, but in an opposition that does not at the same time essentially include a self-critique. Though groups claiming to be the church can be chastised for failing to do so according to Stringfellow's ecclesiological understanding, the true church—which, recall, Stringfellow clearly claims cannot be characterized by invisibility or otherworldliness and of which he has concrete, historical examples—seems to dwell in a moral space outside the sphere of the powers and thus immune to critique of them, whatever the direction of its activism. This tension does not concern the particularity or the relative goodness of any proposed form of resistance, but rather the understanding, including the entailed self-understanding, of what participation in those practices achieves.

This is a tension in Stringfellow's thinking rather than simply an error or a problem, because the texts show a genuine ambivalence. Stringfellow is anything but complacent with respect to the condition and temptations of Christians in the modern world. Moreover, he clearly and repeatedly separates out human acts of resistance from divine righteousness and judgment of the powers. At the same time, there is good evidence to suggest that Stringfellow expects the church in the world to be not only a particular species of institution but different in kind from the powers, however liable it is to sliding back into conformity with them. Stringfellow is caught, it seems, between realistic recognition of the limitations and failings of Christian social practice and a desire for a morally urgent and uncompromising discipleship that cannot be dismissed as out of reach. The equivocation besetting Stringfellow's account of resistance might be seen as the result of certain theological assumptions that, when unrecognized and unchallenged, lead to an unnecessary systemic ambiguity. This book takes its departure from just this possibility: that the tension here evident in Stringfellow—and, I will argue, characteristic of second-generation discourse more generally—results from theological assumptions that are, at best, optional. The argument that follows is composed of several related tasks: making these assumptions explicit, investigating the impulses that lead theologians and ethicists to treat these assumptions as self-evident, and arguing for the possibility of different political theological understandings of Christian resistance that might address these concerns.

The argument of this book proceeds in three steps. First, it claims that complicity is total in scope, which is to say that human persons and communities cannot access[115] positions of exteriority to the powers. Chapters 2, 3, and 4 illuminate and provide evidence for this claim. Chapter 2 draws out necessary resources from two central figures—Karl Barth and Michel Foucault—in order to make this claim and its implications intelligible, while also suggesting and illustrating a method of comparative thought that crosses disciplinary lines. This chapter will begin to describe a maximal reading of the powers that I will call a "total complicity" account and how that reading affects the prospects of resistance. Chapter 3 explores the ecclesiology of John Howard Yoder in order to consider the possibility of voluntary exteriorities, while chapter 4 explicates the work of Walter Wink on the powers as a representative example of intellectual exteriorities. In both cases, I will marshal resources from Barth and Foucault to argue against the candidate exteriority by appeal to the character of human complicity with the powers.

The second step of the argument claims that theorists of the powers have posited exteriorities because of an animating assumption: that complicity and resistance are annihilating opposites. If this assumption is true, then just insofar as one is complicit with the powers, one cannot meaningfully resist them. Thus, resistance would "merely" reorganize the workings of the powers, or delude practitioners of resistance into thinking they had opposed them, or settle for less than adequate responses to them. By means of this assumption, a choice is forced: one holds, with respect to Christian social and political activity, either a despairing view of human existence marred by sin and guilt and therefore disengaged from meaningful social

---

115. I have chosen this phrase mainly to avoid the claim that positions of exteriority, as such, do not exist. I avoid that claim for two reasons. First, I intend for this argument to remain non-dispositive among various views of the fallenness of creation and the moral lives (or lack thereof) of nonhuman creatures, excepting only the powers from this category; whether they have access to positions of exteriority is certainly beyond the concerns represented here and quite possibly unknowable to us, at least anytime soon. Second, I will claim that at least one form of exteriority exists: namely, the righteousness that characterizes God alone. How this relates to the argument that follows will be a subject for later chapters to consider; for now, suffice it to say that refusing humans access to this particular exteriority is a political implication of the understanding of grace explored below.

activity, or a simplistic division of social positions—good and evil, church and world, innocent and guilty—which entitle one (or one's community) to engage in social theory or practice from a morally privileged position. Specifically, it will argue that these critics find in Barth and Foucault's total complicity accounts a blameworthy quietism that, if adopted, would lead to a bias toward inaction for just these reasons.

Finally, the third step argues that this assumption is false: meaningful resistance is not only possible under conditions of total complicity, but actively occasioned by it. Because of one's implication and participation in dynamics of the powers, one has the material to challenge, rethread, and rework these constellations of power. Chapter 6 attempts to show, using the work from Foucault's ethical phase and particular aspects of Barth's ethical writing, how practices of resistance can be developed within a spiritual discipline of repentance that does not depend on eradicating one's complicity with the powers. What results is a newly enlarged picture of the range of possible forms of resistance: smaller, more everyday practices of the self, which we no longer have to see as somehow second-rate, take on more significance in light of the deep traffic between the powers and human persons.

It may help to clarify, from the outset, two points about the argument that follows. First, I intend for my argument to remain non-dispositive with respect to the personal character of the powers. In some accounts, the powers exhibit all the characteristics of spiritual, personal beings; in others, they are representations of the forces of history and society. For the purposes just stated, my interest in questions about the ontological status of the powers is limited to how they function in relation to human activity and agency.[116] That is not to say that this project reads them merely as metaphors for human activity; quite the contrary, the understanding of the first two generations of discourse on the powers and that are employed here depends on their being "animated" in the sense of having spontaneous effects and apparent, agent-like intentions that are not reducible to the sum total of individual human agents. In this respect, it is natural to use the concept of personhood to understand and discuss the powers, whether understood literally or metaphorically; neither possibility is precluded by this argument. Second, though this book interrogates certain kinds of claims on behalf of Christian difference or particularity, I do not intend (as will become clear) to object to this difference or particularity in themselves. Rather than collapse or conceal difference, I have in mind to question certain theological

---

116. There is good reason to think that the New Testament texts depend primarily on this functional character of the powers too, remembering that terms such as *angelos*, *diabolos*, and *satanas* refer, in the first instance, to roles (messenger, slanderer, enemy) rather than to rungs on an ontological ladder.

and metaethical claims *about* Christian distinctiveness. In similar measure, though I raise questions about the implicit understanding of practices of resistance, I do not intend to object to the material elements of any practice, but rather to claims of noncomplicity made on behalf of such practices.[117] As a result, the argument here is distinct from typical complaints leveled against the traditions here considered that they are sectarian or idiosyncratic, as Stringfellow discusses, since differences as such are not the pressing issue, but rather what it would mean in relation to the powers to differ *differently*.

The cumulative effect of the chapters that follow should serve to extend the insights of the theorists of the powers, both those discussed in this chapter and those treated below. In this sense, this book pushes for an internal critique that holds this tradition of thought to account by its own lights. If the first generation of discourse about the powers retrieved its biblical heritage and unearthed its social and political promise, and the second generation extended, systematized, and applied these resources, then perhaps it is time for a third generation: one in which discourse about the powers begins to see its location in terms of other disciplines, to integrate a wider array of topics into a coherent theology, and to reflect on itself critically in order to refine its insights. Most crucially, discourse about the powers that helps contemporary people has to account for (through meaningful, even courageous, acceptance of) the criticism that Christian attempts to help often hurt, that the theological claims Christians make about ourselves are rarely borne out in actual difference from the world, that much theological discourse serves to perpetuate attachments to practices and forms of life that are not emancipatory. The political spirituality that this book seeks to equip, therefore, entails a reorientation of Christian self-understanding in relation to a world of powers, a perception of the world in oneself not unfamiliar in long-standing claims that the human is a microcosmos, but acutely insistent on the fallen character of the cosmos we have internalized.

To a large extent, this project is better situated to call for than to enact such a third generation. Nevertheless, it attempts to sketch a more comprehensive vision of human life amidst the powers by reading this tradition carefully, yet beyond its own assumptions.

---

117. It would seem that the only practices strictly invalidated by my argument (if true) would be practices that have claims to exteriority among their *necessary* motive reasons; there seem to me to be relatively few such claims.

CHAPTER 2

Power and the Powers
Against Exteriority

NEGLECTED ASSOCIATIONS

In his 1924 "Manifesto of Surrealism," André Breton ventures an encyclopedia-ready definition of his movement: "Surrealism is based on the belief in the superior reality of certain forms of previously neglected associations, in the omnipotence of dream, in the disinterested play of thought. It tends to ruin once and for all other psychic mechanisms and to substitute itself for them in solving all the principal problems of life."[1] The object of surrealist art and thinking, in other words, is to make visible and thus to denaturalize one's assumptions about "natural" associations by presenting unimagined, unusual associations. While such a method may be unlikely to solve all the principal problems of life, its use can have unanticipated effects that work to question hidden assumptions.[2]

This chapter seeks to delineate a solution to the characteristic problems of discourse on the powers, discussed above, by using such a comparison in order to reveal—and, ultimately, to reject—an influential assumption. Chapter 1 described the first and second generations of discourse on the powers, arguing that, while they offer helpful ways of enfolding social and political structures into Christian theology, those discourses often presume access to positions of exteriority, from which one or one's community are not complicit with sinful social structures. In this chapter, I hope to show, by means of a comparison between Michel Foucault's analytical work on power

---

1. Breton, *Manifestoes of Surrealism*, 26.
2. Indeed, it is not a coincidence that Foucault corresponded with and used some of the illustrations of René Magritte in his own work. See Foucault, *This Is Not a Pipe*.

and Karl Barth's portrayal of the powers, that an account of the powers can be generated in which those types of exteriorities are ruled out. Chapters 3 and 4 will argue for this account over and against those described in chapter 1, inasmuch as they differ, by demonstrating the forms of misrecognition that take place when voluntary or intellectual exteriorities are posited. Once an account of power without exteriority is thus motivated, I will investigate the assumption that, I take it, leads theorists of the powers continually back to the assertion of exteriorities: that complicity and resistance are annihilating opposites. Chapters 5 and 6, then, will attempt to investigate and disprove this assumption.

To begin with, though, I take it that the juxtaposition of Barth and Foucault is not nearly as intuitive as that between Barth and his fellow Christian theorists of the powers. As a result, some remarks theorizing that comparison, and how it will work in this argument, are called for.

NARRATIVE DISPARITIES AND CONCEPTUAL AFFINITIES

On its face, a collaboration between Michel Foucault and Karl Barth seems unlikely, or bound for various infelicities: equivocations, mismatches of interest and focus, and distortions resulting from what I will call their "narrative disparities," a basic divergence in their understanding of what sort of world we live in. With interests and intentions so apparently at odds, and commitments so seemingly irreconcilable, these two might seem to have little to offer each other by way of help in understanding the powers. Yet, despite and amidst these genuine differences, we can perceive, if we are so inclined, both a kind of "rhyming"[3] between their substantive accounts of power and reasons to think that they might not be the adversaries we would imagine.

Most theological appropriations of Foucault come with severe qualifications about the narrative disparity between Foucault and Christian theology. On the one hand, it is posited that Christianity assumes a prior metaphysical plenitude, or a reconciled or peaceable ontology, or privileged (and therefore unquestionable) revelation. On the other hand, Foucault, himself a certain kind of Nietzschean,[4] is portrayed as allergic to the keystones of Christian conviction. As a result, theologians can make local use of Foucault, but must always remember the "Christian difference." Stanley Hauerwas (discussing David Toole's *Waiting for Godot in Sarajevo*),

---

3. I owe this term to a conversation with Vincent J. Miller, for which I am grateful.

4. Foucault says, for example, that he would use "the genealogy of morals" as a general description of his work in "Prison Talk," 53.

notes that Foucault's account of power is similar to the New Testament's description of the principalities and powers, but approves of Toole's argument that the cross gives Christians hope, "a hope Foucault cannot make intelligible."[5] Because of this hope, and because (purportedly) unlike postmodernists, "Christians have a stake in history," "Christians must be able to narrate postmodernism in a manner that postmodernism cannot narrate Christianity. Or more adequately: we must show how Christianity provides the resources for a critique of its own mistakes in a way that modernity or postmodernity cannot provide."[6] So too David Bentley Hart, who admits that the "theologian might well be tempted to read Foucault as an unwitting phenomenologist of original sin," but that since he "has no judgment to pass on power per se . . . he has no use for the notion of sin. And of course, he knows little of Christian theology's conception of sin in its cosmic aspect: its presence not only in the inner precincts of conscience but within the deep structures of human society and history, the way its intentionality precedes the subjectivity to which it gives shape."[7] Foucault's refusal of Christian commitments—the perpetual presence of a "Christian difference" between his analysis and the use to which that analysis is put—disqualifies him from having any final word in theology: he may be appropriated, but those appropriations must also out-narrate or supplement Foucault in ways he would anathematize.

A more subtle account of how narrative disparities qualify appropriations of Foucault can be found in Jonathan Tran's *Foucault and Theology*. Tran's reservations about Foucault illustrate the point well specifically because Tran otherwise believes that Foucault helps one think about Christian faithfulness and turns to him for a nuanced account of hope, a resource that many theologians would prefer to find in a sacred idiom.[8] Yet, Tran still feels compelled to acknowledge up front that "Foucault thinks the world belongs to power," while "Christians think the world belongs to God."[9] As a result,

---

5. Hauerwas, "Christian Difference," 146–47.

6. Hauerwas, "Christian Difference," 147.

7. Hart, *Beauty of the Infinite*, 68–69. What makes this quotation so strange is that the "deep structures" of sinfulness that Hart attributes to a Christian theological understanding *pervade* Foucault's understanding of subjectivity and structural intentionality. Hart may well argue that Foucault's descriptive cartography of power lacks something essential in refusing Christian (or similar) norms, but this structural similarity, far from being a salient difference, is itself the reason that Christians are tempted to use Foucault in the way he describes.

8. Tran, *Foucault and Theology*, 1.

9. Tran, *Foucault and Theology*, 3. The notion that Foucault thinks the world "belongs" to power will be discussed below. I note here that Tran suggests a basic analogy in the use of "belongs" that doesn't reflect a necessary interpretation of Foucault's texts.

Tran has decided not to include the word "resistance" in his subtitle; doing so would have suggested a world of powers into which God (and Christians) intervene, suggesting ontological priority to the life of the Trinity.[10] Instead, Christians are called to witness, which "seeks to convert the world, if only to [the world's] reality, and incarnates all kinds of languages, including resistance, for that purpose."[11] The content of that witness is the fullness of good that preexists any state of affairs calling for resistance; resistance is therefore internal to—and therefore less significant than—witness, just as Foucault's analysis must fit within (mutatis mutandis) Christian theology for the latter's discursive rules not to be violated. To argue otherwise is to misrecognize God's reign over the world, even in its fallen condition. Thus, Tran warns that his work "thinks about the world as if Foucauldian, though the sensibilities of [that work] are not Foucauldian but rather Christian."[12]

This chapter's use of Foucault in the context of Christian theology, though closely allied with Tran's, departs from his in its methodological self-understanding, in two ways. First, this book assumes a kind of asymmetry between the two terms of comparison. What is striking about Tran's warning is not his claiming responsibility for Christian commitments, but rather the opposition of the two "sensibilities."[13] With these qualifications, Tran signals that he knows that Foucault does not explicitly offer an ontology, or even a coherent sensibility, on par with Christian conviction. Foucault does not produce mere conceptual tools that are endlessly transferable and equally appropriable among diverse discourses; his analyses are often motivated by more robust normative commitments than he is usually given credit for. However, the implication that there is a "Foucauldianism" that competes with Christianity as a technique for accounting for the world overstates the determinacy and situatedness of those normative commitments. To say that one's sensibilities are not Foucauldian but rather Christian suggests not only that the two are mutually exclusive but also that there exists some common genus within which the two are both species. Indeed, there may well be times when a genuine choice is forced between consensus Christian commitments and, for instance, Foucault's understanding of power relations. Yet, there is a more basic asymmetry between Christian theology and the kind of social theory that Foucault offers, which itself has no pretensions to unearth the meaning and orientation of human life. By approaching this

---

10. Tran, *Foucault and Theology*, 3.
11. Tran, *Foucault and Theology*, 4.
12. Tran, *Foucault and Theology*, 3.
13. A similar trajectory can be seen in Tran's apparent ambivalence about Foucault's understanding of power and "the ontology it can invite" (*Foucault and Theology*, 6).

asymmetry from both sides, we will better understand how to read Foucault from a Christian perspective without either distortion or equivocation.

Though more will be said about Foucault's understanding of the role of the intellectual in chapter 4, for now it is important to note that Foucault believes himself to be a kind of cartographer:

> What the intellectual can do is to provide instruments of analysis. . . . What's effectively needed is a ramified, penetrative perception of the present, one that makes it possible to locate lines of weakness, strong points, positions where the instances of power have secured and implanted themselves by a system of organization dating back over 150 years. In other words, a topological and geological survey of the battlefield—that is the intellectual's role. But as for saying, "Here is what you must do!," certainly not.[14]

For Foucault, the intellectual *as such* is responsible for insightful perception that empowers the activist (and, of course, the two roles may be found in the same person). Specifically in that capacity, the intellectual does not close the normative case for their descriptions of social space. As a result, those who participate within that space have the prerogative to amend or interrogate those descriptions: analyses of power are open to revision and discussion from multiple theoretical perspectives. Though these types of social theories are not attempts at simple representation, Foucault thinks that, e.g., his account of the evolution of disciplinary institutions from the spectacular violence of the sovereign to the obscured violence of prisons is vulnerable to criticism and correction on the basis of agreed-upon aspects of the history of the European classical age, without disqualification based on their source. Foucault admits "obsessions" with spatial metaphors for power,[15] and this pervasively spatial conception of the social world entails the possibility of intellectual collaboration, since all those present within that conceptual field may contribute to the map-making process. This specifically discursive nonaggression (for all of Foucault's theorizing of power relations with belligerent imagery!) is what he has in mind in one of his clearest statements against polemics:

> What is tiresome in ideological arguments is that one is necessarily swept away by the "model of war." That is to say that when you find yourself facing someone with ideas different from your own, you are always led to identify that person as an enemy (of your class, your society, etc.). And we know that it is

14. Foucault, "Body/Power," 62.
15. Foucault, "Questions on Geography," 69.

necessary to wage combat against the enemy until triumphing over him. . . . Wouldn't it be much better instead to think that those with whom you disagree are perhaps mistaken; or perhaps that you haven't understood what they intended to say?[16]

For Foucault, suspicions and condemnations built upon narrative disparities are not to be trusted, especially because "the theoretical coordinates of each of us are often, no, always, confused and fluctuating, especially if they are observed in their genesis."[17] Polemics, depending as they do on a construal of those representing another "sensibility" as, at bottom, a discursive enemy, misrecognize the shared social space that is both the subject matter and source of intellectual investigations.

From a Christian perspective, the character of Barth's theology gives us good reasons to think that a discussion between Barth and Foucault, at least on the interpretations advocated here, could be imagined that would neither viciously equivocate nor violate some crucial discursive rules for faithful theology. First, as will be discussed below, Barth thinks, since revelation is nonidentical with its media, God can use as means of revelation aspects of or forms of life in the world (including social theory) that may not seem, at first, hospitable to such revelation.[18] Both as a positive encouragement to listen to nontheological sources and a negative reservation to be placed on the usual Christian sources, this impetus ought to check our impulse to draw sharp disciplinary lines. Second, the peculiar material character of Barth's theology is well-suited for such a comparison. Moving as it does with the logic of the "infinite qualitative distinction" in Kierkegaard,[19] a Barthian theology can systematically and rigorously refuse positions of unquestioned privilege to a Christian religious narrative as such that would, for example, close off the church from empirical observation and criticism or claim a form of unmediated knowledge of God or God's economy of grace. Theology dwells within the immanent frame, operating on worldly

---

16. Foucault and Trombadori, *Remarks on Marx*, 180–81.

17. Foucault and Trombadori, *Remarks on Marx*, 180.

18. See, e.g., mentions of "secular parables of the kingdom" in Barth, *Church Dogmatics* (hereafter *CD*) 4/3 and in 1/1—the famous line that "God may speak to us through Russian Communism, through a flute concerto, through a blossoming shrub or through a dead dog. We shall do well to listen to Him if He really does so." As David Haddorff puts it in summarizing Barth, "as long as secular words do not tempt the Christian community from straying from its task of bearing *witness* to the Word of God, they may be utilized for living according to that task. . . . Secular languages . . . create opportunities for Christian ethics to evaluate the ideological structure of the powers" (*Christian Ethics as Witness*, 303–4).

19. See Barth, *Epistle to the Romans*, 10.

elements as the remnants of revelation; only coming from the other side of the distinction could a narrative simply "out-narrate" others without being out-narrated itself. That is, claims to encompass all other narratives (or methods, or disciplines) can themselves pose an idolatrous threat: only God has the vision to see the world, and that vision is not imparted to humans. Thus, there is no prior reason for a theologian inspired by Barth's theological account of the world not to work with Foucauldian (or other) accounts of how that world operates.

The second respect in which my method of comparison departs from that deployed by Tran can be seen by appeal to Anna Lowenhaupt Tsing's concept of friction. Tsing develops and uses this concept within an ethnography of global connection, but it applies analogously to the kind of collaboration used here, as well. "Friction" is the "grip of worldly encounter" through which a universal aspiration or scheme has purchase on "the sticky materiality of practical encounters."[20] Tsing, attempting to navigate between the kind of universal targeted by postcolonial theory and the forms of particularism often pursued in light of that criticism, calls a universal present and active within a particular situation an "engaged universal."[21] A particular historical moment and deployment gives a universal content and force. Yet, since such moments are populated by overlapping, diverse universals in a global situation, competing universals hardly ever gain unanimous consent. Rather, such universals "travel across difference and are charged and changed by their travels," tested against practical application, contested over and against competing universals, and revised as a result of earnest encounter.[22] Engaged universals are not absolutes: they are norms, such as "social justice," the extent of which people seek to expand, but that can also be challenged and revised within a process of deliberation and implementation.

Tsing explores heterogeneity among universals in the process of collaboration. "Collaboration," as Tsing points out, can mean either united labor and cooperation generally or specifically disloyal cooperation with an enemy. Among the many complexities of global capitalism, unlikely forms of collaboration show us that "we must move beyond the common-sense assumption that solidarity means homogeneity."[23] Instead:

> Differences invigorate social mobilizations. Differences engage political abstractions, making them applicable to local situations.

20. Tsing, *Friction*, 1.
21. Tsing, *Friction*, 8.
22. Tsing, *Friction*, 8.
23. Tsing, *Friction*, 245.

> At the same time, differences are organized by common assumptions about political process. It is impossible to participate in a movement without representing one's demands through its ruling discourses; no one unacquainted with the concept of freedom, for example, can make claims through it. Political mobilizations mount a generalized frame for what will count as politics, including the politics of difference. Difference is thus both a pre-established frame for connection and an unexpected medium in which connection must find local purchase.[24]

To make a difference in the world, engaged universals must present their claims in relation to adjacent discourses and to ruling discourses. Rarely does a universal have occasion to make a public case for itself in isolation from—and without solidarity with—divergent other universals. Representatives of such universals must decide with whom to collaborate and how to translate that collaboration in a way that gets a hold on the practical common concern of the collaboration. Tsing highlights political process as that which sets criteria for this practical traction, discussing forest preservation efforts in Indonesia that drew together a wide range of parties, from local villagers to national and international activists. Yet, her analysis need not only apply to institutions of authority: these demands—the demands of situating one's discourse among one's peers and mobilizing them for practical application—apply to social movements more broadly construed, as well as the practice of intellectual traditions. Progressive activists, claims Tsing, "spend most of their time either searching for seamless consensus or making a point of their irreconcilable differences," underappreciating the importance of "difference within common cause"; a similar point could be made about theologians, some number of whom opt to see these encounters as instances of the traitorous form of collaboration.[25] Against these presuppositions, the most fruitful kind of collaboration may be that which internalizes fraught differences: "collaboration with friction at its heart."[26]

There exists a real possibility for misappropriation of Foucault in a project such as this one. On one hand, it could be argued that the quasi-mythical form of discourse about the powers are fundamentally misaligned with Foucault's outlook on power. Below, I will argue that the mythical character of this discourse—especially the sense in which that character places theology within a narrative of history's unfolding story of the powers—is an asset, both in its own right and with respect to its opening toward

---

24. Tsing, *Friction*, 245.
25. Tsing, *Friction*, 262, 246.
26. Tsing, *Friction*, 246.

Foucauldian analysis. This is the case because, as noted above, that mythology can be read functionally rather than ontologically, without loss to the insights garnered by the discourse. In developing a grammar for a theology of structures, the discourse surrounding the powers need not specify (as it historically has not) that the powers are spiritual beings over and against observable social forces, and this would seem to remove the strictly inadmissible elements of the mythology, on Foucault's terms.[27] On the other hand, there could be a legitimate concern about disciplining Foucauldian techniques with theological mores. As Mark Jordan observes, "theology can be adept at swallowing theories," and "ingesting bits of theory is not the same as bringing a new voice into a disputed question. A voice comes not only with its own shape for speech, but with the resources to reshape itself."[28] This could raise a dilemma: either allow Foucault's techniques their own integrity at the possible expense of usefulness for theological discourse, or adapt them for that usefulness but in the process deny them the voice to speak back to theology. There should be no doubt that, in what follows, I put Foucault's work to use within a theological discourse—though, importantly, a particular theological discourse that I find unusually hospitable to Foucault's work, in contrast to (and in argument with) others. If, despite this, I have succeeded in preserving the integrity of Foucault's positions, it is because the project has judged fairly the basic asymmetry[29] between Foucault's analytics of power and a theological-historical narrative of the powers and, despite that asymmetry, the surprising convergence of Foucault's claims with a particular understanding of one Barthian form of theology.

Barth and Foucault no doubt disagree on a host of important issues, as well as on which issues are important enough to merit attention.[30] This

---

27. Though it is worth nothing that, in my judgment, Foucault was remarkably willing to work on discursive terms not his own, his later work on the ancient world being a good example of this.

28. Jordan, *Telling Truths in Church*, 54.

29. As it was discussed in terms of "sensibility" above, I here use "asymmetry" to claim that the work represented in Foucault's second and third phases as such is nondispositive with respect to a range of possible narrative or traditional locations, so long as those narratives or traditions meet certain criteria that obviously follow from Foucault's analytical claims. A self-critical Christian theology of the world, which is sought after here, seems to me to be well within this range of narratives, even if Foucault would not have affirmed its positive claims about transcendent realities.

30. Despite my belief in their overlapping concerns, I have found only one occasion on which Foucault, the latter-born of the figures, cites Barth: in the conclusion to volume three of *The History of Sexuality*, Foucault notes that later Christian sexual ethics seemed to seek out exemplars of ancient sexual ethics that were similarly austere, a thesis advanced in some corners "which Karl Barth radicalized in making Epictetus a true Christian" (Foucault, *Le souci de soi*, 312). The passage moves on quickly from there, offering no other thoughts on Barth.

argument and its assumptions do not depend on anything like identity between Barth's account of the powers and Foucault's analysis of power. The significant narrative disparities may prove an asset inasmuch as they draw together helpfully distinct sets of resources and prompts. The confluence pursued here comes from their common attempt to describe human social and political life accurately, and to do so in a way that involves a complex picture of subjectivity, agency, and power. This justifies the comparison on the disciplinary level, within which local disagreements can be arbitrated by the common sorts of appeal to theological reflection and social analysis.[31] What this project does not assume is that where Foucault and some version of Christian conviction depart from one another, the theologian has some responsibility to hold to a prior rejection of Foucault in the interests of faithfulness to tradition. Social theory stands under no judgment unaccompanied by the discipline of theology itself; in this, Hauerwas is correct that what theology urgently needs is self-criticism, even though his accompanying claim—that Christianity provides such resources in ways that postmodernity does not—seems itself in need of such criticism.

In this spirit, this chapter will attempt to redraw the lines of debate: rather than pitting Christian theologians on one side appropriating and correcting Foucault, on the other, it will suggest that Barth and Foucault develop a common grammar of power without exteriority that can be used to illustrate and revise other instances of discourse about the powers that do posit exteriorities. To do this, it will first consider Foucault's well-known analysis of power, especially to elaborate on the concept of exteriority itself. Then, it will use this concept to explicate Barth's late teachings on the "Lord-less Powers." While Barth does not use the language of "exteriority," this chapter will argue that it can be applied without doing violence to Barth's account of human agency in light of the powers. What will emerge is a theological description of the powers imbued with the analytical sensitivity of Foucault's work on power, a description that later chapters will seek to motivate by comparing it with existing accounts of the powers.[32]

31. There is a way that we could describe the procedure of anti-disciplinary draws inspiration from queer theory. Thus Lauren Berlant: "Queer theory is a training in paying attention [to intimacies that do not follow normative patterns], the multiplicity of beats and points of convergence that correlate the surprise and contingency of relationality and desire with threat, delight, and ongoingness, world making and world building" ("Properly Political Concept," 686).

32. This should be seen as a kind of response to J. Alexander Sider's call for a theology of the powers that attends to Foucault's analysis of microcapillary distillations and for an appropriate accompanying ethics ("Who Durst Defy?," 254). This project differs from Sider's imagining of such an argument in focusing both on the structural dynamics of Foucault's analytics of power and the personal, small-scale phenomena that

FOUCAULT: RELATIONS OF FORCE, STRATEGIES OF POWER, AND IMMANENT RESISTANCE

Michel Foucault's development of an analysis of power in the 1970s is familiar to many in the academic world but continues to be subject to distorting misunderstandings. Parabolic figures, such as the Panopticon,[33] have come to remind us of Foucault's insights, but the intricate workings of his depiction of power are often lost in the haze of over-familiarity. This section, then, will attempt to redescribe Foucault's work on power from the ground up, focusing particularly on several underappreciated points in Foucault's wider corpus, the neglect of which has had important effects on popular interpretations of Foucault. Though elaboration and defense of this account will continue in chapters 3 and 4, it is crucial for my purposes here to outline how Foucault gets from the theoretical primitive of force to an account of power in which positions of exteriority are ruled out. From that point, one can begin to see the convergence between Foucault's account of power in the modern West[34] and Barth's description of the powers. Even for readers less interested in getting Foucault "right," this re-rehearsal will help build a description of human agency that arises from and is enmeshed with the powers.

Conceptually, the building blocks of this account come from Foucault's understanding of *rapports de force*: force relations. This is clearest in the methodological component within "The Deployment of Sexuality," contained in *La Volonté de Savoir*:

> As for power, it seems to me that it must be understood as a multiplicity of force relations that are immanent to the domain where they are exercised, and that are constituted of their

---

compose those dynamics, but I have agreed with Sider from the start that a theology of the powers "needs to confront very vexed questions of agency and accountability," especially by examining "concepts like action, agency, and responsibility."

33. See Foucault, *Discipline and Punish*, 200.

34. Andrea Rossi helpfully frames the qualification named in the preface above about Foucault's work on the specifically "Western" world, addressed as it is primarily to the task of deciphering the specific features of its politics that work through "conduction," resulting from a particular history (*Labour of Subjectivity*, 14–16). Rossi, too, implies that the description has applications beyond the primary targets of its focus, in large part as a result of the colonizing, globalizing orders that have imposed the politics of conduction. It may well be the case that the analysis offered here does not apply globally today. I present the claims that follow—from my sources, and those I advance—as prompt with which this book's audiences should be confronted as part of a discerning of how one's life is tied up in the political world, which readers will determine for themselves.

organization: the game that, by way of incessant struggle and conflict, transforms, reinforces, and inverts them; the supports that these force relations find in one another, the way they form a chain or system, or, on the contrary, the reactions, the contradictions that isolate them from each other; the strategies, finally, in which they take effect, and whose general design or institutional crystallization is embodied in the state apparatus—in the formulation of the law, of social hegemony.[35]

Though Foucault here makes force the basic unit of power, we should hold at bay its connotations of coercion. At first, the type of force Foucault has in mind is more closely akin to the understanding of force in Newtonian physics: that which acts on an(other) object. Since humans are not only passive recipients of forces but also agents, these forces might act upon us as physical bodies or as thinking and acting subjects. Thus, the tree that is cut down and blocks a walkway, forcing one to walk around or over it, enters into a force relation with the walker just as much (though not as dramatically) as the tree that, having been cut down, comes crashing down on one's house. A force relation, then, is an element of the structure of a relational field as it bears on an agent: the parts of the scene within which one acts and responds to others and the world. Such forces, or potential forces, so densely populate our world that we can rightly call force—in precisely this sense, and not as "coercion"—omnipresent.[36]

Forces, and the relations with agents to which they give rise, are mobile and flexible and, on their own, tend to work on a small scale. We may encounter a similar force relation in a range of contexts: the crossword puzzle, for example, may be a solitary hobby, a pastime while sitting in a waiting room, or the object of a formalized competition (as happens every March in the American Crossword Puzzle Tournament). Whatever the context, a person on one end of the relation, the puzzle-maker, sets a task for the other, who can then participate or refuse. That task has its own rules and character, but the puzzle-doer need not conform to them: she may leave the puzzle half-finished out of boredom, or find a way to cheat, etc. Just as likely, she may never show any interest in doing a crossword puzzle or

35. Foucault, *Histoire de la Sexualité*, 1:121–22.

36. Moreover, as I will reiterate below, Foucault's similar claims about the omnipresence of power ought to be read in this light: power is (at least potentially) everywhere since the force relations that can be arranged into relations of power are everywhere. A failure to appreciate this reasoning, it seems to me, is one of the factors contributing to the popular judgment that Foucault presents a "pessimistic picture" of human life that cannot escape power. Such interpreters seem to have in mind coercion, and not this conception of force, when they read of the omnipresence of power.

never have contact with cultures that create and solve crossword puzzles, and thus never become party to that particular force relation. The task of solving a crossword puzzle may have a range of meanings for the agency of the puzzle-doer or it may have no meaning at all; it may arise in any number of situations, along with a whole field of other possibilities for action in response to other forces. Without being coercive, then, force relations make up the field in which agency is possible: action always occurs within relations of and with forces, even though that action may well be underdetermined by the character of the force in play.

When a set of force relations is stabilized, appropriated, and directed by a particular aim, a relation of power results. Imagine the task of solving a crossword puzzle entering into a new relationship: that of a parent who wants his child to develop certain linguistic and cognitive abilities by solving such puzzles. Insofar as it is social and not exclusively biological, that parental/filial relation is made up of a multiplicity of force relations, directed and regulated, in all likelihood, by the parent through repetition and redirection (forces being arranged such that the one whose action is most intensely regulated and guided is the child). The parent may encourage the child to complete crossword puzzles, command that the child brushes his teeth, and enforce punishments if the child skips school. Each one of these actions creates a relation of force, shaping the field of possible actions for the child. Their common appropriation into a relation of stable roles—one is always the parent, one always the child—and into harmony with each other—they all work to encourage the development of a well-adjusted adult person, say—makes up a relation of power. The adult "governs" the child in the sense of acting so as to encourage some forms of action and discourage others. A host of force relations are used in this process, some of which are coercive, but most of which are not. Though many relations of power exist that do not exhibit this degree of hierarchy, such relations are equally composed of *rapports de force* organized into regular, if flexible, patterns.

From this perspective, we can observe three crucial characteristics of power in Foucault's account. First, power bubbles up from the natural course of social relationships, and it does so constantly. "Power is everywhere," Foucault claims, "not because it encompasses all things, but because it comes from everywhere."[37] It depends upon "the moving base of relations of force that ceaselessly induce, through their inequality, states of power, but always locally and unstably."[38] There is a constant play of relations of force:

---

37. Foucault, *Histoire de la Sexualité*, 1:122. I take this distinction to entail that power's omnipresence does *not* mean that all relations are reducible without remainder to power. Power is constantly an element of such relations, but not exhaustively so.

38. Foucault, *Histoire de la Sexualité*, 1:122. I have translated "socle" here as "base"

here they harmonize to form certain relations of power, there they are in tension, as a relation of power is subject to dispute or in doubt. A sudden illness may abruptly make an adolescent child the caretaker of one of her parents, when the opposite had previously been the case: this is so because that role, caretaker—like so many of our roles—is more precarious than one might typically assume. The peripheral or capillary forms of power that are so often associated with Foucault are these original forms: the small-scale collections of force relations that make up the fabric of everyday social existence. That fabric is constantly unraveling and being rewoven; left to its own, it does not conform to a prior pattern. Its threads can be extremely fine. Yet, their common effect is to connect into a larger whole.[39] To say that "power comes from below,"[40] then, is to claim that peripheral, mundane forms of power give rise to the more complex and visible forms.

Second, power is composed of patterns of forces, rather than institutions—"it is the name that one gives to a strategic, complex situation in a given society."[41] Again, relations of force and power do not tend to cohere into intelligible patterns on their own and do not arise in a ready-made order. However, relations of power can serve a purpose, not because there are prior agents that simply create and deploy them but because they can

---

rather than "substrate" (as Robert Hurley does) to emphasize the "basicness" of *rapports de force*, in this passage and elsewhere.

39. This seems like an important moment at which to mention a common problem in interpretation of Foucault: that power is "all there is." Though more will be said about this in chapter 5, it makes two mistakes about Foucault's analytics of power. First, Foucault explicitly acknowledged that power was one of several "technologies" that humans use to understand and govern themselves; his emphasis on power (which, at times, he seems to concede can be misleading) is in large measure a reaction to the emphases of structuralist linguistics and Marxist critical theory on technologies of sign systems and of production to the exclusion of the type of power that Foucault perceived (see, e.g., "Les techniques de soi," 1604). Though one could claim that Foucault does not properly acknowledge the mutually causal interactions between these technologies, it is clear that Foucault himself believed that social life is composed of qualitative phenomena apart from power. Second, such claims tend to over-interpret Foucault, especially by claiming that he offers an ontology instead of analytics for understanding social phenomena. There are, certainly, implications to Foucault's work that bear on "what is" and "what is not," but as argued below, it is inappropriate to read Foucault as making any such general claims.

40. Foucault, *Histoire de la Sexualité*, 1:124.

41. Foucault, *Histoire de la Sexualité*, 1:123. In this same sentence, Foucault denies that power is a structure; I take it that Foucault's juxtaposition of "structure" with "institution" and "puissance dont certains seraient dotés" means that "structure" here refers to the visible, often institutional and formalized relations between social roles, and not the use of structure that, e.g., Yoder intends in his "Christ and the Powers" chapter. When I use "structure" without further qualification, I intend it in Yoder's sense, which can also be seen as a gloss on Foucault's "strategic, complex situation."

be used strategically.[42] Foucault's claim that relations of power are at once intentional and nonsubjective—which will prove significant in the comparison with Barth's account of the powers below—depends on a repudiation of conspiratorial conceptions of power.[43] While agency exercised from different positions varies greatly in the extent and intensity of its effect, there are no "great actors" in a social whole who decide how to deploy vast networks of power. Instead, as local relations of power arise, they find convergences and supports, or the opportunities thereof, in other existing relations of power. They make alliances—often in accidental and unforeseen ways—that complicate the situation for the actors involved. In this fashion, for example, the modern nation-state has slowly gathered to itself the relations of power that had congealed into systems of education, militaries, and institutions of health. As a relative latecomer with respect to social structures, the nation-state has had to crystallize and combine other, more localized patterns of power into a more complex strategic whole.[44] Moreover, this process has not occurred at the behest of nameable actors, but rather unfolded over the course of a complicated and multifaceted history, such that its intelligibility is only retrodictable. It has acted all along according to an intention, even though no "subject" is at its helm elaborating a conscious strategy.

Third, power has only an indirect relation to coercion or repression. Rather, a relation of power should be defined as "a mode of action that does not act directly and immediately on others, but that acts on their own action." In contrast to a "relation of violence"—which, acting directly on a body or on a thing, "forces, bends, breaks, and destroys,"—a relation of power recognizes the other and preserves the other as an acting subject, opening "a whole range of responses, reactions, effects, and possible innovations."[45] The opposite of power is not freedom; rather, power presupposes freedom. It is only exercised on free subjects, and only inasmuch as they can exercise agency. In fact, "where determination is complete, there is no relation of power: slavery is not a relation of power when one is in chains (it is then a relation of physical constraint), but precisely when one can move or even escape."[46] Power acts first not to dominate, but to colonize, to conscript—to

---

42. Foucault, "Pouvoirs et strategies," 425.

43. Foucault, *Histoire de la Sexualité*, 1:124-25.

44. This is one of the dimensions of Foucault's use of Nietzsche that is underappreciated: Nietzsche is valuable to Foucault in large measure because he was able to think of power outside of a state theory (Foucault, "Prison Talk," 53). Adam Kotsko suggests a way of reading the state back into Foucault through political theology, particularly in relation to *The Birth of Biopolitics*, in *Neoliberalism's Demons*, especially on pp. 35-38.

45. Foucault, "Le sujet et le pouvoir," 1055.

46. Foucault, "Le sujet et le pouvoir," 1056-57.

appropriate another's action for its own or influence it in the direction of its choosing. Its strength comes not from independently overdetermining a situation among subjects (and thereby making them objects) but rather in its dependence on the subjects' own activity to internalize and reproduce its effects. The ultimate victory of a particular regime of power would be to vanish completely underneath the freedom of the subjects on which it acts.

We can summarize these three observations about Foucault's description of power with the more familiar dictum: in the first instance, power is productive. The moments when power becomes repressive, prohibitive, or destructive tend to obscure the wider and deeper range of activities in which power suggests, creates, restores, and facilitates social action.[47] Indeed, power is endlessly fertile, constantly engendering new social dynamics and arrangements, perpetually in motion as it circulates within and among social bodies. Rather than merely prohibiting sexual acts, power endows us with certain dispositions, ways of knowing ourselves and the world, and practices as sexual subjects. Rather than merely proscribing some behaviors and allowing others, power shapes policy into biopolitics, harnessing the energy of populations for strategic use. Power carves out social "channels" through which to funnel agency: it sets up the conditions under which we all will act, and structures the relationships that give action context and meaning. Power generates knowledge, desires, and subjects as well as institutions and structures. And power is everywhere producing these effects because relations of force constantly arise, dependent upon, appropriated by, or working for the transformation of existing constellations of power relations.

This picture of power gives rise to a unique theory of resistance. That resistance is the category opposed to power itself speaks volumes, especially given that concepts such as liberation and revolution were abundantly ready at hand in Foucault's intellectual climate. Foucault acknowledges that relations of power may become so highly concentrated and institutionally organized that they constitute a state of domination or repression that would call for a revolutionary posture. There are occasionally "great, radical ruptures [and] massive, binary divisions," during which resistance is compelled to take the form of opposition, liberation, or revolution.[48] These states occur when an individual or group manages to block the field of power relations, "rendering them immobile and fixed and preventing all reversibility of

---

47. Thus, Foucault posits that "the law is neither the truth nor the alibi of power. It is an instrument, simultaneously complex and partial" ("Pouvoirs et strategies," 424). That which interdicts action from a position of authority is only a remote, latecoming effect of a basically productive phenomenon.

48. Foucault, *Histoire de la Sexualité*, 1:127.

movement" within that field.[49] In such a state of domination, institutional power has so constrained the free subjects upon which it acts that their only way forward qua free subjects is liberation. Nelson Mandela, responding to critics of the African National Congress's use of violence, expressed this dynamic well when he responded that "it is always the oppressor, not the oppressed, who dictates the form of the struggle": the situation of oppression itself, in one dimension, just is the narrowing of viable options for resistance.[50] But more frequently than domination (in Foucault's sense, which is narrower than usual), one encounters a tangle of power that leaves open "mobile and transitory points of resistance, introducing cleavages within society that become displaced, breaking unities and arousing reconfigurations," engaging in the constant play of forces that make up the situation of power relations.[51] That is, resistance—the category more basic than liberation—works on the smaller, less organized scale that is called for by the parallel characteristics of typical relations of power: the scale of force relations.

With this in mind, we can properly understand Foucault's celebrated maxim: "Where there is power, there is resistance."[52] Resistance, at least in potency, always attends relations of power because resistance and power are both constituted by the force relations at hand in a social field. Power and resistance are mutually immanent and homogenous: relations of power arise that make use of force relations for a particular end, and resistances respond by deploying force relations in such a way as to frustrate (or at least complicate) those ends. For Foucault, this must always be the case, since power as such presupposes this strategic situation among free actors. What makes power strong—its ability to seduce or conscript to its own ends the activity of others—also exposes it to just this type of resistance: "by definition, [resistances] can only exist in the strategic field of relations of power."[53] Hence, points of resistance are originally as local and uncoordinated as relations of power, arising in response to situations presented to free subjects. Resistances are thus "the other term within relations of power: they are inscribed within [those relations] as an irreducible vis-à-vis."[54] There is no

49. Foucault, "L'étique du souci de soi," 1530.
50. Mandela, *Long Walk to Freedom*, 537.
51. Foucault, *Histoire de la Sexualité*, 1:127.
52. Foucault, *Histoire de la Sexualité*, 1:125.
53. Foucault, *Histoire de la Sexualité*, 1:126.
54. Foucault, *Histoire de la Sexualité*, 1:127. Hurley here translates "l'autre terme" as "odd term," which expresses well how resistance is unintended by strategic use of relations of power. Since I assume that the connotations of "resistance" suffice to make this point, though, I have chosen to translate it as "other term" to discourage interpreting resistance as heterogeneous to power.

grand refusal or revolt against the entire set of power relations given to one, since they just make up one's network of social relationships. Instead, there are many resistances, each a distinct case: some possible, others necessary, still others improbable; the brutal, the solitary, the concerted, the rampant, the violent, and others.[55]

To say that power and resistance work within the same field, though, is just to say that resistance does not dwell in a position of exteriority to power. In this respect, the less-appreciated second half of Foucault's maxim—"where there is power, there is resistance, and yet—or, rather, by the same token—this [resistance] is never in a position of exteriority in relation to power"[56]—is the negative implication of the first half. Resistance comes from and occurs within the strategic field of relations of power, or the world of force relations. It need not—indeed, cannot—arise apart from this situation. In fact, if Foucault is correct, relations of power depend upon resistances "[to] play within relations of power the role of adversary, of target, of support, of foothold."[57] The "normal" enforces itself through invoking the specter of the "pathological"; the "healthy" is defined over and against the "perverse." The one who resists, then (and every subject does in various ways, with some frequency), does not thereby become exempt from the workings of power or the strategic dynamics within which they take place. Resistance does not make one "other" to the power that one is resisting: that power may co-opt one's resistance, or rearrange itself so as to bypass it, or make other modifications to force relations in order to shift the meaning of one's resistance. This might, in turn, call for new kinds of resistances, which we will discuss later. For now, however, we can decisively say what Foucault denies of meaningful resistance: resistance does not remove one from continuing implication in the relations of power resisted, nor does it determine the final significance of one's standing in relation to power. Resistance, rather than establishing a position of exteriority to power, enmeshes one all the more within relations of power by virtue of its use of the same basic substance: shared force relations that make up the common stuff of our social experience.

Since the term "exteriority" figures prominently in what follows, it is worth pausing over it here to clarify its meaning and implications, especially since this term is used with varying means across discourses. To be in a

---

55. Foucault, *Histoire de la Sexualité*, 1:126.
56. Foucault, *Histoire de la Sexualité*, 1:125–26.
57. Foucault, *Histoire de la Sexualité*, 1:126.

position of "exteriority" with respect to a structure of power would mean that one's self and life, in their entirety, is comprehensibly explicable without reference to that structure of power; such a form of power is simply and totally "other" to oneself. This includes a denial of responsibility: if I attain to an exteriority with respect to a certain form of power, I am not at all morally liable to answer for its character or effects, though I may level judgment against it in a criticism that is in no way also self-criticism. Often, denying just this kind of responsibility motivates claims to exteriority, but exteriority claims exceed questions of responsibility.[58] The one arguing for an exteriority claims not just ordinary blamelessness but blamelessness of a thoroughgoing and absolute sort: one's own character and actions do not belong to the field of activity that makes up relations of power, in Foucault's terms. As an example, consider the positions of a US Senator and an imaginary conscientious protestor in relation to "The Authorization for Use of Military Force Against Iraq Resolution of 2002," which, under US law, permitted the invasion of Iraq in 2003. Let us stipulate that (imaginary) Senator Smith diligently researched both the history of the region and the geopolitical issues in play, listened carefully to the moral objections of her constituents, and, after serious and good-faith deliberation, voted for the resolution. It should be clear that since Senator Smith is straightforwardly (if only partially) responsible for the war that followed from the resolution, she is not in a position of exteriority with respect to that war.[59] Our conscientious protestor, on the other hand, wrote her elected representatives stating reasons against authorizing force, participated in sit-ins and marches, and voted strictly for candidates in the relevant elections that opposed the use of force in Iraq. Stipulating that the decision to go to war and the prosecution of the war itself were blameworthy, it would seem that this conscientious protestor had fulfilled her responsibilities as a citizen to oppose it. Nevertheless—and, crucially, even if she has acted completely responsibly—according to the account offered here, she is not in a position of exteriority to the war, either. Her actions, as well as the identity that she partially shapes for herself in opposing the war, plainly occur within the morass of forces that lead to the war itself. Despite her exceptionally responsible actions, she is involved, and that involvement has effects, both on her and on the forces in play, that exceed her intentions. Though more will be said on the unwieldiness of agency

58. There is more on the distinction between questions of responsibility and questions of complicity/exteriority below.

59. Notice that neither the denial of exteriority nor the assertion of responsibility as such amount to blameworthiness: a similar story could be told about a war (such as World War II), the causes of which are more likely to be seen as just. This will be important later on, since nothing about this explanation of power entails that power is evil.

in the next chapter, I hope this example shows that to assert a position of exteriority, within this account of power, is to deny participation.

Foucault, starting with the concept of force, develops a method[60] for analyzing power that explains how relations of power and points of resistance interact. Far from simple oppositions, those interactions make up the complex game of social strategies and tactics, in which novelty and mobility are the rule rather than the exception. Because power draws energy from the actions of subjects, it is exposed to rearrangement by that same activity. Because resistance exerts its own forces on arrangements of power, it is vulnerable to counteraction and reappropriation by power. Foucault suggests that we specifically should *not* understand this to mean that we are always "inside" a given regime of power with no means of "escape."[61] The refusal of exteriority cannot become resignation to the status quo because power and resistance always make new situations, always shift and change hands, and always depend upon free action and response. Power exists only within relationships, and one's action is never strictly and only constrained by those particular relationships. Rather, whatever relations one undertakes, whatever forces one deploys, one is thereby implicated within relations of power, though those relations admit of varying degrees of stability. Human society is not trapped under the domination of power; human society, with all its differentiating and specifying patterns, is woven from its threads.

LORDLESS POWERS AND SUBJECTED LIFE

With Karl Barth,[62] we reenter the Christian theological discourse about the powers, a discourse that would have seemed alien to Foucault. Yet, having

---

60. This theoretical account of power is properly called a method, though it certainly depends on content-rich claims, because one cannot analyze power without at the same time analyzing particular instances of power: in Foucault's case, the prison system, the emergence of the asylum, the development of sexuality, and other historical phenomena, particularly of the seventeenth and eighteenth centuries in Europe. That is, Foucault's method has a theory of its own, developed as the result of historical and social analysis, which in turn inflects the material analyses, and so on.

61. Foucault, *Histoire de la Sexualité*, 1:126.

62. Let me offer two brief notes on this book's use of Barth as a major source. First, there are theological figures who could, as alternative figures, energize a very similar argument. I have chosen Barth for some material reasons that will be described below, but I do not intend thereby to rule out possibly allied interpretations of other figures. Second, if this book sought to draw on Barth's authority as a canonical figure in political theology, it would be important to establish an understanding of how Barth's thought changes over the course of his career, the grounds on which I can draw from both the *Römerbrief* and the late *Dogmatics*, etc. This literary conversation is an important one,

traced Foucault's understanding of power, I hope that certain themes within this discourse are visible in a new light, one that shows affinities between Foucault's conception of power and Barth's account of the powers that have significant consequences. Though Barth situates his description of the "Lordless Powers," found in the *Christian Life* fragment of *CD* IV/4, within a Christian understanding of the economy of grace, certain conspicuous structural features, as well as material claims about human life and power, set up a fruitful comparison with Foucault's positions.[63]

Barth examines the powers in §78, "The Struggle for Human Righteousness," in which he reflects on the implications of the prayer that God's reign would exist on earth as it is in heaven. So to pray commits Christians to "act in accordance with their prayer as people who are responsible for the rule of human righteousness, that is, for the preservation and renewal, the deepening and extending, of the divinely ordained human safeguards of human rights, human freedom, and human peace on earth."[64] Though only God can truly establish God's reign,[65] human activity may serve as a parable of God's activity by taking an analogous stance toward the world, especially with regard to a type of protest against the prevailing order of the world. Christians are therefore called not only to love and loyalty to God, but into a conflict, a revolt against the shape of the world—the institutionalized

---

and others have made significant contributions to it. Where Barth is critical of his early theology—for example, in its emphasis on negativity that is itself undermetabolized by Barth's own convictions—some account will have to be made here. But in forging an unlikely common cause between Barth and Foucault, I have already departed from the presumption that the theological task is to make representations of subjects as coherent and distinct as possible. My purpose is to forge an argument using fragments left behind by these figures—both of whom contained (and published) multitudes—and not to re-establish the terms on which either figure should be understood.

63. Prather notes that Barth, in *CD* 3/3, discourages "demonology," "noting the impropriety of taking these defeated opponents of God's reign too seriously," especially (speculatively) apart from their concrete connection to human agency in the world (*Christ, Power, and Mammon*, 37). Prather also observes that, by the time of the *Christian Life* fragment, Barth "concedes a kind of 'reality and efficacy' to the demonic powers," however qualified (51). I am less concerned with establishing that I have followed strict dictates from Barth than in the substantive possibility of unduly emphasizing either the powers' demonic character or their role in the economy of salvation. It is possible to do both—and we are in danger of it here!—but this book argues that theologians have somewhat consistently underestimated their extent, and the task of describing this extent and its theological ramifications cannot help but direct us to give a large measure of attention to the powers. The powers are not thereby more important than God—as such, or to this argument. Rather, they make up the arena in which the life of God will have to be won, if it is won at all.

64. Barth, *Christian Life*, 205.

65. Barth, *Christian Life*, 212.

"order" that is really disorder.[66] Disorder "both inwardly and outwardly controls and penetrates and poisons and disrupts all human relations and interconnections."[67] The human fellowship God intends is destroyed, resulting in isolation, rivalry, and violence. Though God alone can establish the just, peaceful relations that disorder fails to attain, God enjoins Christians to resist what prevails in the world.

Yet, for Barth, we have not understood either this calling or the circumstances it addresses without two further qualifications. First, the "militant revolt" called for is directed at a situation, and not against persons: certainly not those outside the Christian community generally, nor even "against the wicked on account of their wickedness and oppression."[68] In this specification, one hears the echoes of the Pauline description of the Christian struggle, being "not against enemies of blood and flesh, but against the rulers, against the authorities, against the cosmic powers of this present darkness, against the spiritual forces of evil in the heavenly places" (Eph 6:12).[69] Second, this situation cannot be identified exclusively with any person or people in their particularity; it is a plight "which is caused by all, for which all are responsible, and which oppresses all."[70] One must see oneself as both responsible for and oppressed by the activity of this enemy. It matters a great deal that we specify this with an account of how structures form and function, lest in this universal inclusion we neglect how the powers work to differentiate, to generate advantages for some and immiserate others, to bind us in forms of horrible intimacy. In this respect, disorder is not primarily unformed chaos, but rather an unjust regularity, a distorting regime of power that sets at odds those whom God meant to be together.[71] For Barth, these differences belie a subjection in common to the forces that pattern the world into disorder. To say, then, that the plight of disorder is that enemy alone with which God commands neither reconciliation nor peace is to put one at conflict with a situation in which one is irrevocably enmeshed.

66. Barth, *Christian Life*, 206.
67. Barth, *Christian Life*, 211.
68. Barth, *Christian Life*, 210.
69. Here I am subscribing to something like Cullmann's view, which prefers to see behind nameable rulers and authorities powers that are not simply human persons (much as Stringfellow does with his concept of the image as principality).
70. Barth, *Christian Life*, 211.
71. Think here of how policing in the United States is institutionalized, even predictable, precisely in its protection of capital and enforcement of structural racism. In the wake of a cursed rage for "order" embodied by National Socialism, Barth knew this well, too.

This understanding of the revolt against disorder opens to Barth's understanding of the "Lordless powers." If, from the human perspective, all are responsible for and oppressed by a situation irreducible to their individual agency, this situation can be described in its own right as subjection to the powers. Following the Augustinian understanding of the disrupting, disordering force of original sin, Barth claims that humanity's alienation from God leads at once to the liberation of human capacities from conscious human control. Just as humans refuse peaceful fellowship with God and each other under God's command, human forces are now set at odds with each other and humans themselves in an attempt at ruthless autonomy:

> Parallel to the history of his emancipation from God there runs that of the emancipation of his own possibilities of life from himself: the history of the overpowering of his desires, aspirations, and will by the power, the superpower, of his ability. His capacities when he uses them, as Goethe describes so vividly and with such frightening profundity in his poem *The Sorcerer's Apprentice*, becomes spirits with a life and activity of their own, lordless indwelling forces. To be sure, he thinks he can take them in hand, control them, and direct them as he pleases, for they are undoubtedly the forces of his own possibilities and capacities, of his own ability. In reality, however, they escape from him, they have already escaped from him.[72]

For Foucault, strategic situations of power, made up of power relations, have their origin in small-scale force relations. For Barth, a formally analogous conceptual history holds: human forces, rooted in created capacities, exceed human control and take on a life of their own, becoming "entities with their own right and dignity" who "act at their own pleasure, as absolutes, without [the human person], behind him, over him, and against him."[73] Foucault's forces are nothing but the elements of the physical world in relation to and in combination with human agency; Barth's forces, though situated within a theological narrative and prehistory, act the same way and are composed of the same elements, despite his anthropological focus. The condition of original sin is not merely humanity's rebellion against God, "but also the rebellion unleashed by it," the disintegration of the human world that results from the alienation of human powers from human will.[74]

The world is the realm of the powers, if not exhaustively so. They may only have a pseudo-objectivity; they may never fully thwart God's

---

72. Barth, *Christian Life*, 214.
73. Barth, *Christian Life*, 214.
74. Barth, *Christian Life*, 215.

providential care for creation. The powers cannot have an autonomous existence—the "ontological godlessness" that they aspire to—and we are thus left to speak of them "only in consciously mythological terms."[75] Yet, the theologian must speak of them because she perceives that they are real and efficacious. "World history," Barth claims, "being the history of [humanity] . . . is also the history of innumerable absolutisms of different kinds, of forces that are truly and properly man's own but that have won a certain autonomy, independence, and even superiority in relation to him."[76] We should understand such "absolutisms" not merely as ideologies (though the category certainly includes those) but as reified abstractions: the representations of human capacities and forces, themselves efficacious though they cannot exist without humanity. Their power is parasitic on human power, but nonetheless real. "There they are," Barth continues, "powerful enough in and in spite of their impotence to be too much for the one who can and should be their lord and to take him to task, to master him who should master them, influencing, determining, and controlling his thought and speech and also his purposes and enterprises for himself and in his common life with others."[77]

Foucault's central claim—that power is productive—finds resonance in Barth's assertion that the powers are the drivers of society, the sources of "great and small conventions, customs, habits, traditions, and institutions."[78] The powers do not merely reflect back what humans choose and desire, but actively generate and proliferate social practices—including choices and desires—that find support among individuals. In this light, Barth can make his strongest statement about their influence: "It is not really people who do things, whether leaders or the masses. Through mankind's fault, things are invisibly done without and above man, even above the human individual in all his uniqueness, by the host of absolutisms, of power that seek to be lordless and that make an impressive enough attempt to exhibit and present themselves as such."[79] From this perspective, we can say that the proximate agents of world history, the engines of the material lives of human communities, are these powers, struggling to set themselves up outside the

---

75. Barth, *Christian Life*, 215–16.
76. Barth, *Christian Life*, 216. As Barth put it in the *Römerbrief*, ours "is a world in which things move towards independence, a world of things existing powerfully in their own right, a world of principalities and powers and thrones and dominations. Like men, the world is imprisoned. As their world, it unwillingly participates in the perversity of men and shares their damaged relationship with God" (169).
77. Barth, *Christian Life*, 216.
78. Barth, *Christian Life*, 216.
79. Barth, *Christian Life*, 216.

influence of God. Human agency, individual or collective, takes place within their frame and, to an extent, as a result of their prior determinations. These powers—the "negative presupposition" of the Christian gospel[80]—make up the substance of social and political orders, and without an understanding of how they work, we cannot fully understand those orders. The prayer, "thy kingdom come," then, has content because these powers make up the world that is the vis-à-vis of God's kingdom: God's kingdom would come from the restoration of human forces to peaceable fellowship with humanity, itself dependent on the restoration of humanity's peaceable fellowship with God.

The powers are themselves heterogeneous, encompassing a range of aspects of human life. Some are political: the demonic in politics that expresses itself as empire—whether monarchical, aristocratic, democratic, nationalistic, or socialistic—is itself inhuman as such.[81] Thus does power no longer protect the right, but rather "subjects the right to itself and makes triumphant use of it. The state no longer serves man; man, both ruled and ruling, has to serve the state."[82] Barth sees Hobbes's *Leviathan* emerging repeatedly in the totalitarianisms of the twentieth century, intoxicating and seducing citizens into identifying with it. Devastated as Europe was midcentury, Barth asserts that "the step from the possibility of adult man to the reality of man under age and under tutelage has proved to be a frighteningly small one. . . . We need to realize that no state of any kind is or has or will be immune to the tendency to become at least a little Leviathan."[83] Another of the named powers is Mammon, the impulse toward self-absolutization on the part of our resources, as well as our productive and consumptive capacities.[84] In its modern form, Mammon is closely associated with money specifically and capital and economic forces generally. Both powerful and unpredictable, money holds sway not just over marketized necessities of life, but also politics and war, the hopes and imaginations of people living under its spell: it would seem that people possess money, but all too often money possesses us. Other spiritual powers—Barth disavows any attempt to survey them all—include ideologies, especially those that posit an absolute or "quasi-divine" normativity.[85] In addition to these "spiritual" or abstract forces, there are also "chthonic powers," those associated in the first place with physical practices and not abstractions. The chthonic powers draw

---

80. Barth, *Christian Life*, 217.
81. Barth, *Christian Life*, 220.
82. Barth, *Christian Life*, 220.
83. Barth, *Christian Life*, 221.
84. Barth, *Christian Life*, 221–22.
85. Barth, *Christian Life*, 225.

humanity "downward" toward a vicious form of mundane existence, rather than "upward" toward idolatry or false righteousness, but they nonetheless subordinate humanity to their influence. Technology, fashion, sport, progress, and others all capture the human imagination and work against the human good.[86] This host of powers tears apart the individual and society among themselves, allowing no true rest or peace during their reign.[87] They illustrate and embody the plight of humanity in the world.

As a result of humanity's captivity to the powers, there is a limit to the efficacy and an irresolution in the character of human activity. In a Christian idiom, building the kingdom of God with human hands is impossible not just because it must come "from above" but also because of the ambiguously tragic nature of human attempts to build it. From our position, the deepest hope for liberation has to come from "outside," a discontinuity with the world that we ourselves cannot achieve:

> The kingdom is not a kind of continuing, prolonging, excelling, and completing of what people may, as commanded, attempt and undertake in a more or less rich understanding of their relationship to it or in some other form of reflection on what is good. . . . It is instead God's own action, which does not merge into the best of human action, for example, that of Christian faith or the Christian church, which does not mingle with it, let alone identify itself with it, which remains free and independent over against it, and which in its purity and freedom is God's gracious, reconciling, and finally redeeming action. . . . It is God's work alone, which as it is revealed to them can be known by people in faith, gratefully hailed and extolled by them, and then attested and proclaimed, but which cannot in any circumstances be made their own operation or promoted, augmented, or perhaps improved by their action.[88]

From this Christian theological perspective, God alone has access to exteriority relative to the world as a whole.[89] For Barth, this means that God's

86. Barth, *Christian Life*, 229–31.
87. Barth, *Christian Life*, 233.
88. Barth, *Christian Life*, 240.
89. I have phrased it this way to be able to hold two commitments simultaneously. First, I want to hold open a widely-subscribed theological conviction that God's life *in se* is explicable (if only to and for Godself) without reference to the powers of the world, and on my definitions, this means that God must have access to exteriority—indeed, God's life is in an important respect characterized by it. Second, however, I have framed this in the slightly abstract and metaphorical terms of "access" because I think the gospel entails that God does not, finally, dwell solely in exteriority relative to the powers, but in fact enters into solidarity with life under their subjection.

action must be understood rigorously according to the category of grace. Though the implications of this concept will be discussed below, suffice it to say for now that the negative implication of grace is the radical nonexteriority of human life and action: all of it, even the actions undertaken in obedience to God's commands, bears the indelible mark of the world, the sphere of the powers. No resistance to their working manages to overthrow them; only God can overcome them.

Still, this distinction between divine and human activity does not authorize indifference, but rather itself calls for this resistance. Indeed, "precisely because perfect righteousness stands before them as God's work, precisely because [humans] are duly forbidden to attempt the impossible, precisely because all experiments in this direction are prevented and prohibited, they are with great strictness required and with great kindness freed and empowered to do what they can do in the sphere of the relative possibilities assigned to them, to do it very imperfectly yet heartily, quietly, and cheerfully."[90] The human person is responsible just because she finds herself within this situation of subjection to the powers, as one has both a passive and an active share in the condition of this world. In spite of this implication and, in some cases, guilt, all people are summoned and empowered to pray for the coming reign of God and to oppose, resist, and revolt against corruption in the scope of their agency.[91] Even though human agency cannot establish peaceable structures of the world itself, Barth believes that one should not be resigned to apathy, for that agency can make a significant, if relative, difference. Not by changing the course of the world as such but by fighting for human righteousness against human unrighteousness, one makes humanity "the proper object of [one's] interest, by making man's right and life and freedom and joy their theme."[92] Inasmuch as this entails a witness against the powers—exposing them, working to frustrate their influence and suggest new and better ways of life—the "little righteousness" allowed to humans calls those who will hear it to resistance. Such resistance, itself a human capacity, always remains within the frame of the world—or, to use Foucault's terms again, within the strategic situation of power—but it nevertheless may make human life so much more free, joyful, and just, and is therefore received as a command of God.

From this vantage point, we can see two advantages to employing Barth in this argument and comparison with Foucault. It is likely the case that one could use other theologians or social ethicists, and arrive at similar

---

90. Barth, *Christian Life*, 265.
91. Barth, *Christian Life*, 267.
92. Barth, *Christian Life*, 267.

conclusions. For example, Reinhold Niebuhr, who writes that "the highest reaches of individuality . . . are dependent upon the social substance out of which they arise," offers an anthropology that entangles sin, social structure, and the nature of hope. That anthropology leads us to a self-critical and measured posture toward reform that resonates with some resources in Barth, and even draws similar criticisms.[93] Likewise, Dietrich Bonhoeffer articulates an ethics of responsibility that asks not how to extricate oneself from involvement in the world, but how to make possible livable lives for future generations, and the personal dimensions of that demand.[94] Without gainsaying the prospects of a similar line of argumentation using either of these figures (or others), Barth offers a unique opportunity here. First, Barth stands in a clear relationship to the later interpreters of the powers in such a way that appeals to his theological resources are also an internal critique of their arguments. Much of the work of the second-generation theorists of the powers draws energy from Barth, and I will claim below that this energy is, in fact, circumscribed in ways that limit its potential. To appeal to Barth, therefore, is directly to engage in contest over the interpretation and implications of the touchstone convictions in play in this discursive tradition. Second, the eschatological emphasis of Barth's thought, particularly the way that its eschatology regiments human moral work and God's grace, opens Barth to clearer comparison with Foucault on the topic of exteriority. Though Barth has much to say about that which lives in the realm of exteriority—the divine—two results of his eschatology save these affirmations from special pleading relative to a Foucauldian social analysis: the clear distinction of exteriority from the elements of this world (as discussed in chapter 3), and the reflexive reserve placed on even Barth's own claims about the realm of the divine (as discussed in chapter 4). Reading Barth alongside Foucault, therefore, offers some tactical advantages in argumentation, even if this does not rule out the possibility of alternative comparisons.

Barth thus gives a maximal reading of the powers that inscribes human agency completely within the sphere of their influence, the world. The normative framing of this narrative—situated as it is within a sequence of creation, fall, and redemption both actualized and awaited—lends moral and theological energy to its call for resistance to the powers. However, the phenomenon as such, for Barth, proves remarkably similar to the description offered by Foucault of the relationship between force, power, and larger strategic situations. Barth renders the mythical picture of human subjection to the powers presented in the New Testament in terms of the social

---

93. See, e.g., Mathewes, *Theology of Public Life*, 239–40.
94. Bonhoeffer, "After Ten Years," 7.

structures, arrangements, and practices that give shape and substance to human life. In this respect, Barth's method neither takes the mythical picture at face value, nor does it simply dismiss that picture as a non-kerygmatic remnant. Instead, Barth expands and recasts the image of human agency, allowing for what Foucault might call "intention without subjectivity." Barth's collateral theological commitments—in this case, to a certain understanding of grace and the relationship between God and creation—lead him rigorously to deny that human activity can succeed in defeating the powers and establishing the reign of God. Yet, Barth takes exactly these commitments to mean that a kind of activism is called for, an activism that will often take the form of resistance. Though the realization of the final defeat of the powers will always remain deferred unto the eschaton, one can fight to loosen their grip on one's social and political circumstances to meaningful effect.

AGAINST EXTERIORITY

Barth's account of the powers thus stands in clear relation to, and near the headwaters of, Christian theological treatments of the powers generally. Foucault, on the other hand, is intelligible without any theological background. Yet, with these two accounts of power and the powers,[95] we can see a claim emerging that, with some translation into their respective idioms and despite their narrative disparities, we can ascribe to both Barth and Foucault. That claim, I will argue, can reorganize our understanding of the issues in play, leading us to see an affinity between Barth and Foucault that is in many ways more significant than the confessional differences.

That claim can be characterized as a rigorous denial of positions of exteriority: the domain of the powers is fully coextensive with human life, and no human attempt to resist their influence or activity can succeed in establishing human life apart from them. Though human life and activity may not be exhaustively explained by the work of the powers, they can never be thought as autonomous with respect to the powers. Though resistance may have dramatic consequences, that resistance never serves to remove human life from the sphere of the powers.

---

95. From here on, I will use "the powers" even in discussions using Foucault (though I will still use "power," as appropriate) on the assumption that the argument of this chapter is successful enough to justify the idea that the two share a single pivot in their positioning of human agency relative to structural power. Though Foucault's analytics of power is originally methodological, it presumes and works upon a plurality of institutions, regimes, and structures that exist as historical phenomena. As a result, the plural and narrative (only in the sense of being historical "actors") aspects of the term are appropriate for Foucault as well as for Barth.

Simultaneously with this claim, we can introduce the language of "complicity" with the powers. In addition to saying that human activity has no access to positions of exteriority, with Foucault, we can say, using Barth's anthropological account of the powers, that complicity is total in scope: all human acts are complicit with the activities of the powers, even when that action seeks to resist the proximate mechanics and purposes of a given structure.[96] That resistance may be effective; it may exhaust all the possibilities available to the one resisting. It may be heroic and beautiful, subtle, thoughtful, or prescient. Yet, because of the dependence of human life and agency upon the powers, resistance always stands in intrinsic, constituting relation to the powers. Resistance becomes embodied in the resources given by the powers and cannot help but to bear their imprint. Thus, even the best resistance—with all of the differences that it makes—does not suffice to eradicate one's complicity with the powers. In what follows, I will call this a "total complicity" account of the powers, contrasted with an "exteriority" account.

Chapters 3 and 4 will defend this claim of total complicity, but a distinction must immediately be made to guard against a significant misunderstanding. In a court of law, one who is an "accomplice" bears some share of the guilt for a crime; complicity as such, in this context, entails blameworthiness, and our typical use of the concept follows this pattern. In its appropriation into this argument, however, "complicity" is distinct from "blameworthiness" in signifying only a relation of implication and not directly imputing moral responsibility for any particular activity of the powers. In itself, complicity means only that we are directly and categorically accountable for our response to the powers, to which we are always already related. To be sure, complicity may become the medium for such blameworthiness: we may and often do mismanage this responsibility. Yet, complicity itself only poses the challenge of responsibility; it does not overdetermine our defeat. On the other hand, if it is the case that complicity is total in scope, then certain types of exculpation are complicated, if not ruled out, beforehand. One cannot rest easy in the thought that a particular exercise of power is simply unrelated to one's own life, for that thought misrecognizes the basic connection created by our complicity. Claims to "innocence" that

---

96. On this way of thinking, it is possible that there exist structures sufficiently remote from one's historical and cultural location that one is not complicit with them in particular (for example, a hypothetical form of economic exchange found only in a remote corner of the contemporary world). However, complicity would emerge with those structures immediately upon contact with one's life, and if the powers are seen as the more abstract, high-altitude patterns (exploitation, possessiveness), one would already be complicit with them in other forms.

depend on one's nonparticipation in such an exercise of power do not suffice to exculpate that one from blameworthiness, since one's complicity may show an unacknowledged responsibility that calls one to act. To say that one is complicit, however, is only to say that one is liable to such blameworthiness because of social relationships to the phenomena of the powers.

In making this distinction, I am attempting to address a well-founded worry that a total complicity account blurs the very real differences in social location and resulting responsibilities among persons. Total complicity, it could be argued, entails a particularly egregious form of victim-blaming, since there are more and less influential people who have contrasting forms of complicity with and possibilities for action in response to the powers. Though chapters 5 and 6 will discuss how a total complicity account still allows for responsible action within the world, several aspects of a response on behalf of total complicity accounts bear mentioning up front. First, it can and should be an aspect of the use of the grammar provided by a total complicity account that it continues to differentiate between persons in terms of the particular shape of their complicity with and responsibility for the powers. Indeed, I see a virtue of this account in its ability to speak faithfully to the personal and small-scale aspects of the powers' working: in short, the world is a stage of powerful others, but those "others" flow in and through us. The dual ethical imperative and possibility occasioned by this set of dynamics is embodied well in the labor strike. Precisely because the value-capturing mechanism of capital works in and through the labor of the worker, the worker—exactly through their differentiation from the boss or owner of capital—is implicated in the system of production, which implication can also be the occasion for changing how that system functions. That relations of power include each of us is a prompt for reflection on the material circumstances of our social and relational lives, a reflection that can detail the form and sites of possible resistance.

Second, there are cases of domination in which the relationship between one's complicity and one's guilt is so attenuated that it becomes urgent to foreground the judgment of violence and injustice. Paying detailed attention to such cases requires reading social life against the grain of the assumption that our outrage and motivation for action require innocence or perfect victims. For instance, Primo Levi explicates Nazi concentration camps as a gray zone, set up to make victims complicit in their own victimization, often producing subjects who are not simply opposed to *but put to the uses of* the perpetrators of injustice.[97] There are two temptations in relation to cases

---

97. Levi, *Drowned and the Saved*. See also the discussion in Rothberg, *Implicated Subject*, 39.

like these that are photo negatives of each other. On the one hand, one can respond by proceeding under the norm to avoid "blaming the victim," and set oneself up not to attend sufficiently to the actual mechanism by which such horrors work themselves out in history and society. On the other hand, an analytical approach to description can imply (or claim!) an inappropriate leveling of responsibility, in which conclusions about the scope of complicity substitute for a pointed and ruthless demand for change. The public witness who exercises the right kind of discernment must refuse both a moralistic analytical tidiness and an informed resignation to the morass of guilt: the scope of complicity does not in principle—and in some cases *must not*, on the basis of the norms of solidarity and common flourishing that motivate this argument—preclude us from naming the beneficiaries, influential agents, and ruling classes within configurations of the powers, and demanding that we proceed differently. As a result, it is practically useful and analytically responsible to maintain a distinction between complicity as the occasion for responsibility, and local judgments of blame, among others, that would direct our application of social pressure and demand.

However, and third, total complicity complicates the roles of victim and perpetrator, powerless and powerful, by insisting that in certain fundamental respects we all are subject to the powers' effects in and through our very selves. The fluidity among social roles—often with deadly high stakes and real ethical significance—still occurs within a larger pattern of human participation in and dependence on the powers as such, and this reality exerts an influence over our social world. All of which is to say: before it is a political and moral achievement, a certain kind of solidarity just describes human social life. The grounds for this book's use of the highly vexed first-person plural "we" dwell in a critical, theological account that theorizes precisely from our lack of common cause and fellow-feeling to a mutual implication in a world of powers that lives within, through, and beyond us. "We," even used to describe my immediate neighbors, live very different lives, and even our differentiated destinies are entangled through the structures that generate and hold the sense-making patterns of our world. These systems are, as Olúfẹ́mi Táíwò asserts, complex and large-scale, but not abstract: they are composed of the practices and patterns that connect the materials of our everyday lives.[98] They organize our interactions by building the world in which they happen,[99] answering to intentions that are only partially explicable with reference to the intentions of actual people. As our ecoconscious households from chapter 1 know, we certainly do not all

---

98. Táíwò, *Elite Capture*, 11.
99. Táíwò, *Elite Capture*, 99.

contribute to our plight identically, but we collaborate, for better or worse, to make a climate in which we all live.

We can now frame the argument of this book in its proper terms. In chapter 1, I considered the significant contributions to Christian social and political thought made by theological accounts of the powers, but raised a concern about the paths of resistance that they tend to suggest. Those paths depend on Christian ethical activity that is not complicit with, and hence occupies space exterior to, the realm of the powers. In contrast, both Barth and Foucault invest their anthropologies with robust accounts of social structures and their influence over human life but without holding in reserve some exteriority from which one can resist the powers. Though one might suspect the relevant differences to be drawn along confessional lines—Barth with his Christian conspirators on one side, Foucault on the other—this total extent of complicity inflects the descriptions of the powers given by Barth and Foucault such that we can perceive a surprising likeness between them. As I will argue below, this view of complicity shifts and recasts the possibilities for resistance in significant ways.

As this book's subtitle suggests, though, I intend for this not merely to be an argument but also a form of spiritual practice. The point of situating this argument theologically is not merely to express the convictions of this book's author, or to appeal to a new audience with deliverances from critical theory or the social sciences. My object is to explicate and make available a way of perceiving and experiencing oneself as alive and free in the world in a way that takes seriously, as an element of our encounter with ourselves, each other, and God, the constraints on and ambivalences of our agency. Ancient traditions insisted that the human poses a microcosmos, a recapitulation of the forms of life that are not finally alien to us. In relation to this point, two elements of this political spirituality come into focus.

First, at least for the persons who are likely to read this book, there is no encounter with a "self" that is unmediated by the forms of identity, meaning, and relation that compose the world, in all its glory and all its horror. In unforgettable words near the opening of his *Minima Moralia*, Theodor Adorno frames exactly this point: the one "who wishes to know the truth about life in its immediacy must scrutinize it in its estranged form, the objective powers that determine individual existence even in its most hidden recesses."[100] A spirituality composed of solidarity does not primarily enjoin warm sentiments about one's neighbors. Instead, it perceives and devotes its resources to living into the stake we have in each other, the fact of our ineradicable entanglement with each other that results from the

---

100. Adorno, *Minima Moralia*, 15.

structures of common life that we share. That spirituality is no less spiritual—no less about love of God and neighbor, nor less reflexively attentive to who one is and is becoming—because it takes place in the street or on strike rather than in a pew. Moreover, if these basic premises regarding our (unequally) shared implication in the powers are true, one is not changing the subject from a properly "theological" rendering of the powers to a "secular" analysis of power: it is, instead, exactly a spiritual practice of solidarity to consider who one is in the perception of and alongside one's neighbors, even beyond confessional location. Any open-eyed turn toward the self is simultaneously a turn toward others in one's world, the common origin of the complex gift of our selfhood.

Second, a political spirituality that can only find itself in and through an encounter with the world has to abandon habits inculcated especially by forms of Christian theology that guide us to look for purity, or righteousness, or exteriority that we can attain through a faithful exercise of agency. We need things that are worth striving for, that call us forward into repentant, loving communion with each other and our world. But the spiritual practice recommended here would direct us away from devoting our energies toward a defense of our innocence, an attempt to separate oneself in location or in narration from our neighbors, or an ever-more fastidious categorizing and accounting of the sins of others. A political appropriation of the concept of *epektasis* articulated by Gregory of Nyssa[101]—counseling an eternal growth in love and spiritual capacity, ever being stretched out by the work of God—would encourage us instead to stamp imperfect figures of love on the social forms that pattern our minds and hearts. This means a rigorous denial to oneself of the pleasures of self-righteousness and condemnation in favor of finding creative new grounds on which to meet a wider range of one's neighbors with a hope toward transformation.[102]

From this book's analytical perspective, exteriorities involve the misrecognition of the character and composition of one's own agency; from the position of its spirituality, the misrecognition of exteriorities entails a lost opportunity to pray and work exactly from the site of "failure," the nonescape that leaves us together, for good and ill. I proceed in what follows from the default assumption that the reader can have a meaningful encounter

101. See, e.g., Gregory of Nyssa, "On the Soul," 244–45.

102. Alexis Shotwell describes this well in ethical terms: "Aiming at individual purity can produce a seemingly satisfying self-righteousness in the scant moments we achieve it, but since it is ultimately impossible, aiming for purity will always disappoint. Orienting ourselves toward flourishing, toward the contingent proliferation of ways of being we cannot predict, toward surprise, opens us to the possibility that the world can go on" (*Against Purity*, 203).

with the possibility that they are complicit with the powers in ways that are elusive, obscure, or surprising. Despite the crucial importance of historicizing and situating these sorts of claims for description of the political world, I intend for the creative work of this book to move with the energy that can come from finding oneself in such unanticipated moments of recognition. There are limits to the extent of the political descriptions that follow: they are taken from reflections on Europe and North America, largely, though the structural powers forming those worlds have been exported elsewhere, often through force and dispossession. I do not address much attention in what follows to strained hypotheticals or narrating obscure, extraordinary cases. This book is invested in the question, "Could one conceivably access an exteriority to the powers?," but it is driven more basically by a question that the reader can ask themselves, for this book is not the judge of its answer: "Do I actually inhabit one?" The argument here is that it is usefully reorienting in one's relationship to oneself to be habituated into answering this question in the negative, even if that habit does not serve every political use, even if it does not alone do justice to every story that needs to be told.

Why should theorists of the powers refuse such exteriorities? Are there not good theological reasons for holding apart some spaces of sanctity amidst the world to which God might call Christians in nonconformed resistance? What evidence do we have for the claims to total complicity that Barth and Foucault make? The following two chapters will serve to motivate the claim of total complicity by arguing against exteriorities, using both theological resources from Barth and social scientific resources from Foucault. Chapter 3 will consider voluntary forms of resistance under the theological heading of ecclesiology. Chapter 4 will consider intellectual forms of resistance under the theological heading of revelation. By considering these topics, I hope that this account of the powers without exteriorities becomes more fully alive with a critical, analytical energy that can help us live out the solidarity with the world that this picture suggests.

CHAPTER 3

Vulnerability and the Visible Church

SEEKING THE OUTSIDE

On New Year's Day, 2011, Toronto couple Kathy Witterick and David Stocker had their third child. After Storm Witterick's birth, the couple sent an email to family and close friends, announcing that they had decided "not to share Storm's sex for now—a tribute to freedom and choice in place of limitation, a standup to what the world could become in Storm's lifetime (a more progressive place?)"[1] While Kathy Witterick, in the media attention that followed, was careful to grant that it would be naïve to attempt to raise a "genderless" child, the couple asserted that they wanted "to give their third child the chance to discover who he or she is, without the parade of pink and barrage of blue."[2] This insistence reiterated their original plea, given amidst what they identify as the "tyranny of pronouns" and the atmosphere of overbearing parents: "Please can you just let Storm discover for him/herself what s(he) wants to be?!"[3]

Even if Storm's parents hold to a nuanced understanding of their child's inevitable collisions with the gender order, a certain motif runs through these pleas: while one might not be able to exist strictly without relation to the domain of gendered life, we can hold out hope that one might set the terms of that engagement, that one could discover for oneself a desired and desirable form of relating to gender, and, in so doing, overcome the limitations of the given order in the name of freedom. Even if one faces questions whose assumptions seem constraining and which garble one's attempt at

1. Poisson, "Parents Keep Child's Gender Secret," para. 9.
2. Poisson, "Outcry," para. 7.
3. Poisson, "Parents Keep Child's Gender Secret," para. 21.

self-expression, that encounter can happen within the frame of one's prior, free decision about oneself: for example, after a young child has made a personal discovery of self-identity. Paradigmatically, the two relevant phenomena—the gender order and the decision about oneself in relation to it—relate to each other, but only externally. One can hold oneself (or be held) outside that order for the purpose of establishing a prior relationship to oneself, in light of which one subsequently engages that order. The inevitability of that engagement results from the omnipresence of gender outside oneself, in the world, but such an engagement can be held at bay, perhaps in a domestic sphere in which a sanctity of personal decision remains.

Storm's parents sought to give Storm, in this gesture, a chance to resist the gender order's ravenous appetite to categorize, mold, and constrain Storm's identity. They are right to do so: the prescriptions, implicit and explicit, of gender performance are often violent and even more often restrictive of meaningful self-expression. Their public critics often react by appealing to bioessentialism or other forms of gendering that make their decision deeply sympathetic to this author. If I wonder aloud about how this attempt at liberation is conceived, it is not because I insist that people accommodate themselves to the patriarchal gender binary and all that comes with it. Instead, one should think carefully about the implications of this case and others like it precisely because of the danger of underestimating the craftiness of gender and of overestimating the success of our attempts to escape it.

A similar dynamic structures certain instances of discourse about the powers, wherein one's decisions about oneself exist at a remove from the influence of the powers and can establish one's relationship to them. Whether or not one can "opt-out" permanently or entirely, one can—and on these accounts, freedom *requires* that one can—make voluntary commitments that set limits to the influence of the powers on one's identity. Perhaps one must establish some kind of relationship to dominant regimes of gender and sexuality; on these accounts, such relationships can be the object of our own unconditioned decision, an expression of subjectivity undetermined by the powers. Perhaps one cannot avoid some forms of participation in a society whose political institutions pursue war and other violent means to their ends; on these accounts, though, one's pacifism or nonviolent witness (say, to the "peaceableness" of the kingdom of God) suffice to distinguish one's own activity from the activities of the ruling authorities. Inasmuch as these decisions are personal, voluntary determinations of one's own relationship to the particular constellation of the powers one faces, we might call them "moral exteriorities."[4]

However, as this chapter attempts to demonstrate, these moral commitments do not exist in and of themselves. Rather, they are typically communicated and nurtured by larger communities, from which we emerge and without which no commitments are possible. Thus, articulations of these forms of exteriority constantly oscillate between moral forms and communal forms in a way that would equally justify the term "communal exteriorities." Such communities are formed when people who make similar commitments with regard to the powers come together in fellowship and mutual encouragement, for the sake of cultivating these commitments in others or activism rooted within them, for their reinforcement or for pedagogy, and so on. The self-understandings of such communities, I will argue, tend toward the assumption that on the basis of the voluntary commitments of their members in the face of the powers, these communities—or at least, the ideal communities that they imperfectly embody—stand outside the influence of the powers.[5] Such a self-understanding imagines nonconformed moral community as an alternative to the domain of the powers, as "other" than the world.

Since attempts at this type of exteriority, then, can vacillate between individual and collective expressions, I will use the term "voluntary exteriorities" to gather both these moral and communal exteriorities. A theorist who posits a voluntary exteriority argues for a position from which, because one or one's group successfully determines the forms which their relations to the powers will take, that one or that group cannot be seen as complicit in at least some of the activities of the powers. On these accounts, voluntary, conscious commitment suffices to distance one or one's community from the domain of the powers—whether absolutely or partially—such that one or one's community can critique the powers without simultaneously performing self-critique.

Theologians who hold to the possibility of voluntary exteriorities tend to argue that the "church" (the "true church": at least a part of the gathered community of self-identified Christians) dwells in exteriority to the "world."

---

4. That is, these voluntary commitments themselves are forms of exteriority: it could perhaps still be the case that no person dwells in that "other space" fully or purely. However, inasmuch as one does opt for these forms of nonconformity, one obtains a position of exteriority.

5. Notice that here I only intend those communities that are both formed by and understand themselves as forms of resistance to the wider world. Clearly, there are many forms of human community that are not defined vis-à-vis the world in these ways, and they are not the subject under examination here.

As discussed above, the world is the jurisdiction of the powers, taken in their totality: the object of reprobation and rejection in the Johannine literature[6] and elsewhere in the New Testament. In such theologies, the church is not only called to but achieves some measure of opposition to the world; the church is somehow exceptional, a particular site of God's redeeming activity as it becomes a nonconformed community. While these theorists frequently concede that the line between church and world divides not only groups of people but also the impulses, habits, actions, and convictions within each person—and that each member inhabits the church only ambiguously as a result—they nevertheless regard one as non-complicit just to the extent that one does, in fact, identify with the church.

This chapter argues that, in fact, these depictions of voluntary exteriorities in general—and what I call "ecclesial exceptionalism" in particular—neglect the forms of complicity with the powers that remain despite the efforts of one or one's community to oppose or refuse them. To do this, it examines the ecclesiology of Mennonite social ethicist and theologian John Howard Yoder. Yoder's account will be helpful because of its explicit connections between the narrative of the powers and ecclesiology. I will show how Yoder's understanding, especially in its emphasis on the "otherness" of the church, represents a form of voluntary exteriority. Then, I will introduce resources from Barth's ecclesiology to delineate an alternative account of the church in which, despite the church's apparent relative differences from other structures, it is decisively a part of the world. I will compare these two authors' descriptions of baptism in order to display the stakes for understanding willful human activity. Foucault's account of the human person as constituted from social material both before and after particular exercises of "agency" will illustrate the reasons for siding against any form of exceptionalism. Finally, I will examine the larger picture of agency that is produced by this refusal of voluntary exteriorities and its stakes in terms of our thinking about the possibilities and demands of meaningful resistance.

A PEOPLE CALLED TO OPPOSITION

First, it is important to name certain facts: John Howard Yoder committed grievous violations against women, and he did so despite numerous calls to stop and interventions from sources he should have heeded. The field of Christian ethics is still grappling with how to relate this fact to the reception of his work, particularly as we wrestle with how enmeshed his crimes

---

6. See, e.g., 1 John 2:15–17 and similar passages. This usage ought to be distinguished from the "world" in the sense of cosmos or creation as such.

were with his thought.[7] There is a persuasive case to be made simply to set his work aside in favor of others whose lives exemplify a more effective commitment to justice, or at least until some consensus emerges about the appropriate way to interpret his thought in light of his actions. I include him in this section to contribute to this conversation, not to ignore it, because I think that Yoder's thoroughgoing belief in the attainability of the "outside," and his resulting (eschatological) confidence that he stood apart from the usual dangers and demands of the gender order, is deeply relevant to that conversation. Many arguments about how his thought set the stage for his behavior have focused on the social practice of revolutionary subordination. Another important dimension of this work is considering his abuses in light of his theological conviction about exteriority to the relevant orders of gender and power (akin to his brand of ethical perfectionism), to which we now turn.

Yoder was skilled at marshaling historical and theological resources to cast Jesus's ministry as a directly political intervention. Once understood, according to Yoder, the political character of Jesus's person and work inflects the whole of Christian doctrine. The synoptic gospels' dependence on the *Torah* and Deuteronomic histories, with their full vision of Israel as embodying God's demands of mutual social care, is no longer occluded by a spiritualizing reading that tends toward supersessionism.[8] The temptations Jesus faced, both in the wilderness and throughout his ministry, are best understood as the persistent possibility of violent revolution as a way around the demands of nonconformed discipleship.[9] The cross of Christ thereby takes on its historically appropriate political overtones.[10] Yoder's reinterpretations—or, better, retrievals—of Christian commonplaces in terms of what he believes to be their immediate and historical political significance multiply, both in *The Politics of Jesus* and in his other works. Yet, the central and organizing dynamic of Christian and Christoform social ethics is the opposition between church, the voluntary community of disciples, and world, the sphere of influence of the powers.

Yoder gathers the diverse group of New Testament references to the powers with the notion of "structure." In everyday use, "structure" means a visible institution with a nameable membership; at other times, it refers to

---

7. See Goossen, "Defanging the Beast"; Guth, "Doing Justice"; Cramer et al., "Theology and Misconduct." See also the final section of the preface to Pitts, *Principalities and Powers*, xv–xvii, for another reckoning with the use of Yoder. I have also learned much about this topic from Stewart-Kroeker, "What Do We Do?"

8. See, e.g., Yoder, "Implications of the Jubilee," in *Politics of Jesus*, 60–75.

9. Yoder, *Politics of Jesus*, 96.

10. Yoder, *Politics of Jesus*, 125.

coherent patterns within human dynamics visible to an analyst. What these uses have in common, however, is that they highlight "patterns or regularities that transcend or precede or condition the individual phenomena we can immediately perceive."[11] Reading Colossians 1:15–17, Yoder identifies the powers with the regularity, systems, and orders that govern creation, holding all things together in Christ.[12] Originally a gift of God, these powers were meant to mediate God's creative power by organizing reality in lieu of continuous divine interventions, making reality knowable to creatures and dependably consistent. The powers are meant to represent the language of the universe, the participation of the disparate elements of the universe in the divine purposefulness.

Yoder draws on an influential Dutch theologian, Hendrikus Berkhof, to translate the scriptural language of the powers into the terms of modern phenomena, and especially institutions.[13] Berkhof attempts to name the powers in several places. In his first list of "world powers"[14] (an exegesis

11. Yoder, *Politics of Jesus*, 137–38. It is clear enough here that Yoder prefers a "demythologized" understanding, in which the powers are not superterrestrial beings but rather the kinds of phenomena regularly treated by the social and natural sciences. In this he agrees with Berkhof that "whether they be conceived as persons or as impersonal structures of life and society, they form a category of their own" (*Christ and the Powers*, 26). The defining mark of the powers, for both Yoder and Berkhof, is *not* what kind of beings they are but the function they serve, as Berkhof argues from the translation of the Greek word αγγελοι with "messenger" rather than a term that denotes a class of beings. As Prather observes, Yoder offers not a strict exegesis of the Pauline concepts, but rather focuses on what they illuminate from the standpoint of modern treatments of power, including by going beyond those treatments in theological reflection (*Christ, Power, and Mammon*, 73).

12. Yoder, *Politics of Jesus*, 140–41. Yoder points out here that *synestēken*, often translated as "hold together" or "subsist," has the same root as the modern word, "system." We could say that in Christ all things "systematize"; creation coheres into intelligible patterns and structures that we can then name "powers." Pitts nicely describes this angle of Yoder's work as offering "theological insight into the logic of social being" (*Principalities and Powers*, xxxiii).

13. Yoder, *Politics of Jesus*, 142. David Simon, creator and writer of the television series *The Wire*, describes that series as "a Greek tragedy in which the postmodern institutions are the Olympian forces." The police department, educational system, drug economy, and government bodies are those "throwing the lightning bolts" at individuals who cannot rise above their influence by the sheer force of their agency (Simon, "Interview," para. 8). To the extent that this description of drama is palatable to a contemporary audience, so, too, should be a depiction of the powers: that depiction ought to be dismissed for its mythical expressions in terms of angels and demons no more than Simon's description of his work in terms of Greek deities. Though Simon adopts a tragic posture that, by appeal to the economy of grace, might be rendered optional, a similar hermeneutic is at work.

14. Which, importantly, he argues "rule over human life *outside of Christ*" (Berkhof, *Christ and the Powers*, 20). The way in which the church is understood as the body of Christ, and how this leads to claims of voluntary exteriority, I will explore below.

of Colossians 2), Berkhof includes human traditions, public opinion, and religious fasting or feasting—all "human commands and teachings" (Col 2:22).[15] Berkhof's second summary list includes time, space, life and death, politics and philosophy, public opinion and Jewish law, religious and cultural traditions and "the fateful course of the stars."[16] A third list enumerates these and includes the administration of justice and the order imposed by the state.[17] Berkhof argues that the powers often unite groups of people while separating them from God's intentions, using examples that are both intuitive—race, class, state, and *Volk* in Nazism and Communism—and unfortunate—Chinese ancestor reverence, Japanese Shintoism, Hinduism in India, the *polis* of the Greeks, the Roman state.[18] Yoder generates a further taxonomy of Berkhof's named powers that includes religious structures, intellectual structures, moral structures, and political structures, a totality that he acknowledges is overwhelmingly broad.[19] Yet, that broadness results from the dependence of life on such structures; without them, neither society nor history could exist. That is to say, in Yoder's words, "*we cannot live without them.*"[20]

But both creature and world have fallen, and the powers no longer express only the creative and redemptive purposes of God. In mythical terms parallel to the original sin committed by Adam and Eve, the powers rebelled by refusing modest conformity to God's purposes and arrogating to themselves the claims of absolute value characteristic of idols.[21] The powers behave as though they were the "ultimate ground of being" and accordingly demand from humanity appropriate worship.[22] This self-assertion—comprised of claims both to value and independence—is a distortion of their original, life-giving form. Though not limitlessly evil, for they continue to structure creation into a world, they subject creation, and especially humanity, to a form of slavery: enthrallment to their strength and their demand for infinite regard. Indeed, because of their role in God's intentions for creation—that is, because they are fallen creatures—their claims to value have a surface plausibility. Humanity is subjected precisely to the structures and values that are necessary for meaningful life, but without reference to what

15. Berkhof, *Christ and the Powers*, 20–21.
16. Berkhof, *Christ and the Powers*, 22.
17. Berkhof, *Christ and the Powers*, 29.
18. Berkhof, *Christ and the Powers*, 34–35.
19. Yoder, *Politics of Jesus*, 142–43.
20. Yoder, *Politics of Jesus*, 143; emphasis original.
21. Yoder, *Politics of Jesus*, 142.
22. Berkhof, *Christ and the Powers*, 30.

lies beyond them: God.[23] In this way, because the powers barricade the way to a genuinely free and loving dependence on God: "*we cannot live with them.*"[24] True human freedom—dependent, as human life is, on the powers—seems unimaginable in this fallen condition.

God decisively responds to plight of the fallen world in Christ, and that single response has two dimensions. The first dimension resembles what has been traditionally named God's work in the "orders of creation":[25] even in a fallen condition, the powers dwell within the sphere of God's sovereign providence over the course of events in the world. Namely, despite their rebellion, the powers serve God's purposes by preserving human life so as to prepare humanity for the advent of the redeeming work of Christ.[26] It is important to note that the powers have no autonomous value apart from this redemption and the church. The divine act of creation does not impart such value apart from the full economy of redemption. Yoder emphatically seeks to distance himself from accounts of the natural world that fail to affirm that "in Christ [all] values find their meaning and coherence."[27] Yet, if God is going to redeem humanity as such and not transform humans into something else, "the powers cannot simply be destroyed or set aside or ignored. Their sovereignty must be broken."[28] Thus, something akin to Calvin's "theology of patient resistance"[29] is in effect in Yoder's account of the world: God's rule in Christ extends beyond the borders of the church and into the world of the powers, which have their own role in the economy of grace despite their fallen character.

Still, Yoder consistently focuses on the second dimension of God's response to the fallen powers in Christ. That dimension includes the life of

23. Yoder, *Politics of Jesus*, 142–43. It is useful to invoke here Augustine's conception of sin as choosing the lesser good over the greater, or "enjoying" what should be "used," and vice versa. The powers, necessary to life and order, fall as a result of their overreach.

24. Yoder, *Politics of Jesus*, 143.

25. It is easy to neglect this point in Yoder's work, since his emphasis lies on the work of Christ in the church. Yoder's criticism of the "orders of creation" language is not that it posits providential work outside the church, but that it restricts such work either to the First Person of the Trinity (see *Politics of Jesus*, 144n7), thus separating Christ's work of redemption from the Father's work of creation and preservation, or fails to include religion and ideology among such orders (*Politics of Jesus*, 144). Yoder, rather, has his own notion of the relation between these orders and the *extra calvinisticum*, Christ's work *etiam extra carne*, which, he believes, retains the tension between human fallenness and divine providence within a specifically Christological account.

26. Yoder, *Politics of Jesus*, 142–43.

27. Yoder, *Politics of Jesus*, 144.

28. Yoder, *Politics of Jesus*, 144.

29. Oberman, *Dawn of the Reformation*, 258.

Christ in the flesh and his continuing work in and through the church; here Yoder weaves the directly Christological political discipleship described above into the narrative of redemption that uses the grammar of the powers. Jesus breaks the sovereignty of the powers "by living a genuinely free and human existence."[30] Willingly subjecting himself to the powers but refusing to affirm their self-glorification, Jesus set himself on an inevitable course toward crucifixion:

> Therefore his cross is a victory, the confirmation that he was free from the rebellious pretensions of the creaturely condition. Differing from Adam, Lucifer, and all the powers, Jesus did "not consider being equal with God as a thing to be seized" (Phil. 2:6). His very obedience unto death is in itself not only the sign but also the firstfruits of an authentic restored humanity. Here we have for the first time to do with someone who is not the slave of any power, of any law or custom, community or institution, value or theory.[31]

Christ's triumph over the powers lies in exposing, unmasking, and disarming them on the cross and showing that their most feared weapon—death—can be overcome by the power of God. In the Paschal Mystery, God, in and through Christ, decisively and finally defeats the powers by absorbing their strongest blow and emerging victorious nonetheless. Christ's freedom thus refutes the powers' claim to the inevitability of their force, breaking their hypnotic spell over humanity, and provides the example of a new, nonconformed way of life. With this understanding, the confession of "Christ as Lord" can be taken in its properly doxological, rather than metaphorical, sense: as a statement about Christ's designation as God's viceroy over creation and about the sovereign victory over the powers.[32] The shape of meaningful resistance is taken from the image of Christ's freedom with respect to the powers.

The site of meaningful resistance is the church: quoting Berkhof, Yoder asserts that "the very existence of the church, in which Gentiles and Jews, who heretofore walked according to the *stoicheia* of the world, live together in Christ's fellowship, is itself a proclamation, a sign, a token to the powers that their unbroken dominion has come to an end."[33] The question of passive or aggressive resistance is therefore moot, in the first instance, as the existence of the church in a world of powers is itself "a superlatively positive

---

30. Yoder, *Politics of Jesus*, 144–45.
31. Yoder, *Politics of Jesus*, 145.
32. Yoder, "Serve Our God," 131–32.
33. Yoder, *Politics of Jesus*, 147–48.

and aggressive fact."[34] As Yoder says, again citing Berkhof, "Clairvoyant and warning words and deeds aimed at state or nation are meaningful only insofar as they spring from a church whose inner life is itself its proclamation of God's manifold wisdom to the 'powers in the air.'"[35] Hence the "otherness of the church" consists in proclaiming God's liberation and in refusing to be a community held in bondage: the church is *now* the community created by the cross, and not the sword.[36] Christ has defeated the powers; the church need not attack them. Rather, the church focuses its energies on avoiding their seductive illusions, and by its very existence, the church exemplifies the end of their uncontested reign.[37]

We have arrived at the voluntary exteriority that shows itself as ecclesial exceptionalism: the "otherness" of the church is the cornerstone of Yoder's thinking about the powers. On the apostolic meaning, "world" signifies neither creation nor nature nor the universe but instead their fallen form.[38] In other words, the world is domain of the powers, the structured whole of created reality that they make up. The church, through baptism, discipline, morality, and martyrdom, stands in marked contrast to this "world," as is evident in the pre-Constantinian expectation that members of the church not serve the world and, therefore, the state.[39] Despite this alterity, the church addressed itself to the concerns of the world based on its conviction, all apparent evidence (such as persecution) to the contrary, that Christ was also Lord over the powers. After the "Constantinian"[40] moment, the two visible realities—church and world—were fused, tragically and faithlessly.[41] As Marva Dawn describes it, the work of the church is "to proclaim the message of Christ's victory over the powers *by being a community liberated from their dominion.*"[42]

Yoder therefore attempts to retrieve the apostolic quality of the church's "otherness." If the normative view of the New Testament, on Yoder's reading, does not suffice to convey that apostolic quality, then we will have to learn

---

34. Yoder, *Politics of Jesus*, 148.
35. Yoder, *Politics of Jesus*, 148.
36. Yoder, *Politics of Jesus*, 148–49.
37. Yoder, *Politics of Jesus*, 150.
38. Yoder, "Otherness of the Church," 55.
39. Yoder, "Otherness of the Church," 56.
40. Yoder takes care to avoid making the claim that this transformation happened at the behest or even as a direct result of Constantine. "Constantine" is Yoder's symbol or label of the founding of Christendom, whatever one's evaluation of Constantine himself.
41. Yoder, "Otherness of the Church," 56–57.
42. Dawn, "Biblical Concept," 171; emphasis mine.

from history that "the church's responsibility to and for the world is first and always to be the church."[43] The meaning of history consists not in the rearrangement of the balance among or the dynamics between the powers but in the formation of an alternative community eager to do the work of God.[44] The world must be named and relegated to its proper place as structured unbelief, the space that God's patience has given to humanity within history. Christians who participate voluntarily in the church have a unique calling; Christian ethics—or discipleship—is for Christians. There may be social roles that the powers both render and consider necessary, but Christians are not to take these roles on.[45] If the interplay of the powers cannot accommodate, say, an ethic of love for enemies, this is not because of the impossibility or otherworldliness of the Sermon on the Mount but rather because that ethic is intended for people who freely choose to imitate Christ. Therefore, the "Christian soldier" represents not an uneasy compromise of values or the twofold nature of inner and outer person, but a simple oxymoron. What the world needs from the church is for the church to express and continue Christ's redemptive work through its spoken and embodied witness, not to take responsibility for managing and improving the work of the powers. Though the mission of the church consists in familiar acts of service of the neighbor, this service always imitates a Christ who unfailingly refuses the ways of the world.

In its emphasis on otherness, Yoder's ecclesiology portrays the church as what I have termed a voluntary exteriority. It is true, for Yoder, that the world unfolds under God's care. And the ultimate destiny of the world is redemption in God's kingdom, as the church is called to be today what the world called to be ultimately.[46] Such assertions might suggest that Yoder believes the church is only *called* to be, and not necessarily that it *is*, a position of exteriority; that this ecclesial-political eschatology is not realized but only realizable. However, a preponderance of the relevant textual evidence undermines this qualification.[47] The interlocking descriptions Yoder offers

---

43. Yoder, "Otherness of the Church," 61.
44. Yoder, "Otherness of the Church," 61.
45. Yoder, "Otherness of the Church," 62–63.
46. Yoder, *Body Politics*, ix.

47. There is relevant counterevidence, though. For example, Yoder claims that in holding to certain duties more strongly than others do, he does not intend to claim (nor is he in fact claiming) that he is "either in thought or in action more 'pure' than others," and "the question is not whether one can have clean hands but which kind of complicity in which kind of inevitable evil is preferable" (Yoder, "'Patience' as Method," 40). For the reasons presented here, I believe that this sentiment, though important, is just too difficult to square with the balance of Yoder's ecclesiology.

of God's agency in establishing the church, the agency of the church itself, and the membership of the church show that in his view, the church cannot but be such a voluntary exteriority.

First, the very being of the church is so closely identified with the work of God in history that it must, to some degree, dwell in exteriority. The church is the "political novelty that God brings into the world," in which human divisions are broken down "not by human idealism or democratic legalism but by the work of Christ."[48] The church, then, does not merely prefigure the kingdom of God as an analogy, but "is itself the beginning of what is to come," not only as promise of the coming kingdom but, in its character and orientation, a manifestation of that kingdom.[49] As Reinhard Hütter puts it, "eschatology turns into history in the form of the concrete and visible 'new order' of the church."[50]

Second, the church, by virtue of its own noncomplicit agency, acts from a position of exteriority; the exteriority of God's agency in and through the church is communicated to human ecclesial agency.[51] As a result of the work of Christ and the gifts of the Spirit, the covenant community is free from serving the powers and is able to deploy the criteria of good and evil that it finds in loyalty to Christ.[52] Whatever sense of reserve applies to the church's current form, its agency in the world, insofar as it lives out its calling as covenant community, represents and advances the kingdom itself.

Third, though finally subject to no sure confirmation other than faith, the exteriority of the church can be glimpsed in the character of its membership. Yoder redefines the Pauline formula "justification by grace through faith" in hopes of loosening the grasp of the Lutheran interpretive categories that lead readers to assume that justification is radically disjointed from "any

---

48. Yoder, "People in the World," 91.
49. Yoder, "People in the World," 125–26.
50. Hütter, "Church," 47.
51. James Cone, interestingly, makes a parallel claim throughout his career (though not on behalf of the "church," as Yoder understands it) when he argues that the "forces of liberation are the very activity of God" (*Black Theology of Liberation*, 3). Though Cone's early work is steeped in Barth, he tends toward this identification of God with the liberating activity of the oppressed as part of a larger theological program committed to eradicating oppression. While I take Cone's sense of the urgency of liberation with utter seriousness, I do not think this identification is the only way toward a robust theology of resistance to the powers.
52. Yoder, *Politics of Jesus*, 94. Pitts argues that the crucial dynamic for Yoder lies "between service and domination, not withdrawal and participation," and this point is well-taken (*Principalities and Powers*, 144). However, the trajectory of Yoder's argument implies that the nondominated service is an attempt to claim the noncomplicity that would come from successful withdrawal.

objective or empirical achievement of goodness by the believer."[53] Among the early Christians, the perpetuation of divisions threatened the new and inexplicable kind of community of Jews and Gentiles that the church was meant to be. The work of Christ is to break down the wall of division between these people, making peace between those who have been estranged; God's justification is to be understood as the right, because reconciled, relationship between social groups once alienated from each other.[54] The church, as a place where the divisions of the world do not hold, *is* the work of God, for Yoder: the new humanity is revealed in the inexplicable unity between those whose allegiances can be reconciled no other way.

Inasmuch as one participates in the believing, covenanted, nonconformed community that is the true church, it is safe to say that Yoder believes that one thereby dwells in a position of exteriority to the powers.[55] Perhaps no one dwells in such a space with their entire being; the habits of heart that the world instills in us are difficult to break and our success is ambiguous at best. Still, that participation offers an avenue for noncomplicit social engagement, a possibility to confidently claim that one's own works and intentions are also those of God. The church is quite capable of self-criticism on this model, but, when it fulfills its calling, it can perform a criticism of the powers that is not also a self-criticism.

What makes Yoder's version of exteriority specifically voluntary should be clear: membership in the church cannot come from historical accident of birth into Christian circumstances but only from freely undertaken commitment.[56] Once reinvigorated with the serious moral demands of discipleship, ecclesial life and unbelief cannot coexist. Yoder insists, with Menno Simons and Martin Luther, that one of the unmistakable qualities

53. Yoder, *Politics of Jesus*, 213.

54. Yoder, *Politics of Jesus*, 220–21. Thus, the relationship between divine justification and reconciliation between persons (what we might see as the social dimension of sanctification) "is not a sequential relationship," as Luther might have it.

55. Marva Dawn's appreciative remembrance of Yoder in the postscript to "The Biblical Concept of 'the Principalities and Powers'" conveys something like this imagination: "John did not let the academic institution become a 'power' in his life," she writes, using a construction that repeats in the short addendum (185). Twenty years later, it is overwhelmingly evident that, whatever vicious habits of academic culture Yoder avoided, he most certainly did allow the hierarchical structure of the academy—in some of its very worst forms—a place in his life and relationships. That failing should not at all be laid of the feet of Dawn, who means here only to appreciate a mentor; rather, it is one important fact in relation to the claims made by Yoder himself about holding oneself apart from the powers.

56. Here I clearly side with Richard Bourne, who suggests that Yoder does little work to avoid problematic understandings of voluntariness and that Barth can serve as a useful corrective to this problem. See Bourne, "Governmentality," 110.

of the true church is brotherly and sisterly love: church attendance, after all, can be forced or half-hearted, while unfeigned love cannot.[57] Church practices—such as discipline—become abusive in the absence of a clear and responsible voluntary commitment to the ecclesial life; they depend on members having committed themselves to certain standards in trust.[58] The free church stance that Yoder represents not only disestablishes Christianity as a state religion; it also refuses to enjoin the demands of the Christian life on all people. The post-Constantinian church is and ought to be the congregation of those who have freely undertaken the voluntary commitment to follow Jesus, brought together by their participation in the work of God to create a new humanity that will prove a sign and implement of the kingdom.

The object here is not to rehash the familiar argument about Yoder's "sectarianism." Depictions of the church on which it is a voluntary community called to a particular way of life requiring intentionally formative practices do not in themselves constitute a claim of exteriority. The issue is not the distinctiveness of the church from other religious communities or in relation to the wider world itself, but rather the theological claims made on behalf of that distinctiveness: whether they suffice to remove the church from the influence of—and therefore from complicity in—the world, such that one cannot participate in both at the same time.[59] And if that is the case, then our impetus toward resistance will be channeled almost exclusively through identification with the church and its practices. Should we come to believe that the church "manifests the firstfruits of true liberation from the dominion of the powers,"[60] as Mark Theissen Nation paraphrases Yoder's belief, then alternatives—both performed by Christians otherwise than in foreordained communal or sacramental practices, and those pursued by all others—are at best second-rate. These stakes are significant for determining how one ought to be disposed toward Christian resistance and the claims one makes on its behalf, and they do not depend on a relative preference for classic types of "church" or "sect."[61]

57. Yoder, "People in the World," 82.

58. Yoder, *Body Politics*, 5. Statements like this make Yoder's personal history of abuse all the more enraging, whether or not that history can reasonably be interpreted as failing to meet his own standards.

59. In the words of Paul Martens: "Despite the claim that [church and world] exist simultaneously, there is a 'radical break' between them. Because a particular social manifestation is attached to each aeon, one cannot participate in both at the same time" (*Heterodox Yoder*, 42). This section of Martens's book (44–49) is very helpful for understanding the precise claims of Yoder's distinction of church from world.

60. Nation, *John Howard Yoder*, 116.

61. In missiology, Joon-Sik Park makes an illuminating distinction: for Yoder, mission is not withdrawal from the world, but overcoming it (*Missional Ecclesiologies*,

VULNERABILITY AND THE VISIBLE CHURCH

The symbol of the church's voluntariness and the first among its sacramental practices is the believers' baptism. As one might expect, Yoder's characteristically Anabaptist understanding of this sacrament is deeply rooted in his theological vision. Where citizenship within a society or membership in a family once meant that one's Christian identity was decided by others, the Anabaptist tradition maintains that Christian discipleship in the world always demands explicit, adult commitment. Inherited social definitions—whatever class and category prevail in a given context—are no longer defining marks of the person, for baptism grafts them into a new people.[62] As the sign of induction and membership into the covenant community, baptism "*is* the formation of a new people whose newness and togetherness explicitly relativize prior stratifications and classification."[63] Baptism ushers one into a new, set apart way of being.

Storm's parents believed that their child could contract into the gender order on their own terms as an exercise of freedom. Analogously, Yoder argues that through baptism, one makes a conscious decision to join a nonconformed community, the church, that relates to the totality of the world—the sphere of the powers—from a position of exteriority. Called out from a life under the dominion of racism, one enters a covenanted community in which God reconciles people of different races and ethnicities to one another. Called out from participation in state violence, one witnesses, along with one's church, the coming kingdom in which the ethic of love for enemies is second nature to all. The believer may always have habits that call for repentance and may retain citizenship in both the heavenly and worldly kingdoms. Yet, just to the extent that one dwells in ecclesial space, one participates in God's activity to transform creation into new creation outside the domain of the fallen powers. The church is an exception: while every other structure bears the indelible stamp of the world, the church, as body of Christ, is formed by and for the reign of God. In the church, the eschaton is present among us; what is coming for the world in its totality dwells in the loving reconciliation of the new humanity.

96–101). If the stakes of this debate were settling the question of sectarianism, it would be important to evaluate the prospects and pitfalls of withdrawal. Instead, it is identifying the church with Christ's "overcoming" the world that sets the stage for my reflections.

62. Yoder, *Body Politics*, 28.
63. Yoder, *Body Politics*, 33.

CHURCH, WORLD, AND DIVINE FREEDOM

For Karl Barth, baptism into the church is no less important than for Yoder: baptism with water is the first step in the Christian life of faithfulness that corresponds to the faithfulness of God.[64] Similarly, baptism cannot be coerced or compulsory, but rather must occur as a free expression of fidelity.[65] Like Yoder, Barth defines baptism as a sign of the response to a call for disentanglement from certain social dynamics, a "breaking of all rules, customs, sequences, and arrangements."[66] Moreover, Barth, like Yoder, disavows "sacramentalistic" conceptions of baptism. For Yoder, baptism might be called "sacramental" in that God's activity and human activity simultaneously and noncompetitively dwell within the action. But over and against historical accretions of mechanical and magical substantial understandings, the ritual is specifically an ordinary human behavior. The result of baptism, on Yoder's account, is not the impartation of an invisible and mysterious grace but rather the constitution of a visible social group.[67] Barth likewise contends against the sacramental tradition that baptism with water communicates no inexplicable and invisible grace—it is the fully human work of confession and mutual association[68]—but takes his criticism significantly further. On his conception, baptism is not the means or instrument of grace itself; rather, it responds to the mystery of Jesus Christ. Baptism cannot be properly called a "sacrament," then, even in Yoder's sense.[69]

This departure matters because baptism symbolizes, obliquely, the possibility of escape: membership in a particular community of resistance, for an ecclesial exceptionalist, constitutes otherness to the world and makes possible the identification of one's action with God's action. Insofar as one is a faithful member of that community, one has removed oneself from the influence of the powers. Barth's theological reasoning about the church shows us a way of thinking about the world that calls this exceptionalism into question.

Barth rigorously maintains that the human decision to be baptized has as its presupposition and precondition divine activity to effect change in the person; in other words, baptism with the Holy Spirit, whether it come sequentially prior to or following water baptism, is the assumption of baptism

---

64. Barth, *CD* 4/4.
65. Barth, *CD* 4/4:97.
66. Barth, *CD* 4/4:130.
67. Yoder, *Body Politics*, 44.
68. Barth, *CD* 4/4:69.
69. Barth, *CD* 4/4:99.

with water.[70] Baptism has a transcendent *telos*, one beyond the capacities of those who partake in it and the power of their common action. Divine and human agencies do not overlap here; instead, human action is directed and hastens toward a divine fulfillment that it cannot achieve.[71] The divine work in baptism is deferred, not necessarily temporally, but by the interval of God's free decision. Those called to baptism must never try to appropriate to themselves God's action.[72] Even if God's action reliably corresponds to human action, we should understand that correspondence in terms of a kind of free agreement with the decisions made by the human person. To put it in ecclesial terms, baptism proclaims but does not itself establish the fellowship of the church.[73] Where Yoder argues that the constitution of the church is God's work in and through a freely confessed baptism, Barth insists that baptism itself represents neither the constitution of the true church nor the activity of God.

Understanding the difference between Barth and Yoder on baptism allows for an understanding of the wider divergence in play. For Barth, the church is awakened, quickened, and illuminated by God's grace through the election of Jesus Christ. Yet Barth applies what I will call a "double reserve" to the church that distinguishes his ecclesiology from that of Yoder: the essential *invisibility* of the church, simultaneous to its visibility, and the distinction between Creator and creature that interrupts the attribution of Christ-like qualities to the church. His application of this double reserve can be rephrased without essential loss in terms of a denial of the type of ecclesial positions of the exteriority posited by Yoder. Barth thus offers a genuine ecclesiology without exteriorities: an account in which the church has a role in the economy of grace that does not depend on the church's opposition to the world.

The first form of reserve that Barth imposes on the church is its simultaneous visibility and invisibility. For Yoder, the retreat into "invisibility" was an aftereffect of the Constantinian fusion of church and world, which veils the original visibility of the church as a voluntary communion of believers and leads to a displacement of faithfulness onto an invisible elect. Barth holds no less fervently to the noncoercive character of church membership and to the historical, empirical presence of the church. It is a phenomenon of world history as susceptible to historical, psychological, and sociological

---

70. Barth, CD 4/4:37.
71. Barth, CD 4/4:67.
72. Barth, CD 4/4:68.
73. Barth, CD 4/4:78.

analysis as any other.[74] In a gathering perceptible to the outsider "its cultus, teaching, preaching, instruction, theology, [and] confession" take place in definite relation to the conditions of the surrounding world.[75] It is acted upon by and reacts to other human phenomena; it forms and is formed by its context. From one angle, therefore, the church belongs fully and visibly within the immanent frame: "world-occurrence" is "the sphere in which [the people of God] has to exist with . . . resoluteness."[76]

In contrast, the same essence of the church is also properly invisible to the world. On Yoder's understanding, the church is set apart from the structures of the world because of its visible social ethics, which are uniquely determined by the gospel. We might say that Barth conceives the church such that it is not "of the world" on account of God's free and gracious relationship to it; the church's distinctness lines up not with any of its features as such but with its invisible relationship to God. The church has a calling, perceptible only to faith, as the living community of Jesus Christ that results from the working of the Holy Spirit.[77] This dimension of the community is *not* identical with any characteristic of the empirical church:

> There is no direct identity between what the community is and any confession, theology or cultus; any party, trend, group or movement in the being of the community as it may be generally perceived; anything within it which can be demonstrated or delimited or counted or formulated in a purely human way; or, of course, any of the individuals assembled and active within it. There is nothing within it which does not prompt, which may not itself be, the question whether and how far it has a part in what the community is. There is nothing within it which does not continually have to receive again this part, which does not have to be believed in its participation.[78]

In this way, the invisible essence of the church is related dialectically to all of its visible elements: as visible and creaturely communion, it has no particular claim on this status as gathered and commissioned by God. The "secret," the "mystery" of the church is not itself but instead its head, Jesus Christ.[79] Likewise, its activity is only set apart from the world through the prior activity of the Spirit. Discussing the graced holiness of the church, Barth clarifies

---

74. Barth, *CD* 4/1:139.
75. Barth, *CD* 4/1:139.
76. Barth, *CD* 4/3.2:39.
77. Barth, *CD* 4/1:144.
78. Barth, *CD* 4/1:144.
79. Barth, *CD* 4/1:152.

that the church "is not itself [that] which by its special activity in the world marks itself off from that of other societies[, which means that] it does not lie in its power or under its control to give to its own activity the predicate 'Christian.'"[80] By introducing the concept of invisibility to his ecclesiology, Barth misdirects claims to ecclesial exceptionalism: what is exceptional, because outside the world, is the sovereign God. Any claims about the church's unique status hold true only for faith and from without. The exclusiveness it might be said to generate is relative, provisional, and teleological,[81] withdrawing from sight once we consider the church in its own right.

The promised destiny of the church is for its invisible essence—its received character as people of God—to be made into visible expression. The visible and invisible elements of the church are funded by a single essence and emanate from the same center, and therefore cannot be separated. God molds the visible community in such a way as to explicate and represent its invisible hope and destiny; its invisibility is to its visibility as potentiality is to actuality.[82] Just as a finite potency requires an outside agent to actualize it, the invisible being of the church depends on the leadership and impulse of Christ to press the visible church into conformity with it.[83] Unlike most cases, however, this invisible being does not belong to the created essence of the church but is the result of its election and calling. Not only does realization depend on divine agency, but the very possibility of it is impossible for the visible community: it arrives "by grace and not by nature," promised and given as free gift.[84] That is, the church is only the true church in accordance with its invisible essence within a history "whose subject is God," working for and to and with specific humans.[85] Equally, "to the extent that it is anything in itself, it is the phenomenon of the mere semblance of a church, and it is only this semblance, and not the true church, that we shall see" when we consider its own status.[86] In this light, it makes sense to claim that the characteristic sin of the church is bearing witness to itself rather than to God: whatever it has, it does not possess by right.[87] When it acts in accordance with its proper place, it serves as a site of transparency to God's presence, expressing in its visibility an invisible election. Hence, the invisible

---

80. Barth, *CD* 4/1:182.
81. Barth, *CD* 4/1:153.
82. See, e.g., Barth, *CD* 4/3.2:46.
83. Barth, *CD* 4/3.2:46.
84. Barth, *CD* 4/3.2:47.
85. Barth, *CD* 4/2:3.
86. Barth, *CD* 4/2:4.
87. Barth, *CD* 4/2:10.

potential, being, and goal of the church depend on the agency of God, who freely makes the visible community a conduit for an invisible sanctity. Just as the dark letters of an electric sign can only be seen when electrical current is run through it, the church depends on the Holy Spirit to illumine and quicken it from within.

The second form of reserve appropriate to Barth's description of the church runs along similar lines: its distinction from the Creator as itself a creature. By reasserting the role of grace and by clarifying the body metaphor, Barth carefully regiments his conception of the church as the body of Christ in order to preserve its full creatureliness. As Nicholas Healy argues, this use of somatic language depends upon recollection of the crucifixion: the body of Christ is properly dead without the resurrection in the power of the Spirit; thus, the identity between the visible and invisible elements of the church depends on the resurrection.[88] In these ways, the church is not by nature[89] the body or expression of the divine Word in the same way that Jesus Christ himself is. Furthermore, despite Barth's consistent talk of the "being" of the church, the church possesses no essence that might be identified as the body of Christ; that it is the body comes always from without, from a displaced center.[90] This is the case because the church, even in its invisible dimension, "is not Christ, nor a second Christ, nor a kind of extension of the one Christ."[91] On the contrary, though it is his earthly-historical form of existence, "it is not, as He is, the Word of God in the flesh, the incarnate Son of God."[92] Accordingly, the church's claims for its role in the economy of grace are always to be tempered by the awareness that it is a creation and, even in its expression of and association with Christ, never becomes divine.

As a result of this double reserve, then, Barth leaves the church in no position of exteriority; any criticism, from its perspective, of the world is simultaneously self-criticism in expectant hope of God's coming kingdom. What for Yoder is a direct, if imperfect, transfer of normativity from Jesus's human social practices to the church's social ethics becomes here misdirected and refracted. The church can become a site of normative witness, if God acts to make it so, but this normativity never adheres to the church

---

88. Healy, "Logic of Karl Barth's Ecclesiology," 256. Healy here deals with Barth's claim that "without the Holy Spirit the body of Jesus Christ and in it all humanity can only be dead" (Barth, *CD* 4/1:151).

89. I intend to invoke here the distinction deployed by Cyril between sonship "by grace" and "by nature" (Cyril, *On the Unity of Christ*). Humans might all become "children" of God by grace; the uniqueness of the Word incarnate is his sonship by nature.

90. Healy, "Logic of Karl Barth's Ecclesiology," 257.

91. Barth, *CD* 4/3.2:47.

92. Barth, *CD* 4/3.2:47.

VULNERABILITY AND THE VISIBLE CHURCH

itself. It is provisional and temporary; it is not exclusive, as other parts of the world might become temporary sites of witness to God's grace.[93] Most importantly, for our purposes, the church is *always* a part of the world. It might be the part that God deigns to use as a witness most often. It might be the part that exists in appropriate creaturely self-consciousness. But it never attains to a position of exteriority from the world, and thus the powers. Thus, the Barth of the late *Dogmatics* did not depart in this from his earlier work, in which he proclaims:

> Indeed, we sense once again that the meaning of so-called religion consists in its relation to life as it is really lived, living in society and not in separation from it. A separated, holy realm is no holy realm. From the secure port of our specifically religious location—once praised often and loudly—we look with longing out at the world because we sense that, as many theologians are once again beginning to sense, that there can be no "inside" so long as there is an "outside."[94]

Christians live immersed in society, not "in separation from" society; the church can give its members no position of exteriority that would exempt them from complicity.

In comparing Barth and Yoder, we are faced with a choice between two ecclesiologies, but more importantly, two views of the possibilities for nonconformed communities. As "free church" accounts, both distinguish the church from society's institutions and make membership in the church voluntary and noncoercive. Both emphasize the centrality of community in the Christian life as a social form of eschatological expectation. Both argue that the church exists in a relevant social and political context that makes its witness matter for the world. Where they differ is their account of the way that church and world are distinguished. For Yoder, church and world are two orders enclosed within God's providential guidance; within that enclosure, the church participates in Christ's redemption as the bearer of the new community, while the world is the object of God's enduring patience. Church and world exist in annihilating opposition: inasmuch as one is complicit with the powers that constitute the world, one does not inhabit the space of the church, and vice versa. For Barth, the church and the institutions and orders surrounding it are enclosed within the world, both as good creation and as fallen into confusion. At its best, the church receives the grace of God to become that part of the world that bears witness to God as a

---

93. See, e.g., the passage about "secular parables of the kingdom" in *CD* 4/3, cited in chapter 2.

94. Barth, "Christian in Society," 37.

self-conscious creature. Yet God never removes it from the moral sphere of the world, nor is it granted an independent normativity that it could steward as its own proper possession. The church awaits not its extension and purification according to its own ethos, but rather the arrival of a kingdom discontinuous with even its exalted form. Its visibility is at the same time its vulnerability, including its vulnerability to complicity.

How, then, shall we arbitrate between these two conceptions of the church? For their differences deeply depend on different emphases and positions in eschatology and in soteriology, and comparison, as a result, can only serve to elucidate and elaborate on their disagreement. What criteria might we use to prefer one or the other without question-begging, importing some prior systematically theological preference?

Fortunately, the contours of the ecclesiologies just described render them vulnerable to a social scientific assessment of the kind that Foucault can offer us.[95] That is, if Yoder is right, then there exists a visible, nameable community that is not complicit with the powers, discernible by all, even if confessed only by a few. Whether one subscribes to the norms derived from the imitation of Christ or not, Yoder's ecclesiology depends on the church's ability, by living out those norms even to a degree, to elude complicity with the powers. Yoder's ecclesiology seems to leave no recourse to invisibility. However ambiguously the visible church lives its call, it is in this visibility the one and only church. But if Barth is right, we should expect to find that the church is everywhere and always complicit, even if it preserves a peculiar witness to the kingdom of God. The disparity between ecclesiologies can be adjudicated by means of an account of how the powers operate within or without the church. If it can be established that the church could, in fact, attain to a position of exteriority, one could hold out hope for Yoder's view, should one desire. However, if it can be established that no such position of exteriority can ever be possible for the visible church, we would have sufficient reason for siding with Barth's rigorous refusal of ecclesial exceptionalism.

---

95. For an interesting attempt to cast Yoder as a genealogical figure, offering something like Foucauldian reflections on historical particularly, see Blum, "Foucault, Genealogy, Anabaptism." The concerns of that chapter are adjacent to this one, but do not address the theological claims Yoder makes on behalf of his historically particular communities in the same way.

POWER AND THE SELF

Clearly, Foucault has no ecclesiology as such. Likewise, he would no doubt pose a host of questions to both of the theological accounts sketched above. The object of turning to Foucault is not to claim that he agrees with Barth's ecclesiology, but that Foucault gives us reasons to prefer Barth's account to that of Yoder, at least with regard to the question of voluntary exteriority. These reasons will fall into two basic categories: the subject's identification with and formation by dynamics of power both logically before and after particular instances of her agency. Foucault might persuade us that when that agency is seen in its full context, we will not be able to defend claims to voluntary exteriorities. In this respect, we can rightfully and unequivocally say that Barth and Foucault both oppose an opposition between church and world specifically or voluntary exteriorities generally and for analogous reasons that, though they differ, can be held together in a critical theological ecclesiology.

Foucault's account of productive power and agency is sufficiently well-known and well-discussed that we do not need to rehearse it in full detail here, especially given his picture of structures of power described in the previous chapter.[96] What follows instead is more narrowly a story of the will's frustrations: how voluntary action is not only hemmed in by power, but also expresses power's perhaps alien intentions. That we have no interiority to hold outside the world, no sense in which we can "choose" not to be implicated, will recast how we think about the agency of the resisting subject.

Foucault's encounter with figures such as Nietzsche, Bataille, and Blanchot represented for him a call to question the subject, "its primacy and its originating function." Foucault answered that call by relentlessly interrogating what he took to be the canonical Western account of subjectivity: that power is a capacity held by subjects, transacted through decisions and withheld at will.[97] Just as the Toronto couple would have it for their child, the subject sets the terms for their encounter with the world. But Foucault holds that this picture substantially obscures the workings of power, and to understand power's full domain, we must question the frequently assumed priority of this subject. Accordingly, he shifts the emphasis on understanding agency, in the first instance, from the figures of sovereignty—state

---

96. Readers interested in more detailed treatments of this aspect of Foucault could consult the works of Foucault cited in chapter 2 above, or could start with O'Farrell, "Power and Culture"; Dreyfus and Rabinow, *Michel Foucault*; Schirato et al., *Understanding Foucault*; Cremonisi et al., *Foucault and the Making of Subjects*; Deleuze, *Foucault*; Carrette, *Foucault and Religion*.

97. Foucault and Trombadori, *Remarks on Marx*, 46.

institutions and the individual person—to the complex mechanisms of power that precede them, logically and temporally.

It is all too easy to reify "the subject" in ways that misremember or misrecognize the actual shaping of particular subjects. What is called for, on Foucault's understanding, is the remembering opened by attention to the material facts of our lives, which will reveal that individuals are constantly undergoing or exercising power.[98] As we perceive the expansive domain of power, we come to include within it the spaces—bodies, desires, and other realms of "privacy"—supposedly deprived, held outside of its influence. The innocence of will that Yoder implies, able to dispose of oneself apart from and over against the structures of the world, is incredible if the dynamics of power named by Foucault in fact hold. Our desires have a history, and relations of power envelop those desires, both giving rise to them and making use of them for purposes unintended by the individual. The person who patronizes a tanning salon, to take one of Foucault's examples,[99] is not primarily subjected to power through government regulation of the salon or in the pressures of economic exchange and participation, though these dynamics certainly exist. Rather, power suggests and gives life to the desires of the individual as such, making impossible any untroubled claim to the "mine-ness" of one's desires.

Foucault also gives us reasons to think that the meaning and effects of our voluntary action are underdetermined, due to the cleverness of the powers. He describes how this happens in two ways that he endows with jargon-laden names, but that are not foreign to our everyday experience.

First, what he dubs "functional overdetermination": that the flow of the world of power shifts beneath our feet, rearranging itself to accommodate our attempts at resistance on its own terms.[100] In the simplest possible terms: the machine would love to sell you a Rage Against the Machine T-shirt made by sweatshop laborers in Bangladesh.[101] The term "fake news" emerged into popular discourse in the fall and winter of 2016, especially as a straightforward but crucial way to describe internet-based hoaxes such as the allegations that a Washington, DC, pizza restaurant was hosting a child trafficking ring.[102] Seeing the new popularity of the term and its potential as a means of dismissing news sources that would challenge him, President

---

98. Foucault and Trombadori, *Remarks on Marx*, 98.

99. Foucault, "Body/Power," 57.

100. Foucault, "Confession of the Flesh," 195.

101. The phenomenon of "commodifying dissent" is particularly apropos here: see, e.g., the treatment of consumer culture's reaction to the "voluntary simplicity" movement in Miller, *Consuming Religion*.

102. See Fisher et al., "Pizzagate."

Donald Trump and his sympathizers quickly appropriated it for use as a cudgel against practicing journalists. The durability of the powers over time means that they play a complex game in relation to our efforts to tell the truth and to resist, which often changes those efforts' meaning in order to frustrate them.

For a more complex and larger-scale example, take the reception of the legacy of Martin Luther King, Jr. in the United States. The witness of the "radical King" was quickly, after his death, sanitized and harmonized with whiteness.[103] With his murder reframed as a sacrificial death and his thought and organizing reduced to a dream of conflict-free harmony, his moral authority could now be used to legitimate a narrative of colorblind racial progress. In Vincent Lloyd's terms, "King sought to build a national consensus against segregation, but in doing so, his image and legend came to be carefully managed by the powers that be, even as those powers came to accept integration."[104] In the terms of this argument—and recalling Michelle Alexander's description of shifting racial caste represented in chapter 1—the powers adjust apparently to accommodate resistance, handing a real victory to those seeking reform, but strenuously reorganizing in order to account for the new situation. White supremacy can no longer take the form of Jim and Jane Crow; it must transform according to the criteria laid out by the agency of those resisting—judging now only the "content of one's character"—which results in purported colorblindness. Once that price is paid, the militarism, the class conflict that will soon result in the financialization of the economy, and other powers targeted by King's witness can slip by largely unnoticed. The civil rights movement indeed achieved something real—movingly, meaningfully real!—in forcing white supremacy to retreat from institutionalized segregation; Foucault's vision helps us see how the powers nevertheless rearrange themselves in response to our agency to ensure we do not arrive "outside." Thanks to structural dynamics like these, invoking King has become so politically fraught that writer Mychal Denzel Smith recommends that Americans simply take a vacation from talking about his legacy, image, and authority.[105]

Simultaneously, "strategic elaboration" colonizes more and more space for the patterned regularities of the world, even if that regularity is disordered by violence.[106] The powers push, despite our best efforts at nonconformity, to repeat and reproduce themselves. As Cynthia Hess processes the

---

103. See, e.g., West's introduction to *Radical King*.
104. Lloyd, *Black Natural Law*, 89.
105. Smith, "Paved with Good Intentions."
106. Foucault, "Confession of the Flesh," 195–96.

dimensions of Yoder and Christian nonviolence, she challenges the picture of self-possessed agency that Yoder champions:

> Research studies on trauma . . . challenge the notion that all persons enjoy the wholeness or coherence that Yoder assumes. They suggest, using Yoder's terminology, that sometimes the violence of the powers can embed [itself] so deeply in people that they experience a fracturing of their identities which makes it difficult to sustain the internal coherence necessary for living a life of Christian discipleship.[107]

The violence of the powers, once visited upon victims, can become a gruesome, unwelcome companion, complicating the agency that we might like to hold outside of its influence. For Foucault, the overt, devastating violence of trauma is a species of the wider category of structural imposition on more and more space, including inner space.

In broader terms, this tactic is evident in the ever-expanding domains of the current economic regime, variously labeled neoliberalism, or financialized capitalism, or one of a host of other names. The agency of government at every level faces pressure from the ability of capital to leave a place in pursuit of a more favorable tax regime, causing a uniform push toward austerity; as the 2018 competition for Amazon's HQ2 demonstrated, attracting capital pushes in the same direction. The speed and transience of capital have begun to pattern labor markets: as Ruth Milkman outlines, a new "precariat," a class of workers existing outside the protections won by twentieth-century organized labor, live under "open" employment relations, with weak regulation and prevalent standards.[108] "Flanked by an army of unemployed," as Guy Standing describes, the temporary labor available to the precariat deprives them of a stable expectation of work, distant even from the occasionally career-building lower rungs of the economic ladder.[109] Foucault also perceived in the late 1970s that the logic of markets and the free flow of capital was being extended to new dimensions of life, such as crime, public health, and the family, especially in applications of Chicago School economics, which constituted a growing influence of this logic's power.[110] All of these dynamics mean that one who attempts to resist a form of power will find herself swimming against the flow of an increasing flood.

What is intended to liberate may enable a more total domination; what is meant for resistance may only more deeply empower the status quo.

107. Hess, *Sites of Violence*, 27.
108. Milkman, "Introduction," 2.
109. Standing, *Precariat*, 15–16.
110. See especially Foucault, *Birth of Biopolitics*.

Activity meant to rearrange the world according to the image of an outside always meets with the world's ability to assimilate it, transforming it into a new inside. And that activity is itself often patterned after the world in ways that are invisible to us. One's actions feed back into the social machine, reverberating through the agency of others to purposes outside one's control. No one is spared, and no one can find a position outside. If meaningful freedom, especially in the form of resistance, depends on the possibility of positions of voluntary exteriority, then this is a dark picture of human possibility indeed.

Power, then, encompasses individual agency: any attempt to give rise to a voluntary exteriority misrepresents the origins and destiny of human work. To an Anabaptist such as Yoder, who claims that a believer should seek baptism freely, of his or her own volition, we could pose a range of Foucauldian questions. What are the understandings of Christian discourse at work in both the communal and personal understandings of baptism? What are their origins, and how have they configured the "game of truth" in which this voluntary association is implicated? What social factors govern the statements made about baptism and the church? Why does the candidate want to be baptized; what is at stake in doing so? What will this baptism mean within a larger, if still local, social whole? How is such a choice intelligible in terms of the relations of power historically characteristic of this religious tradition? These questions and countless others suggest that the types of activities that one might undertake in order to attain to a voluntary position of exteriority are fraught with elements that are beyond the control of any individual and inevitably entangled with the world. Baptism, as the free church traditions practice it, may well entail no coercive force. But that does not suffice to prove that power is not implicated in its practice. Foucault's view of the subject lets us see that no actual, visible person or community can ever act without complicity in at least several of the predominant power structures at a given time. If by "church" we mean gathered and freely confessing living persons, then claims that the church has acted to make itself somehow separate from and opposed to the world are ruled out just to the extent that this account of subjectivity is convincing.

Incidentally, Foucault does have a prominent concept for understanding alternative space: the famous heterotopia.[111] A heterotopia is not a position of exteriority: Foucault identifies those with utopias. "By contrast," as Mark Jordan elaborates, "a heterotopia is a real place, traced out within an existing society, in which larger social settings are represented, contested, and inverted. A heterotopia is a sort of outside that is permitted on the

---

111. Foucault, "Of Other Spaces."

margin of the inside."[112] Societies still exercise control over heterotopias, but they allow for an encounter with the negative space left by exteriority. As a boundary, heterotopias have the otherness of liminality, of representing limits and their transformative power, not the otherness of exteriority. We might say they are the part of the world that represents the world to itself, occasionally (or perhaps more than occasionally) through disruption. The object of this chapter has been to suggest that the church at its best, as Barth describes it, is somewhat like a heterotopia in this sense, constantly striving to be just on this side of the outside. Foucault helps us to prefer Barth's ecclesiological account over Yoder's, since Barth does better justice, within his own theological idiom, to the phenomenon of the complicity of the church with the life of the world.

INSIDE AND OUT, VOLUNTARINESS AND COMPLICITY

The same criticism of the particular claims of ecclesial exceptionalism could be made of voluntary exteriorities more generally. If Foucault is correct that power works not just to dominate or repress individuals but also behind, before, and through them, then one cannot simply opt out of participation in power dynamics. What will challenge Witterick and Stocker's plan to allow baby Storm to make self-expressive decisions about the gender order is that those decisions themselves cannot but be formed and reformed by that order itself. Others' knowledge of Storm's biological sex may be withheld for a time, and in the space created by that ignorance, Storm may experience fewer pressures. But no one can engage in a process of self-discovery independently of the cultural artifacts circulating in a specific place and at a specific time. Both that act of discovery and its material expressions of gender, whatever they turn out to be, will result from a prevalent gender order from which Storm cannot simply be exempt. The spaces of decision, which might seem outside the influence of the powers, prove to be enclosed within the world as the sphere of their operation. Voluntariness and complicity cannot become simple opposites, then; voluntary responses to the powers are themselves categorically enabled by the powers. The condition of the possibility of human action is also the grounds of its tethering to an immanent frame.

Voluntary exteriorities, either moral or communal, are often posited as occasions of noncomplicity with the powers. In theology, claims to voluntary exteriorities have often taken the form of ecclesial exceptionalism.

---

112. Jordan, *Convulsing Bodies*, 165–66.

By examining this ecclesiology, we have shown how these types of exteriorities—and, a fortiori, ecclesial exceptionalism—misread human agency with respect to the powers. This is why an ecclesiology in which the church dwells fully with and within the world does better justice to human agency and complicity. In the larger scope of this book's argument, denying voluntary exteriorities is an essential step toward redirecting our spiritual practice of resistance away from attempts to locate ourselves outside the powers' influence, as if we could live simply in opposition to them. We can frustrate their apparent purposes; we can try to gum up their works, slow them down, and refuse to be held in their thrall. And there are good reasons to encourage participation in countercultures, communities of conscious ethical practice, nurturing enclaves for those subject to the powers' violence, and alternative forms of social space. But if we channel our attempts to resist through imagined exteriorities, assigning value to those attempts insofar as they achieve something like nonparticipation, we misunderstand the ineradicable intimacy—sometimes the horrific and violent intimacy—of structural influences on our agency. The apparent contradiction between Yoder's confidence in his own access to an order of redeemed gender politics and how his violations repeated the harmful forms of the present one could be understood as just this species of misrecognition.

Such a misunderstanding matters for how we live among the powers. In the shadow cast by alleged exteriorities, we may fail to see a range of other possible forms of resistance. After all, if there are methods through which one can simply escape implication in white supremacy or patriarchy, then those methods take on the imperative force that comes from reacting to generations of abject horror. But if there are no intrinsically successful strategies, no spaces that are, finally, safe, then we are returned to an incredibly expansive realm of responsible action, in which the urgency of resistance can be embodied through a universe of creative practices. If that responsibility extends not only to any social space we might occupy, but also into the full depth of who we are, then that universe includes how we relate to ourselves as places in which the world is acting. The shape of our agency, formed as it is by the powers, calls for the political spirituality that will be described in chapter 6.

That picture of agency does not rule out Yoder's principled theological pacifism or the Toronto couple's admirable attempt to give their child a wider array of possibilities for gender expression. It rather recasts the pride of place given to alleged exteriorities, not least because the forms of optimism that give rise to them are much more closely allied to cynicism than one might assume: the former trusts in the success of strategies for avoiding complicity; the latter, having experienced profound disappointments, is too wise to believe in them. There is a theological account of human life among the powers—and, more importantly, a form of spiritual practice—that harnesses the endless critical force of cynicism and the holy, undomesticated energy of optimism. Before outlining those practices, though, we should consider the role of theological accounts themselves, including this one, since we may turn to them as another possible hope of eliminating complicity in the absence of voluntary exteriorities. Thus, the next chapter will consider a parallel argument in relation to intellectual exteriorities.

CHAPTER 4

Healing Vision

INTELLECT AND DISTINCTION

In the April 29, 2011, edition of *The New York Times*, film critic Dan Kois complained about the faux-connoisseurism required in his field. Suffering through the instances of "slow cinema" produced by auteur directors (Kois names Kelly Reichardt's *Meek's Cutoff* and Andrei Tarkovsky's *Solaris*) for the sake of validating one's critical credentials seems little better to Kois than his daughter watching the cartoon *Phineas and Ferb*.[1] Too young at six years old to understand the humor, Kois's daughter watches the cartoon "aspirationally," and since she "understands the rhythm of jokes," she laughs at the appropriate moments despite not seeing the humor.[2] In much the same way, Kois feels compelled to watch art and independent films that he recognizes his peers respect, but with a hollow appreciation: motivated only by wanting to be recognized himself by those whom he recognizes, and not by any enjoyment of these films. He mourns the "sophisticated cineaste [he] might never become," but, it seems, is content to conclude that the films he finds boring are, in fact, boring.[3]

This moment of honesty provoked a response from the *Times*' regular film critics, Manohla Dargis and A. O. Scott. Scott sees contemporary "anti-art bias" as an unknowing defense of the corporate status quo.[4] Dargis argues that, rather than "slow cinematic" films, she finds those like *The Hangover Part II* boring, filled as they are with well-worn plots featuring

1. Kois, "Eating Your Cultural Vegetables."
2. Kois, "Eating Your Cultural Vegetables," para. 5.
3. Kois, "Eating Your Cultural Vegetables," para. 18.
4. Dargis and Scott, "In Defense of the Slow and Boring," para. 2.

recycled gags and characters.⁵ Dargis seems to express their sentiment most strongly:

> Thinking is boring, of course (all that silence), which is why so many industrially made movies work so hard to entertain you. If you're entertained, or so the logic seems to be, you won't have the time and head space to think about how crummy, inane and familiar the movie looks, and how badly written, shoddily directed and indifferently acted it is. And so the images keep zipping, the sounds keep clanging and the actors keep shouting as if to reassure you that, yes, the money you spent for your ticket was well worth all this *clamor*, a din that started months, years, earlier when the entertainment companies first fired up the public-relations machine and the entertainment media chimed to sell the buzz until it rang in your ears.⁶

Having labeled Kois a "cheerful conformist" earlier in the piece, Dargis's implication is clear enough: slow cinema is countercultural by requiring *thinking*, challenging the corporate machine that churns out mass-produced sequels and retreads.

Nor are Dargis and Scott alone in this pattern of thinking. In response to criticisms emerging in the 1970s that labeled the Frankfurt School as guilty of "resignation," Theodor Adorno makes a strong case for the liberating power of critical thought. For Adorno, "if there is any chance of changing the situation [of social power], it is only through undiminished insight."⁷ While life is easier for the individual who capitulates to the collective with which he identifies, "the uncompromisingly critical thinker, who neither superscribes his conscience nor permits himself to be terrorized into action, is in truth the one who does not give up. . . . [T]hinking is not the spiritual reproduction of that which exists. As long as thinking is not interrupted, it has a firm grasp upon possibility."⁸ So too does Noam Chomsky, in his justly famous essay, "The Responsibility of Intellectuals," claim a crucial role for critical thought. "It is the responsibility of intellectuals," Chomsky asserts, "to speak the truth and to expose lies."⁹ This is specified later on in the essay, as Chomsky describes the public's basic concern as the role of intellectuals in the creation and analysis of ideology.¹⁰ Other examples abound: the role of

5. Dargis and Scott, "In Defense of the Slow and Boring."
6. Dargis and Scott, "In Defense of the Slow and Boring," para. 6.
7. Adorno, "Resignation," 200–201.
8. Adorno, "Resignation," 202.
9. Chomsky, "Responsibility of Intellectuals," para. 4.
10. Chomsky, "Responsibility of Intellectuals."

the intellectual—and, by extension, of elite knowledge—in social criticism is a topic perennially fascinating to critical theorists (not least because it is effectively self-study).

But the demand for a political critique of knowledge manifests in many places, not just among knowledge workers of various sorts in the intellectual classes. That paramount critical text of our era—Greta Gerwig's 2023 film *Barbie*—employs a perfectly explicit form of this critique, despite its glossy portrayal of the aesthetics of "cheerful conformism." A group of politicized Barbies and their real-world allies, responding to the takeover of Barbieland by the newly reactionary Kens, seek to raise the consciousness of other Barbies who have fallen under the Kens' reactionary spell. America Ferrera's character, a real-world woman named Gloria, delivers a pained speech about the impossible double-binds of performing femininity under conditions of patriarchy. The recitation of a feminist complaint itself conscientizes the duped Barbies who hear it, snapping them out of their ideological slumber. "By giving voice to the cognitive dissonance required to be a woman under patriarchy," one of them says, "you robbed it of its power!"[11] The protagonists then carry on in the articulation of critique, as if spreading a liberatory contagion: any Barbie can be made to recognize her situation and, in that recognition, unforget an empowering practice of life. That a summer-blockbuster comedy believes it can count on its (adult) audience to metabolize this structure of critique between comic beats and among brightly colored sets bespeaks its widespread familiarity. Under conditions in the US wherein organized progressive critique is largely limited to the expressive institutions of some parts of the academy and the culture industry, and in a time when that critique can feel impotent in the face of political machinations to enforce gender and sexual hegemony—*Barbie* wrapped shooting less than a month after the June 2022 release of the *Dobbs* decision overturning *Roe v. Wade*—it makes sense that discursive tactics, such as complaints lodged on social media, feel like the last, best option for political mobilization. After all, surely part of the complaint has to be the dearth of films that take women and girls to be paradigmatic agents—a situation in which *Barbie* bears a representational and political burden that the property is ill-equipped to manage. The film copes with its own impossible situation by enlisting a familiar account of freedom through re-narration.

Generally speaking, accounts functioning this way hold that one's agency is co-opted by power as long as one is trapped in the ideology that wins consent for power's prevailing structures. That is, insofar as one fails to see the hegemonic social and political orders for what they are, one cannot

---

11. Gerwig, *Barbie*.

help but to reproduce those orders. To use the terms of the previous chapter, voluntary exteriorities are impossible under the conditions of subjection to misrecognized ideology. Instead, those who wish to resist power are directed first to a clear-eyed representation of its nature and workings, to a finer picture of the relations of power that make up a given society. Once obtained, this knowledge gives one the strategic insight one needs to resist power, perhaps through the sorts of nonconformity suggested in accounts that depend on voluntary exteriorities. But perhaps even that knowledge itself counts as a kind of "transcendence" of social orders: the capacity to think and imagine new ways of being (and being social and political)—especially beloved of academics and others in knowledge-producing and -regulating classes—might be seen as a kind of spiritual freedom that allows one to hold oneself in reserve. I will call accounts that depend on critical thought for effective resistance to power theories of *intellectual exteriorities*.

In the previous chapter, I argued that even highly engaged forms of voluntary resistance to the powers do not suffice to establish a position of exteriority. A theorist of the powers could conceivably grant this point, but still hold out hope for access to exteriorities based on the freeing power of critical thought itself. In Christian theological discourse specifically, this kind of liberating thought is often discussed as one version of God's revelation to creation. To see the world as it is—to be able to name the powers for what they are—grants one a certain power over them, or at least grants one a degree of freedom with respect to how they work. The theorist of the powers may despair for the possibilities of successful resistance based on her own agency, but, through the power of God's gracious revelation, believe that she is delivered to a new kind of freedom from their influence and, with that freedom, possesses a new range of critical possibilities. Like those who encounter demons in some of Christianity's canonical stories, she hopes knowing a demon's name means having power to channel God's command of it.

In this chapter, I will consider the implicit claim that critical thought causes a rupture with one's complicity, that thinking succeeds in interrupting the reproduction of that which exists. As an example of this gesture, I will explore the momentous trilogy of the powers written by Walter Wink—*Naming the Powers, Unmasking the Powers*, and *Engaging the Powers*. Where Yoder was especially concerned to situate the church in relation to the story of the powers in salvation history, Wink emphasizes the methodological and epistemological assumptions that prevent contemporary thinkers from perceiving the powers as they really are—that is, seeing their techniques at work, through which one can perceive and resist their spiritual essence. For Wink, the situation of modern humanity before the powers calls for a clearer vision, both of ourselves and of the ancient world in which the character of the powers was properly shown. I will argue that Wink's understanding thereby depends on a conception of revelation to establish an intellectual exteriority from the sphere of the powers. To argue that this claim to an exteriority is mistaken, I will use resources from Foucault's work on the relationship of power and knowledge: if knowledge itself is produced by power, it is not possible for knowledge to disentangle one from power. I will then appeal to Barth's notion of the instability of revelation in the situation of human religion. Barth's account offers a description of revelation that, like Wink's account, gives us some understanding of the human situation in ways that aid critical resistance, but that neither domesticates divine "knowledge" nor creates positions of exteriority.

This literary exercise, however, stages in an explicit, theological form an examination of a technique that is widely prevalent. To take an example: longstanding protests against racialized police violence reached new audiences in 2020 after the high-profile murders of George Floyd, Breonna Taylor, Tony McDade, and many others. One of the byproducts of this moment in the movement was intensified production and circulation of the heralded "antiracist reading list," a canon of recent works that critically analyze white supremacy largely for an educated, mostly white, mostly Anglophone audience. Insofar as reading and discussing the books on the antiracist reading list introduced new audiences to techniques of analysis that surface racializing forms of power and domination, their circulation is one form of constructive response to racial injustice. I held these hopes, too, as I myself created, circulated, and read texts from such reading lists. But the antiracist reading list—as books on a shelf, perhaps prominently displayed in a Zoom background; as citations one can casually offer in conversation; as cornerstones of the curriculum of a series of church group meetings—is in grave danger of operating as a fetish object, a guarantor of the nonracism of its circulator and possessor. In that capacity, the books on the list need not even be read—and one might reasonably wonder how many of the paperback copies of Kendi and DiAngelo sold in 2020 have meaningful creases in their spines.[12] Even if any particular version of the reading list is completed, the knowledge it both imparts and symbolizes does not deliver one from one's complicity with racialized domination, and therefore cannot itself be the end, what is produced by the political contestation over racial capitalism that continues. However well-intended the attempt—perhaps especially subtly in the most conscientious!—the process of coming to know,

---

12. See Jackson, "What Is an Anti-Racist Reading List For?"

and representing oneself as knowing or coming to know, repositions one in continuing relation to the structures of power that the knowledge describes.

Sara Ahmed named this dynamic more than a decade before social media made practices of repentant reading and confession more widespread. Her concern about "whiteness studies," an academic subfield that attempts to respond to black critique by accounting for the history and practices of whiteness, is that "declarations of whiteness" and other attempts at antiracism are nonperformative.[13] For Ahmed, declaring one's whiteness or even "admitting" to racism does not suffice to establish evidence of an antiracist commitment, not least because the declarations themselves can, in fact, reproduce the relations of power that they seek to challenge in unforeseen ways.[14] She documents several channels through which these unhappy performances flow. One of these is the assumption that racism is habituated "unseeing," the unwitting prejudice that is overcome in the practices of altered perception that culminate in confessions of identity, such as "I am/we are white."[15] A parallel technique congeals around institutions' production of diversity and antiracist statements: later responses to complaints of discrimination or mistreatment can be filtered through a sense of pride, for which such statements are evidence, that one or one's institution has public commitments of justice-oriented character—"that's not who we are." As a result, "organizational pride in being good at hearing messages prevents the message getting through. Such a speech act does exactly what it says it does not do: it refuses to hear complaint in the very moment it says that it does hear complaint."[16] When power is conceived as working largely through concealment, then claims to awareness, ranging from self-awareness to public declaration, take on an outsized importance. When these strategies for coping with power are removed from dialectical motion with other forms of practice, they start to block meaningful transformation by the reassertion of goodness or exteriority.

Ahmed incisively diagnoses part of the problem: racism is not simply about ignorance, or even stereotypical knowledge, and driving it out cannot

---

13. Ahmed, "Declarations of Whiteness," 13. The familiar caution is necessary: by "performative" here, Ahmed does not mean something like "demonstrative" or "for show," but rather the way that certain speech acts enact the realities that they signify. The "non-performativity" of antiracism, therefore, means that it does not work the way that it narrates itself to work.

14. Ahmed, "Declarations of Whiteness," 4.

15. Ahmed, "Declarations of Whiteness," 6. See also Ahmed, "Nonperformativity of Antiracism," 107.

16. Ahmed, "Nonperformativity of Antiracism," 111.

be accomplished by speaking into a presumed silence.[17] "Race, like sex, is sticky: it sticks to us, or we become 'us' as an effect of how it sticks, even when we think we are beyond it," she warns.[18] This is one of the features of how, in this book's vocabulary, racism is specifically structural as part of the generative milieu for subjects. Antiracist declarations are unhappy performatives—attempts to take on a commitment that fail, even impede, the mobilizing of that commitment—because the conditions are not in place that would allow those declarations to do what they say. Much more than perception into what is ideologically mystified, antiracism requires "working with racism as an ongoing reality in the present. Antiracism requires interventions in the political economy of race, and how racism distributes resources and capacities unequally amongst others."[19] Attending to that political economy implicates subjects differentially, a reality often defended against by the good commitments symbolized by the antiracist reading list. Ahmed, in contradistinction to these defensive techniques, perceives the stickiness evident in her own implication in this system: "The critique I am offering, as a Black feminist, is a critique of something in which I am implicated, insofar as racism structures the institutional space in which I make my critique, and even the very terms out of which I make it. . . . What we might remember is that to be against something is precisely not to be in a position of transcendence: to be against something is . . . to be in an intimate relation with that which one is against."[20] Critical attention expresses precisely a form of relationship, a nonexteriority, without which the criticism does not get off the ground; critical knowledge not only responds to, but often depends upon, the very systems that it seeks to critique. These sorts of doubling, subtly shifting ironies work to incorporate "knowledge" into the processes of power.

This book, too, is implicated in that which it criticizes, including on the grounds of the conditions of possibility of its work and the institutional location of its production. Despite my efforts to read the longstanding theological and theoretical canons included here against themselves in various ways, the citational politics entailed in doing so perpetuates the currency that they have in church and academy. The system of theological education in which this book participates depends largely on students taking on debts

17. Ahmed and many others would hasten to specify that this "silence"—and the parallel "invisibility" of whiteness—only describes predominantly white spaces; to racialized others, whiteness can seem omnipresently visible and loud. See, e.g., Ahmed, "Declarations of Whiteness," 1.

18. Ahmed, "Declarations of Whiteness," 13.

19. Ahmed, "Declarations of Whiteness," 14.

20. Ahmed, "Declarations of Whiteness," 12.

to receive entry and earn credentials, debt that is increasingly undefrayed by the forms of employment that the sort of training I provide enables.[21] Under the political economic circumstances that prevail in the US, the fact that I am given the time and resources to, say, write an academic book about power depends upon a whole network of relationships of mutual implication: the workers who clean the graduate school I attended and the seminary where I teach, those across the globe who farm the food that I lack the skills and resources to grow myself, and immeasurably many more. I write this largely from Washington, DC, and its suburbs, the contemporary imperial core, and I have regular contact with people who manipulate its levers of power. The list could go on. And even if the sorts of confessions contained in this line of reflection hit the mark, that recognition alone does not itself impede the flows of power as currently constituted, nor does it enable easy reforms that draw us near to an end of the work of transformation. Such confessions are forms of self-knowledge, the absence of which can distort our collective work, and they do not contravene the opportunity provided by faithful, attentive analysis. But critique as a posture is fated to get stuck in contradiction if it cannot be pushed to a reflexive negativity,[22] one that understands the difference that even negation fails to achieve.

This chapter, then, aims to explore the theological dimensions of social and political knowledge. It will not solve all the epistemological problems implicated in this exploration; much less is it a complete theological epistemology. Instead, it recommends a fragment useful for a certain kind of spirituality, a relation to one's own process of knowing. Such a provocation enjoins us to seek empowering knowledge of the world that is the fabric for our living, but also insists that we see our knowing itself as woven into that fabric. A political theological positioning of revelation, then, can be a prompt to a political epistemology of solidarity, an encouragement to coming to know together for the purposes of collective transformation, and not for the sake of personal moral distinction or innocence.

---

21. The opening lines of Adam Kotsko's *Neoliberalism's Demons* puts this quite well: "Every academic critique of neoliberalism is an unacknowledged memoir. We academics occupy a crucial node in the neoliberal system." A quick survey of the tensions between serving the "meritocratic" order under conditions of increasing precarity leads Kotsko to claim that "we academics live out the contradictions of neoliberalism every day" (1).

22. I owe my understanding of this term to David Newheiser; one accounting for it can be found in *Hope in a Secular Age*, 18.

VISION HEALS

As Walter Wink began his trilogy about the powers in the late 1970s and early 1980s, he took a sabbatical to live in Chile, with some time spent as well in Argentina, Brazil, Bolivia, Peru, Costa Rica, and Nicaragua.[23] Experiences ranging from fear of military dictatorships to sympathy with the victims of political torture and the relatives of those who had "disappeared" to "the everyday crush of oppression" in the abandoned places of these countries led Wink to the brink of despair: "The evils we encountered were so monolithic . . . that it scarcely seemed that anything could make a difference."[24] Reading Wesley Carr's 1981 *Angels and Principalities* in this context convinced Wink both that the language of principalities and powers could give him some purchase on these situations and that something was amiss about the prevailing use of this language.[25] Carr's thesis, according to Wink, that "the Powers are good altogether, and not the demonic forces they have been pictured to be, [and that therefore] they cannot be made to serve the needs of Christian social ethics," fundamentally misconstrues the relevant New Testament evidence.[26] Wink therefore begins his trilogy with a full accounting of that evidence in *Naming the Powers*.

According to Wink, when contemporary theologians describe the New Testament's understanding of the powers, we tend to do violence to that understanding because of prior commitments to methodological materialism.[27] Consequently, we cannot be disturbed in the right way by the biblical conception of the powers: we tend to assume that the biblical authors misrecognize and misunderstand the exclusively material phenomena of power through superstition, assimilating the invisible, unknown forces of power "only by personifying them and treating them as if they were

---

23. Wink, *Naming the Powers*, ix.

24. Wink, *Naming the Powers*, ix. I have not found a place where Wink accounts for the role of US colonialism in creating and aggravating these situations, nor a description of what sorts of distorting effects his role as a tourist/observer has in the contexts he narrates. Though I appreciate Wink's contribution to discourse about the powers, this lack of attention to the preconditions and effects of one's own knowledge is symptomatic of the problem diagnosed in this chapter.

25. Wink also refers to his reading Stringfellow's *Free in Obedience* in 1964 as an impetus for his study of the powers, but Carr's work seems to have spurred him to larger and more critical consideration of the first generation of work on the powers (see *Naming the Powers*, 6).

26. Wink, *Naming the Powers*, 6.

27. Wink, *Naming the Powers*, 3.

conscious willing beings."[28] This type of demythologization[29]—reducing the powers to merely mythical representations of institutions, social systems, and political structures—leaves a remainder that materialists cannot properly appreciate. As well, Wink argues that it does not suffice to take the powers as (merely) the personification of social structures.[30] That, too, would neglect the full composition of the powers. The first problem the theorist of the powers must address is the prejudice against such spiritual phenomena caused by presumptions in favor of reductionism; such presumptions irretrievably flatten the insight of the New Testament's portrait of power. We are cut off from a clear vision of the social and political battlefield, "our eyes and minds held captive to a way of seeing and thinking that can only regard such entities as mere fantasies conjured up by the prevailing belief system."[31] A whole realm—and one with considerable effects on our lives—is veiled by this blindness.[32]

That realm is called various names by Wink—including the "intermediate," the "cosmic," and others—but is most properly labeled *spiritual*. If we are open to the possibility of a certain kind of spiritual realm, we will be able to appreciate the New Testament's understanding of the powers:

> The "principalities and powers" are the inner and outer aspects of any given manifestation of power. As the inner aspect they are the spirituality of institutions, the "within" of corporate

---

28. Wink, *Naming the Powers*, 3.

29. Wink seems to waver on whether or not "demythologization" is an appropriate approach to the New Testament. Here, and in other places (typically early in the trilogy), he identifies it with the reductionism that he makes the target of significant criticisms. Yet, elsewhere, he is happy to refer to Satan as an archetype of human experiences of evil, and to follow what he calls a "functionalist approach" in approach to the question, "Is the angel of the church [in the case of those mentioned early in Revelation] then *real?*" (Wink, *Unmasking the Powers*, 25, 71). I highlight his use of this word, fraught with ambiguity as it is, to point out that Wink does not understand his rejection of a certain kind of reductionism as an affirmation of something untethered to public, material analysis. For this reason, though, I will preserve what I perceive to be his distinction of materialism from reductionism. That he offers no objection to varieties of materialism that include accounts of emergent "spiritual" phenomena suffices to show that his problem specifically lies with the reduction of social and political life, without remainder, to its material aspects.

30. Wink, *Naming the Powers*, 103.

31. Wink, *Naming the Powers*, 4.

32. Another angle into what is challenging about Wink's account of knowledge about the powers could focus on his heavy reliance on the metaphors of vision/blindness and how that reliance is tangled up in ableism. Insofar as such an argument would press the point of a misunderstanding of human capacity and grace, I take my approach here to be allied with it.

structures and systems, the inner essence of outer organizations of power. As the outer aspect they are political system, appointed officials, the "chair" of an organization, laws—in short, all the tangible manifestations which power takes. Every Power tends to have a visible pole, an outer form—be it a church, a nation, or an economy—and an invisible pole, an inner spirit or driving force that animates, legitimates, and regulates its physical manifestation in the world. Neither pole is the cause of the other. Both come into existence together and cease to exist together.[33]

In describing the powers in this way, Wink means to heal the division between one-sided materialism and one-sided spiritualism. Indeed, the powers are generally encountered in and through embodied forms; demons in the New Testament, Wink claims, are often portrayed as fearing and abhorring "decorporealization," as in the case of the Gerasene demoniac.[34] Wink does not seek to readmit just any spiritual phenomena into the contemporary scene. The powers exist within their concretions in institutions, systems, or officeholders, and need these concretions as a self needs a body.[35] Yet, the spiritual dimension must be conceived with its own integrity, since in some cases the material forms of power may only be explicable on the basis of prior spiritual forms; they are "just as much the creation of the Powers as their creators."[36]

Two results follow from Wink's insistence on attention to the equal poles of materiality and spirituality. First, Wink elides "power" with "the powers," claiming that "all manifestations of power [should be] seen under the dual aspect of their physical or institutional concretion on the one hand, and their inner essence or spirituality on the other."[37] There are no exclusively material phenomena of power: all such phenomena are animated by an individuating spirituality. Second, while it is worth recognizing that human institutions have human origins, that recognition is itself only partially illuminating. In fact, "these institutions are not simply subject to human fiat. They possess a spirituality, an inwardness, that is highly resistant to change."[38] The intransigence of the powers comes in part from their irreducibly spiritual aspects, inexplicable in themselves on appeal to the human agency that has a role in their creation and perpetuation.

33. Wink, *Naming the Powers*, 5.
34. Wink, *Naming the Powers*, 5, 106.
35. Wink, *Naming the Powers*, 145.
36. Wink, *Naming the Powers*, 103.
37. Wink, *Naming the Powers*, 107.
38. Wink, *Naming the Powers*, 135.

Much of the trilogy's second volume, *Unmasking the Powers*, explores these powers, using the concept to understand contemporary life. For example, the horrors of the twentieth century meant that, in a sense, "we had killed Satan": systematic evils visited upon humanity on a huge scale "virtually outstripped the symbol and [became] autonomous, unrepresentable, beyond comprehension."[39] As the representation of Satan increasingly became identified with a personal spirit-being (and, hence, more incredible, even comical, to some modern minds), the evils of the twentieth century became increasingly vertiginous, creating a symbolic deficit. On Wink's view, this situation is uniquely threatening since "without a means of symbolization . . . evil cannot come to conscious awareness and thus be consciously resisted. Like an undiagnosed disease it rages through society, and we are helpless to produce a cure. *Evil must be symbolized precisely because it cannot be thought.*"[40] For Wink, the first question to be asked is not, "Does Satan exist?," but rather, "What it is about the human experience of evil that has led many to posit Satan?"; the metaphysical question only arises when a political tradition has lost touch with the basic experience of radical evil, which leaves it susceptible to this symbolic confusion.[41] In service of rehabilitating Satan within a political theology of the powers, Wink traces a figural history through the Hebrew Scriptures and through the New Testament. What results is a spiritual account of social life:

> *Satan is the real interiority of a society that idolatrously pursues its own enhancement as the highest good.* Satan is the spirituality of an epoch, the peculiar constellation of alienation, greed, inhumanity, oppression, and entropy that characterizes a specific period of history as a consequence of human decisions to tolerate and even further such a state of affairs.[42]

As one among the powers, Satan has both outer and inner, material and spiritual reality. As the symbol for extreme evil, Satan represents the spirit of social alienation from God, "the great system of mutual support in evil . . . the image of unredeemed humanity's collective life."[43] Yet, though we deliver ourselves into Satan's clutches, the history of evil does not begin with our misuse of agency, since we enter a world already organized for evil.[44] The outer reality of Satan exists in the condition—here understood

---

39. Wink, *Unmasking the Powers*, 10.
40. Wink, *Unmasking the Powers*, 11; emphasis original.
41. Wink, *Unmasking the Powers*, 26.
42. Wink, *Unmasking the Powers*, 25; emphasis original.
43. Wink, *Unmasking the Powers*, 24.
44. Wink, *Unmasking the Powers*, 31.

as the traditions of intellectual and social arrangements in which we find ourselves—that is itself the precondition for our reaffirmation of Satan.

For all that, however, human choices determine whether or not Satan's work will be destructive or constructive of faithful humanity. Wink believes that Satan, according to God's plan, is "the heavenly sifter, the setter of choice," who might on occasion tempt simply with evil but, more frequently, tempts us away from the best with the good.[45] Thus, Wink can claim that "Satan is not gentle; if we relate to him unconsciously we can be destroyed. Satan plays for the highest stakes of all, but for those who bring the light of the image of God to the struggle for choice, Satan is 'Lucifer,' light-bearer—a very brilliant servant of God."[46] To label the nuclear arms race of the Cold War "satanic" is to see a choice forced upon humanity by its scientific prowess, and one with deadly high stakes. Understanding the character of Satan, for whom the task is not to promote the welfare of one regime at the expense of another but to sift, we realize "that the [Cold War] struggle is not between the administrations in Washington and Moscow, but that *both are on the same side.*"[47] With respect to the human element of the temptation toward total destruction, the situation takes on a logic of its own, one presumably not held in mind by any of the human decision-makers but discernible to those who see it as a moment of divinely set choice. From this vantage point, Wink can speculate that "perhaps in the final analysis Satan is not even a 'personality' at all, but rather a function in the divine process, a dialectical movement in God's purpose which becomes evil only when humanity breaks off the dialectic by refusing creative choice."[48] In faithfulness to God, one can sublimate Satan, transforming Satan "not through the denial and repression of our evil, but by naming it, owning it, and lifting it up to God."[49] Human society can integrate what Satan does by means of appropriate recognition and forging the right kind of interrelationships to our own evil.[50]

Likewise, Wink names among the powers the demons of Satan's cohort. In interpreting the demonic, Wink seeks a third way between what he sees as liberation theologians' exclusive focus on demonic structures of power and the popular view that ordinary, perhaps necessary, malfunctions

---

45. Wink, *Unmasking the Powers*, 17–18.
46. Wink, *Unmasking the Powers*, 20.
47. Wink, *Unmasking the Powers*, 28; emphasis original.
48. Wink, *Unmasking the Powers*, 33.
49. Wink, *Unmasking the Powers*, 40.
50. It is not clear to me precisely how this relates to the existence of nuclear arsenals, but I understand the impulse to relate all things to God's creative and redemptive intentions.

in human development count for apparently demonic phenomena.[51] Appropriately enough, Wink thus claims that a "truer understanding of persons sees them in cybernetic or systemic terms, as the network of relations in which they are embedded. This means that the individual can never be considered in isolation from the political, economic, and social conditions in which the person was gestated and by which the person has been to a significant degree formed."[52] But the demonic is not "merely the consequences that follow in the wake of self-idolizing institutions; it is also the spirit that insinuates itself into those whose compliance the institution requires in order to further its absolutizing schemes." In a moment with Foucauldian overtones, Wink writes:

> Such systems cannot govern by force alone; indeed, force is always a counsel of last resort and a sign that a Power is losing its grip on people's minds. When a demonic institution is functioning normally, it does so by the enthusiastic and willing consent of those it is in the very act of oppressing, or at very least, with their terrified compliance. The policeman steps off the corner and into their heads. The Powers rule from within.[53]

Demons here are phenomena in which a person internalizes and repeats the inner spirit of the fallen structures of power in a given society. They are the psychic and libidinal dimension of power, as inscribed onto personal subjectivity. Yet, there is mutual influence between inner demons, embedded in the psychic life and practices of the person, and outer demons, which have collectively material existence and expressions. Such forces can "erupt into a frenzy of violence in the permissive context of a riot, revolution, or war.... A megalomaniac like Hitler would get nowhere if he not were riding the cresting wave of resentment from millions of would-be megalomaniacs longing to be released from the restrains of truth and civility."[54] These are psychoses sometimes barely restrained in the organized social world, the depths of unintegrated chaos that circulate through a collective sensorium.

To use the familiar idiom in relation to the demonic: this is possession. Sometimes persons can be possessed by a force alien and extrinsic to the self, a form of captivity to an internalized oppression ("outer personal possession"). There are also "inner personal demons," whose effects are visible in the struggle to integrate a repressed aspect intrinsic to personality, which aspect is only made evil by its rejection. Finally, there are "collective

---

51. Wink, *Unmasking the Powers*, 41.
52. Wink, *Unmasking the Powers*, 42.
53. Wink, *Unmasking the Powers*, 43.
54. Wink, *Unmasking the Powers*, 43.

possessions," when a group or nation is enthralled by a demon capable of binding them, then bending them to the service of death.[55] For the first type, Wink analyzes Girard's description of the scapegoat as the retroactive occasion for collective identification and exclusionary violence. For the second, Wink discusses the aspects of personality that cause fear and a split in one's self-identification. For the final type, Wink offers the examples of Nazism in Germany and institutionalized racism in the United States, which have a life of their own, flowing in and out of particular subjects.[56] If Satan represented the role of total denial (or, at least, the possibility thereof) in God's economy of grace, Satan's hordes represent the particular but vicious instantiations of this denial. The demons possess and oppress humanity in ways that complicate the boundaries between personal and public.

Wink's account of the powers, in sum, reasserts at every turn what he believes to be obscure to modern modes of perception: that our patterned ways of life, in both their personal and political aspects, are not only material practices, susceptible to a natural history of the kind that a social scientist would give, but are also spiritual practices, calling for a position within a theological account of human collectivity. Their spiritual aspects are no mere epiphenomena: they themselves generate the material practices as often as they arise from them. Our underappreciation of this spiritual dimension threatens our ability to name the powers accurately, and thus to resist them meaningfully. Attacking what is often the symptom rather than the disease, social critics mistake the material face of social structures for their whole and thereby neglect the hold they have on people, the sway they exercise over human imagination, the agency over human affairs they exert that cannot itself be explained by collective human agency. Instead, "only by confronting the spirituality of an institution *and* its concretions can the total entity be transformed, and that requires a kind of spiritual discernment and praxis that the materialistic ethos in which we live knows nothing about."[57] Still, the powers are not simply evil; as well as Satan and the demons, Wink names among the powers the "angels of the churches" addressed in the early chapters of Revelation and the ordering elements of the universe beyond the social world that make life possible. Wink's interpretation of the powers is, therefore, the kind of maximal reading argued for in this book: the scope of the powers is coextensive with, and perhaps even exceeds, human life and existence, even if they do not exhaust the meaningful aspects of human life and existence.

---

55. Wink, *Unmasking the Powers*, 43.
56. See Wink, *Unmasking the Powers*, 46, 57, 64.
57. Wink, *Engaging the Powers*, 10.

As his trilogy progresses into its final volume, *Engaging the Powers*, Wink begins to refer to the powers collectively as "the domination system." On Wink's use, the domination system includes a network of powers congealing around their own idolatrous self-preservation, with Satan as the system's world-encompassing spirit.[58] Like Yoder and others, Wink holds to a tripartite thesis concerning the theological role of the powers: they are good; they are fallen; they must be redeemed.[59] The powers in their created form are good, and even now "can be not only benign but quite positive."[60] Yet, we can only affirm institutions to be good if we simultaneously understand them to be fallen. Wink is concerned to do justice to the full story of the powers in God's economy of grace by seeing to it that they are "honored, criticized, resisted, and redeemed."[61] In these respects, Wink's "domination system" carries roughly the same meaning as the wider political theological use of "world": the sphere of influence of the powers, created to be the realm of human and other created agency, fallen yet redeemed by Christ's saving activity. Indeed, Wink does name the domination system with *kosmos* (world), *aiōn* (age), and *sarx* (flesh), the dimensions of fallen creation that adhere—not necessarily coherently—into networked systems of force, of focal interest to the work of the church in the world.[62]

Wink does not identify the church simply as the site of resistance to the powers, but rather names "the angels of the churches" among them. Like demons, such angels have a function manifested by their personality and vocation, an inner spirit.[63] Such an angel "becomes demonic when the congregation turns its back on the specific tasks set before it by God and makes some other goal its idol," succumbing to the domination system.[64] Frequently, churches abandon their vocation for a reason related to their unique spirituality, and to do so is to repeat the fall of the powers within ecclesial walls. Only a form of grace can "bring the churches into line with the will of God. . . . They cannot be transformed . . . unless they encounter that Otherness as judgment and accounting: God must suddenly appear to the congregations as *outside* their ken. They must experience a jolt of recognition: we are out of phase with the will of God."[65] Thus, in a Barthian

---

58. Wink, *Engaging the Powers*, 9.
59. Wink, *Engaging the Powers*, 10.
60. Wink, *Engaging the Powers*, 10.
61. Wink, *Engaging the Powers*, 10.
62. Wink, *Engaging the Powers*, 51.
63. Wink, *Unmasking the Powers*, 71.
64. Wink, *Unmasking the Powers*, 78.
65. Wink, *Unmasking the Powers*, 80.

turn of phrase, Wink asserts that "we must do everything we can to foster change, and we can do nothing. God calls us to transform the church, and yet only God can bring that transformation about."[66] If Yoder over-identifies the church with the realm of God's gracious activity, thus creating a space of voluntary exteriority to the powers, we cannot say the same about Wink. God stands as judge of the church as much as the world—God, the otherness at its heart and the holiness it is called to embody but cannot on its own strength. If we are to find a claim to exteriority in Wink's description of the powers, then, it cannot be the simple opposition between church and world that constitutes ecclesial exceptionalism.

Wink opens his consideration of resistance with the question, "If the Domination System is so insufferable, why do people tolerate it?"[67] The outer manifestations of the powers—those identifiable people and groups that serve as their embodiments—are few and, considered on their own, often not possessed of overwhelming force. Wink says that the routine failure of the many to cast off their oppressors, who are few, is "the greatest political mystery ever."[68] The marginalized, Wink believes, must be convinced to allow themselves to be marginalized; six million whites could not otherwise subjugate twenty-nine million other South Africans, nor could women, who compose a demographic majority in the United States, fail to push through an Equal Rights Amendment if they united and considered their true interests. The powers must enlist the help, or at least the compliance, of those they seek to subjugate, and it would seem as though their dependence upon this help and compliance would severely constrain their destructive potential. The only explanation possible for the invidious character of the powers, then, is that most people are caught in a powerful delusion, without which they would not acquiesce to their oppression.[69] For Wink, resistance to the powers thus entails dispelling this delusion and unleashing the reconciling power of a true vision of human social and political life:

> Exposing the delusional system is the central ascetical task in our discernment of the Powers. For the Powers are never more powerful than when they can act from concealment. To drop out of sight and awareness into the general surroundings, to masquerade as the permanent furniture of the universe, to make the highly contingent structures of current oppression appear to be of divine construction—such is the genius of their deceptive

---

66. Wink, *Unmasking the Powers*, 82.
67. Wink, *Engaging the Powers*, 87.
68. Wink, *Engaging the Powers*, 87.
69. Wink, *Engaging the Powers*, 88.

art. . . . The mighty prefer, therefore, to rule by means of invisible constraints: unseen filaments tied to the public's arms and legs, and imperceptible spiritual brain-implants causing the masses to will to be what has been made of them.[70]

The machinery of power has coercive force at its disposal—militaries, police forces, strategies of economic oppression—but it operates most efficiently and preserves the veneer of legitimacy when it annihilates resistance by conscripting those who might resist through delusion—as Gramsci would say, hegemony is the crucial structuring force of domination. The prime condition for resistance, then, is exposing these delusions as delusions and removing the powers' most significant weapon for oppression.

A central figure of resistance, then, is the "seer," typified in John of Patmos, the supposed author of Revelation. The seer does not possess esoteric knowledge, but rather "the gift of seeing reality as it really is. Nothing is more rare, or more truly revolutionary, than an accurate description of reality. The struggle for a precise 'naming' of the Powers that assail us is itself an essential part of social struggle."[71] Resistance depends on vision, silencing the siren song that lulls us into compliance and seeing the powers for what they are. Such a seer cannot merely read off the spirituality of the domination system from simple observation, however, since the seer too has internalized its demonic spirit.[72] Rather, the seer can discern that spirit, and by naming it, externalize it, which allows the seer to expel the spirit as a lie. "The seer," therefore, "locates the source of the chanting [the slogans of the powers] outside, and is set free from it."[73] The seer can interrogate the givenness of the current embodiment of the powers in the domination system, freeing imagination from its habitual ascription of necessity to the status quo. Denaturalizing the powers is the cornerstone of resistance, since "an empire [such as the domination system] is, by its very nature, a system in a permanent crisis of legitimation. It is not a natural system, but an artificial amalgam held together by force," hence its use of propaganda.[74] While delusional assumptions remain unrecognized as such, "they are seldom effectively transcended."[75] The key that unlocks successful resistance is clearness of vision, a description of how things are that simultaneously shows how things are contingent, or how things could be.

70. Wink, *Engaging the Powers*, 88.
71. Wink, *Engaging the Powers*, 89.
72. Wink, *Engaging the Powers*, 89.
73. Wink, *Engaging the Powers*, 89.
74. Wink, *Engaging the Powers*, 93.
75. Wink, *Engaging the Powers*, 96.

HEALING VISION

Simultaneously, Wink assumes that all are complicit in this delusion from infancy and all, therefore, are responsible for it.[76] It is true that no power is mighty enough to destroy our capacity to recognize truth.[77] But despite a persistent if quiet internal witness that something is amiss, the spirituality of domination thrives as external cult and inner devotion. This leaves one with a responsibility to allow oneself to be converted to a true understanding of prevailing social and political arrangements and an ethical response to them. Since the powers do not rule by delusion alone, such a conversion is costly and inflicts harm on those who will so resist, in the required transformation of one's habits and dispositions, to start. Along with a liberating vision, "there must also be a *healing of the servile will* in their victims. Along with the revolutionary analysis and praxis, there must be therapies."[78] Perhaps more appropriately, that vision itself is not merely a vision of the external order but also one's place within it. Such a vision involves not only seeing the powers for what they are, but also the "*sense of powerlessness*" that is always "*a spiritual disease deliberately induced by the Powers to keep us complicit.*"[79] One is complicit by virtue of one's spiritual slumber, here interpreted as deluded acquiescence to the domination system's hypnotic spell.

The road to eradicating this complicity, then, begins with the emancipation of one's mind. Faith's victory over the powers, for Wink, lies "not in immunity to their wrath, but in emancipation from their delusions."[80] A real freedom from the demonic is possible, enabled only by the truth. The model of the revelations that came to John exhilarate us because they suggest the possibility of becoming disenthralled, of awakening from the world as if from a bad dream.[81] In the clearest statement of this pivotal claim, Wink posits:

> Vision heals. Mere awareness of the state from which we are fallen is not enough to effect systemic change, but it is its indispensable precondition. Apocalyptic (unveiling) is always a protest against domination. Liberation from negative socialization and internalized oppression is a never completed task in the discernment of spirits. To exercise this discernment, we need eyes that see the invisible. To break the spell of delusion,

76. Wink, *Engaging the Powers*, 96–97.
77. Wink, *Engaging the Powers*, 98.
78. Wink, *Engaging the Powers*, 102; emphasis original.
79. Wink, *Engaging the Powers*, 103; emphasis original.
80. Wink, *Engaging the Powers*, 103.
81. Wink, *Engaging the Powers*, 103.

we need a vision of God's domination-free order, and a way to implement it. For that, we look to God's new charter for reality, as declared by Jesus.[82]

The situation of human life among the powers calls for "eyes that see the invisible," a vision that points the way toward God's new order. The true revolution requires revelation: what is in plain sight must be revealed through the gracious gift of new spiritual eyes through which to see. That gift itself dispels the false spirituality of the powers, resigned as it is to their putatively natural and necessary character. Once unburdened of the false spirituality of the powers, one can begin to live into God's new order.

God's new order is free from domination in all of its forms: inequality, racism, sexism, even some forms of law, and—apparently its central difference from the current system—violence. While a fuller treatment of Wink's political theology would require a comprehensive exploration of these elements of critique that Wink takes to draw energy from God's kingdom, at least a sketch of his eschatology is necessary for our purposes here. Wink connects eschatology and resistance in his final exhortation, positing that "we are to struggle with all our might and courage for [the end of the domination system], yet we cannot make it come. The conditions of its arrival are beyond our control, yet we have a fairly clear idea what they are; and as a sufficient number of people are attracted to God's domination-free order, and commit their lives and fortunes to bringing it about, it will happen, because it has been happening, and it is happening now."[83] Christians can begin living in God's "counterreality" now since God's reign has come near in the acts and words of Jesus. This counterreality "makes choice possible, exorcises the old conditioning, and holds out to us a new world waiting to be claimed by us."[84] Wink believes that the New Testament bears witness to the present reality of this kingdom and the prospect that one could choose to live into it. Though there are still forms of reserve applied to this eschatological living—we may establish a relatively more egalitarian and flourishing ways of life, but these will fall short of the fullness of the reign of God[85]—there is still an injunction to embody another order amid the powers. This call to embodiment is also a demand for resistance: "resistance to evil and death, to the Dragon and its Beasts, is the only way to live humanly in an inhuman world."[86] Wink's eschatology, then, is inaugurated

---

82. Wink, *Engaging the Powers*, 103–4.
83. Wink, *Engaging the Powers*, 319.
84. Wink, *Engaging the Powers*, 319.
85. Wink, *Engaging the Powers*, 320.
86. Wink, *Engaging the Powers*, 321.

HEALING VISION

by the gift of the eyes of faith and embodied by choosing a "partnership society." "What *ought* to be," in other words, "for those with eyes of faith, already *is*. Living by faith entails maintaining, through creative imagination and communal reinforcement, a vivid sense of God's counterreality as more real than apparent reality itself."[87] This partially realized eschatology leads Wink to identify the reign of God with certain instances of resistance. In the sufferings of those resisting the powers in South Africa, Myanmar, or South Korea, there are people "who are now beginning to *see* and *act* free from of the Domination System" and "the reign of God has already begun!"[88] In these ways and despite Wink's occasional assertions that the kingdom transcends human efforts, the eschaton overlaps with the current age where healed vision allows people to resist the powers' dual dimensions.

Having traced Wink's account of the powers through the course of his trilogy, we can see how his project is itself, in both method and substance, an attempt at resistance. Most people born into the contemporary domination system start from a default assumption of reductionist materialism, which is actually a form of spiritual blindness. Though they may understand the observable phenomena of structures of power, those structures possess and are animated by an inner spirituality that is an essential aspect of their being and activity. Moreover, this blindness is itself an effect of the powers' influence over human life: the demonic influences over social and political life would have us think that they are tragic but necessary, that responsibility requires ceding territory to their ways, and that they, after all, are nothing but reflections of ourselves. The institutional and visible church, itself among the structures that can become demonic, is no exception to the spirituality of the status quo and the blindness to the true form of the powers that Wink describes. This blindness can be dissipated, however, by the gift of revelation that is bestowed upon the one who has genuine faith. Revelation takes the form of healing vision, a penetrating vision into the true state of political and social orders; without vision of this sort, resistance is doomed merely to rearrange the material traits of structures of power while leaving their inner spirituality intact. Consumed by this vision of God's opposition to and redemption of the world, however, one can resist the domination system, thus claiming territory—if even for a fleeting moment—for God's kingdom on earth. Wink's work itself seems like just such an attempt at the kind of truth-telling that would enable such effective resistance to the powers and inaugurate God's new order.

---

87. Wink, *Engaging the Powers*, 323.
88. Wink, *Engaging the Powers*, 323.

This narrative about the possibility of resistance to the powers constitutes a claim to an intellectual exteriority. Wink posits an opposition between the type of knowledge that reconciles one with the fallen form of the powers and the knowledge that sets one against their demonic influence. The former is the false consciousness that leads one to complicity; the latter is the precondition for resistance. Furthermore, the healed vision that leads to genuine resistance comes as a gift from God in a moment of God's inaugurating God's reign on earth, not in full, but in reality and despite the captivity of the world to the powers. To receive this revelation, then, is to attain a measure of exteriority from the powers: breaking the spell of belief in their putatively natural character allows one to reform the integrated whole of the social structures that oppress and subjugate humanity. Indeed, one's agency is always mixed up with God's agency in such activity: grace continually props up human insight and resistance. Yet, there is a vision of the invisible—of a world free from the distorting influence of the powers—accessible to humanity through grace. The one who can see the powers for what they are has, by that token and in the same measure, transcended them. The path to meaningful resistance runs through revelation: one is complicit up until the point of one's spiritual liberation through revelation.

The theological character of Wink's account accounts for some of the impulses behind this claim to an intellectual exteriority: as we have seen at every stage in this book's treatment so far, the idea of a God who creates a world distinct from Godself often inclines the theologian to identifying those things they believe to be sanctioned by God with God's original relation of exteriority to the world. But the long trajectory of Wink's argument holds a formal identity with other such claims, such as the practices of declaring whiteness described by Ahmed as unhappy performatives. The critical point we will press in alliance with Foucault, then, is not about revelation as such, but about what humans are like as social and political knowers: how our intellectual activity relates to the circumstances of power that enable it.

POWER AND KNOWLEDGE

Like Wink, Foucault takes an intense interest in the relationship between knowledge and power. Foucault is also invested in understanding the social world in order to inform active practices of resistance. These shared interests, however, cannot obscure their divergence on the question of intellectual exteriorities. Foucault, working in a different idiom, has some very similar insights to Wink, but by radicalizing them, Foucault extends them into self-reflexivity. In the process, he develops what we can use as a criticism of posited intellectual exteriorities.

First, though, one might object that Foucault—who only pays attention to the world in the ways that a materialist does, on Wink's description—is exactly the kind of social theorist against whom Wink levels the charge of reductionism. After all, if Foucault denies the kind of spiritual or intellectual exteriority for which Wink argues, that may simply provide evidence for Wink's claim that contemporary social scientific outlooks reduce reality to what is empirically observable (and inferences based thereupon) in a way that distorts both social theory and critical resistance. Indeed, Foucault thinks that his interest in power is even more "materialist" than the Marxists of his day, and criticizes those who "occlude the question of the body, in favour of consciousness and ideology."[89] It might seem now, as was the case when this comparison was set up in chapter 2, that there is simply a clash of orthodoxies in play here: reductionist materialism and a Christian account of the spirituality of the world, attempting to out-narrate one another.

There is good reason, however, to think that Foucault, despite being a certain sort of materialist, is not guilty of the kind of reductionism with which Wink takes issue. Inasmuch as Foucault's work has or implies an ontology, it is materialist on almost any definition. However, recall that, for Wink, the problem is not disbelief in spiritual substances or personal spirit-beings, but rather a reduction of the powers to the mere personifications of our own visible social practices. The error of reductionism is a failure to recognize the inner dimension of power, that which is inexplicable by the particular form of its outer manifestation. In a real (though non-biological) sense, the powers must be seen to have a life of their own—to generate their outer manifestations as often as they are generated by them. Yet, for the reasons outlined in chapters 2 and 3, this is a close analogue to what Foucault does hold regarding power. Foucault describes power such that it has a "mind of its own," a knack for strategies that cannot be controlled or even simultaneously perceived by single agents. At every turn, Foucault argues against conspiratorial versions of power, in which a few who possess some species of authority control the levers of the entire social machine. Power finds surprising resonances and appropriates unforeseen relations among social phenomena to create an ever-shifting landscape of forces. Foucault specifically does not claim that the intentions and activity of power are reducible without remainder to representations of human collectivities: in fact, Foucault is quite clear that the strategic elaborations power undertakes often undermine those collectivities, or provide unexpected results, or work

---

89. Foucault, "Body/Power," 58–59.

in subtle and barely detectable ways. Consequently, if the problem Wink's account of the powers is meant to address is indeed reductionism, and not simply materialism, then there is no prior reason to dismiss a rejoinder from Foucault.

The difference-making absence from Foucault's account of power is not the spiritual dimension as such, but rather the unalloyed normativity that Wink brings to his account (it is not coincidental that many of Wink's test cases admit of little moral ambiguity). For Wink, the vision that heals is a gift imparted by the revealing God. A true vision of God's kingdom is, by that fact, not subject to human revision or criticism. The "seer," the one who sees the powers for what they truly are, has this knowledge by the power of divine inspiration, as does the author of Revelation. Thus, the difference between Wink and Foucault, tradition-specific rhetoric aside, is not in their accounts of the nature of the powers, but rather in the character of their normative responses to them. In Wink's trilogy, the appropriate response to the powers is fairly clear and subject to a set of prescriptions: types of diagnoses (such as the forms of possession), rules for engagement (such as nonviolence), and other forms of resistance that are tightly connected with the descriptive account there on offer. Yet, I will argue that one of the virtues of Foucault's depiction of knowledge and power is a rigorously critical attitude toward such forms of normativity and a resulting underdetermination of prescriptive responses to power.

Like Wink, Foucault seeks to investigate power and knowledge because putative bodies of "knowledge" are oftentimes strategies of power that constrain human possibilities. Though examples abound, the central subject of criticism in the first volume of *The History of Sexuality*—"scientia sexualis"—illustrates this point nicely. Historically speaking, scientia sexualis, along with its supposedly Eastern counterpart, "ars erotica," is one of the two most prominent procedures for rendering sex meaningful.[90] These are ways of understanding not just sex, but the sexual self within social sexual norms—in other words, broadly discursive regimes of generating the "truth" of sex. Practices of "confession," from the early Christian monastic context to contemporary psychoanalysis, become second nature to those acculturated to a scientia sexualis. That acculturation is so intense "that we no longer perceive it as the effect of a power that constrains us"; rather, we feel its prodding so acutely that we are led to believe that when we do not confess, it is because "the violence of power weighs it down" through repression.[91] This incitement to discourse promotes normalization and self-monitoring:

---

90. Foucault, *History of Sexuality*, 1:57.
91. Foucault, *History of Sexuality*, 1:60.

HEALING VISION 123

constantly attempting to discover the truth about our sexuality, those living under this regime deploy the categories and prejudices of our extensive sexual knowledge. Thus, the idea that sexual discourse is subject to power primarily in the form of repression cannot account for all of the ways in which one is constrained by the regime of scientia sexualis, being responsible for "a proliferation of discourses, carefully tailored to the requirements of power; the solidification of the sexual mosaic and the construction of devices capable not only of isolating it but of stimulating and provoking it . . . ; the mandatory production of confessions and the subsequent establishment of a system of legitimate knowledge and of an economy of manifold pleasures."[92] The culture of scientia sexualis represents itself as liberating us from repression, when in fact it imposes a host of burdens on the "sexuality" that it engenders, including a usable self-knowledge that recruits one into circulating categories for sexual identity. This form of knowledge is an effect of power, a fruitful inquiry into which "must define the strategies of power that are immanent in this will to knowledge."[93] Foucault seeks out an accurate description of the phenomena of power, and does so especially by applying a form of suspicion to their self-representations, as Wink does.

Yet, Foucault seeks to highlight the mutual implication of power and all forms of knowledge. Where Wink saw delusion generated by the explanatorily prior powers, Foucault posits their simultaneous emergence. The scientia sexualis is a prime example of this. "The essential features of this sexuality," Foucault posits, "are not the expression of a representation that is more or less distorted by ideology, or of a misunderstanding caused by taboos; they correspond to the functional requirements of a discourse that must produce its truth."[94] The scientia sexualis as a discursive practice generates an object, "sexuality," that cannot be dismissed as an illusion. It is not merely a representation of a given human sexuality against which we can "check" its representations for proper correspondence. Instead, this sexuality is generated by the requirements of a certain game of truth. To understand the character of the prevailing idea of sexuality is not only to understand the image it presents on its own terms, but to see it as shaped by "[an] 'economy' of discourses—the intrinsic technology, the necessities of their operation, the tactics they employ, the effects of power which underlie them and which they transmit—this, and not a system of representations, is what determines the essential features of what they have to say."[95] Structures

92. Foucault, *History of Sexuality*, 1:72.
93. Foucault, *History of Sexuality*, 1:73.
94. Foucault, *History of Sexuality*, 1:68.
95. Foucault, *History of Sexuality*, 1:68–69.

of power are not given existents, which only later attempt to misdirect one's proper recognition of them, such that one could get at the truth about them by distrusting their self-representations. Structures of power emerge and work precisely by generating the knowledge that is appropriate to them; power and knowledge are simultaneous aspects of a single set of phenomena. That is, knowledge, like power, is a flow through an arrangement of force relations.[96] It is not subject to later, destructive distortion by the powers; it is itself a product of the powers, a channel through which they flow.

This conception of the mutual implication of power and knowledge lies behind Foucault's concerns about critiques of ideology. On Foucault's understanding, ideology "always stands in virtual opposition to something else which is supposed to count as truth."[97] On the prevalent conceptions of the twentieth century, moreover, it "stands in a secondary position relative to something which functions as its infrastructure, as its material, economic determinant, etc."[98] Foucault worries that these assumptions behind ideology critiques mislead the theorist into believing that the problem consists "in drawing the line between that in a discourse which falls under the category of science or truth, and that which comes under some other category," when it would be more productive "[to see] historically how effects of truth are produced within discourses which in themselves are neither true nor false."[99] For Foucault, discerning truth and falsity in a particular case is a social practice that involves the applications of ready-at-hand judgments, dependent in the first instance not on an independent picture of how things are but on contingent facts about social existence. Thus, "'truth' is to be understood as a system of ordered procedures for the production, regulation, distribution, circulation and operation of statements. 'Truth' is linked in a circular relation with systems of power which produce and sustain it, and to effects of power which it induces and which extend it. A 'regime' of truth."[100] Knowledge is first a kind of know-how: a skill of dealing in a particular way with social forces, the need for and character of which is generated by those forces themselves. Knowledge "about" the state of things happens within this larger context of practices and skills that emerge from relations of power. Therefore, "the political question . . . is not error, illusion,

---

96. Foucault believes that this applies to certain types of knowledge and not others (e.g., mathematics).

97. Foucault, "Truth and Power," 118.

98. Foucault, "Truth and Power," 118. It matters here that Foucault often sees himself as pushing on the (perhaps crude) Marxist conceptions of ideology and knowledge that circulated in his milieu.

99. Foucault, "Truth and Power," 118.

100. Foucault, "Truth and Power," 133.

alienated consciousness or ideology; it is truth itself."[101] The powers ought to be seen not as hiding behind illusions but as giving us our discursive practices themselves from the very beginning, as shaping the practices of truth-seeking and communication themselves. The extent of their influence over our imagination and perception is total, not because any particular version of the truth is necessary and determined in advance, but because the intellectual criticism we would use to generate such statements is itself woven through with power.

To say that the extent of the powers' influence over truth is total is not to deny that we have truth-seeking and truth-telling practices that can guide us usefully. (In other words, from the description of truth procedures as inextricably flowing with power, it does not follow that, intensively, those procedures *only* circulate power.) In keeping with the form of the animating assumption that this book seeks to challenge, that would entail that only an innocent truth—the truth insofar as it corresponds unproblematically with the world, the truth as what is left when the distortions of power are subtracted—actually allows us to commune and communicate with the world around us. This sort of assumption leads to the quick and easy association of Foucault in popular representations with some version of "postmodern relativism," the evidently self-contradictory idea that all truth claims are mere subjective reports or exercises of social force. We should here translate Foucault's dictum that power is not bad, but rather dangerous, into a technique for political epistemology. Thinking with the theological patterns established by analysis of the powers can help: the powers are not strictly evil, and even describing them as "fallen" can obscure their purposive character. The powers are created to form bare potency into life—life that knows, in some forms. They rebel against the communion of love they were created to enact, but can only do so by warping, by inverting, by obscuring the vocations given to them by God.

Daniele Lorenzini explains the shifts in Foucault's analyses of knowledge in ways amenable to a critique of knowledge's implication in power that is thoroughgoing without falling into such a bad contradiction. Through the 1960s and early 1970s, Foucault makes this point variously, often trying out contrastive pairs—truth-demonstration and truth-event; knowledge-savoir and knowledge-connaissance; archeology and genealogy—in search of the distinction that will describe how discursive practices are epistemic and how, in pursuing epistemic goals, they are also political techniques. As Lorenzini describes it, when Foucault introduces the idea of an obligation to truth in the 1979–80 seminar, *On the Government of the Living*, he

---

101. Foucault, "Truth and Power," 133.

invites the distinction that makes sense of this aspect of the phenomenon of knowing politically: the related pair of "games of truth" and "regimes of truth."[102] A game of truth is a regulated system for the production of truth claims, establishing the distinction between true and false statements in a given field. A regime of truth is the political arrangement, which cannot be the local truth-of-the-matter itself, that enforces obligations humans have to the truth and its effects.[103] Reconciling accounts on a spreadsheet is a mathematical game of truth: certain results are true; others are false. The social relations of power that translate an unbalanced account line on a spreadsheet into the eviction of a home or the repossession of a vehicle make up the regime of truth: structures of ownership and property enforce a form of submission to translating the game of truth into enacted relations within the world. "While *acceptance* of the truth," Lorenzini clarifies, "can be explained at the level of the game of truth . . . by relying on its formal structure and rules, *submission* to the truth (giving the truth the right and power to govern one's, and others', conduct) must be addressed at a different level, that of the regime of truth."[104] Objections to Foucauldian critiques of knowledge on the basis that they make "truth" impossible, therefore, tend to miss the point by asserting the validity of particular games of truth where Foucault directs attention to the regimes that employ their results.[105]

Yet the purpose of that distinguishing movement, though it preserves a method of describing the register in which we take claims to be true, is not simply to assign practices of truth to one or another side of a ledger. Foucault intends to interrogate the "therefore" that connects them: "it is true, *therefore* I submit."[106] Games of truth are not insulated against distortions from exercises of power; especially in domains that involve qualitative or normative judgments, everyday claims of bias suffice to show as much. Games of truth mediate our epistemic engagement with the world at the same time that they are themselves mediated through regimes of truth. Foucault shows even more interest in how we become subjects through our experiences of selves and others by means of political structures of truth: how we thematize ourselves, making ourselves the subjects we are (insofar as we really are those subjects!) by taking to be true—and therefore submitting to—certain versions of the truth. In this form of human sociality mediated by truth,

---

102. Lorenzini, *Force of Truth*, 34.

103. Lorenzini, *Force of Truth*, 35–36.

104. Lorenzini, *Force of Truth*, 38.

105. Here, I take it that a certain technique that one could find inspiration for in Foucault could look a lot like contemporary forms of pragmatism. Lorenzini observes parallel moments in Wittgenstein, intuitively (Lorenzini, *Force of Truth*, 46–49).

106. Lorenzini, *Force of Truth*, 51.

there are subjections, like Foucault's famous critique of confessional ways of knowing oneself, enlisting oneself within pastoral and therapeutic discourses. But, illustrating the underdetermination of forms of power and their possible reappropriation by resistance, those same pathways between truth and subjectivity are the domain of spirituality, Foucault's understanding of which will be more clearly the subject of chapter 6 below. For now, suffice it to say that the enduring potency of Foucault's political epistemological technique is not its comprehensiveness, and certainly not its having explained all "knowledge" by means of a reduction without remainder to "power." Rather, Foucault clarifies a field of critique wherein the relations that structures of power attempt to obscure in the name of truth may show up, giving us an occasion to ask questions about what the powers would like us to accept in unaware silence.

If we take on some version of this Foucauldian technique, then we cannot turn to vision for an exteriority to power. Wink's attempt to gain critical leverage on the powers by means of exposing their delusions through revelation, like critical theoretical attempts to resist power through critiques of ideology, cannot accomplish what it intends to. That attempt depends on the identity of Wink's critique of the powers with revelation—perhaps mediated and revisable in some particulars, but in its basic orientation, stamped with a divine judgment that guarantees its own nondeceived character. This is a mystifying discontinuity, one that uses the concept of revelation to exempt itself from the influence of the powers—an intellectual exteriority. Wink's insights may indeed be faithful, empowering, useful in resisting domination. But Wink's assumption that knowledge falls on the side of delusion, on the one hand, or (more rarely) revelation, on the other, misrecognizes the theological situation of his own theorizing. Whatever knowledge Wink's theological technique produces will itself also be implicated with the powers, dependent on the practices and procedures that they sustain. The theorist is constantly involved in an economy of knowledge and power, such that the knowledge he generates with an eye to resistance may be reappropriated or reconfigured to calcify relations of power. This has happened repeatedly in the history of theology, including the recent history of theology committed to resisting structures of domination.[107] There is not "*one* knowledge" or "*one* power," nor "*knowledge* or *power* which would operate in and of themselves."[108] Rather, there is a system, a network of power from which forms of knowledge constantly emanate. Thus, "there is no foundational

---

107. For just one description of this, see Althaus-Reid, "Gustavo Gutiérrez."
108. Foucault, "What Is Critique?," 60.

recourse, no escape within a pure form."[109] One cannot retreat from complicity with the powers by means of coming to know them in immediacy; the powers are always already there within the process of their representation.

Analysis can empower resistance, though, even if it does not do so in a way that grants exteriorities. In Foucault's words, "it's not a matter of emancipating truth from every system of power (which would be a chimera, for truth is already power) but of detaching the power of truth from the forms of hegemony, social, economic and cultural, within which it operates at a given time."[110] The theorist can, as Wink claims, suggest that the current form of the powers is neither necessary nor natural, and in so doing, at least present the possibility of transformation. By making particular, contingent constellations of power and their history explicit, the theorist can invite a joint deliberation that calls them into question. Thus, a notion of critique emerges: "critique is the movement by which the subject gives himself the right to question truth on its effects of power and question power on its discourses of truth. Well, then!: critique will be the art of voluntary insubordination, that of reflected intractability."[111] The subject needs no divine right to exercise that prerogative to question truth and power. Even though one cannot escape power categorically through critical knowledge, one can use games of truth to analyze particular relations of power, especially as used by those in authority. Here it is useful to remember that power is a broader and explanatorily more primitive term than authority: to say that one cannot escape power is not to say that one is condemned to live under any particular regime, that there is no horizontal transcendence. We have no guarantee ahead of time that attempts at reform motivated by this account of critique will succeed, or even that they will not make matters worse. Moreover, it will never be the case that, as a result of critique, one will simply not be governed except by the sorts of structures that one likes. Foucault, though, does believe a certain form of critique can be seen as "the art of not being governed quite so much."[112] The normative trajectory of the theorist's work can encourage flexibility and fluidity amid particular patterns of power so as to make them more livable, more capable of claiming practices and ends once ruled out.

This amounts to a disavowal—theological, as well as theoretical—of a "truth" set apart from the economy of the world, a truth that can serve as normative guarantor of our critique. The result is a dialectical non-identity

---

109. Foucault, "What Is Critique?," 63.
110. Foucault, "Truth and Power," 133.
111. Foucault, "What Is Critique?," 47.
112. Foucault, "What Is Critique?," 45.

between our claims to knowledge, even those the theologian believes come from revelation, and whatever reality principle they answer to. By the same token, for Foucault the social theorist has no definitive authority with respect to social relations, or to how to achieve justice within them. Rather, the intellectual has a certain role with respect to activism: cartography. To revisit Foucault's conception, the intellectual "no longer has to play the role of an advisor.... What the intellectual can do is to provide instruments of analysis."[113] Those inclined to resist the powers do not need, from the theorist (as such), normative prescriptions; that responsibility belongs to all (the theorist included) inasmuch as they are "those who do the fighting."[114] This should lead us not to overidentify the role of the theorist with the source of normativity, not least because to do so abrogates the responsibility of all to find a creative and liberating response to power. Instead, the theorist can give "a ramified, penetrative perception of the present, one that makes it possible to locate lines of weakness [and] strong points"—a map of the present configuration of relations of power that can equip those who resist.

This social map is itself an instance of power: it grants no exteriority, no transcendence from that which it claims to represent. The choice of the map as metaphor is itself evocative, since the map is knowledge graphed as a response to and easily subsequently appropriated by structures of power (and often, historically, by agents of domination). Maps, like all knowledge, are sites of contention, resulting in contrasting, often competing, forms of salience, way-making and -finding, and historical preservation. One map of the same physical territory may chart what is lost to colonizing violence; another may authorize, enable, and direct that same violence.[115] The representation, however, may expand the range of options salient at a particular historical conjuncture, the alternatives among which actual persons can choose. It is meaningful to ask about whether and how a map is accurate according to cartographic games of truth, but it would obscure the uses to which mapping is put to leave the matter there.

If we follow Foucault on this point, what possible conception of revelation can follow? A common intuition holds that just this kind of normativity is required in order to make this concept intelligible. Is Wink correct that modern accounts of knowledge and resistance like the one given by Foucault rule out central Christian convictions, such as revelation? Playing by Foucault's rules for speaking about knowledge, could one so much as claim to have received revelation from God? The predicament of human

113. Foucault, "Body/Power," 62.
114. Foucault, "Body/Power," 62.
115. For a story about the former, see, e.g., Fields, "Decolonizing the Map."

life among the powers is only intensified if one cannot even be sure that one's critical resistance gets them right in important respects. As a result, it seems like Wink's fear—that we would fail to resist the powers effectively if we were to give up the uniquely Christian insight into their workings—is validated by Foucault's radical position. However, Barth's account of revelation gives us reasons to hope that we can avoid this species of pessimism as we describe a spiritual practice of relating to one's own political theological knowledge.

REVELATION AND INSTABILITY

Once again, one would expect Barth to side with Wink's Christian account rather than with Foucault. And we have good reason to believe Barth would do just that: a constant theme in his work is the repudiation of the desire to hear "other voices" than that of God revealed in Christ by the power of the Spirit. Like Wink, Barth believes that Christian life and thought depend on revelation, and we abandon that starting point at the peril of losing not just Christian distinctiveness, but the true object of theology in all its uniqueness.[116] There are ways that the confessional line—drawn between Wink and Barth on one side, and Foucault on the other—really does name meaningful differences. Barth asserts a doctrine of revelation that Foucault simply would not accept, and this difference affects their view of power and resistance is a way that cannot simply be ignored.

However, in many centrally important aspects, consistent features of Barth's developing account of revelation[117] can accommodate Foucault's in-

---

116. Barth, *CD* 1/2:97.

117. As discussed in chapter 2, the notion of "Barth's account of revelation" makes synchronic what is surely diachronic: the elements and positions in Barth's discussions of the doctrine shift over the course of his career. By the time of the *Church Dogmatics*, the trinitarian structure of revelation is clear in a way that is not evident in the *Römerbrief*. As Johnson notes, some of the tendencies of his work in the 1920s had implications Barth would later avoid: for example, the idea of the impossibility of knowledge of God seems to rest on a prior, rational notion of the possible ("Reappraisal," 9). This development also bears the marks of Barth's encounter with Roman Catholic theologians, such as Peterson and Przywara, and Barth's allergy to the *analogia entis* offered by these theologians is one of the driving forces of Barth's changing account of revelation (see also Barth, *Anselm*).

However, as with his theological development as a whole, there is an underlying consistency that makes this phrasing a tolerable shorthand for a series of insights into revelation. It is clear as early as the *Römerbrief* that the human incapacity to know God is not simply the result of a Neo-Kantian account of the limitations on knowledge, but also as part of the character of God's deity and the grace involved in revelation. As McCormack points out, even the "external limitation" on the human witness to revelation,

HEALING VISION

sights on the connection between power and knowledge in ways that Wink's cannot. This is so because Barth maintains a sharp distinction between revelation and knowledge. Revelation is the presence of another world within our own. "In so far as our world is touched in Jesus by the other world," Barth writes, "it ceases to be capable of direct observation as history, time, or thing."[118] Rather, what is left behind—what we can call "religion"—is "the crater made at the percussion point of an exploding shell"—not the exploding shell itself, but its lasting impression.[119] In his later idiom, Barth would simplify, "where we think that revelation can be compared or equated with religion, we have not understood it as revelation."[120] Revelation never becomes human knowledge in the form of religion; revelation always stands in judgment of religion (and religious knowledge) as in itself unbelief.[121] In this way, "our position is rendered critical and uncertain . . . our brokenness is broken. Paul against 'Paulinism'! The Epistle to the Romans against the point of view adopted in the Epistle! The Freedom of God against the manner of life which proceeds inevitably from our apprehension of it!"[122] What religion is good for, in Barth's view, is a kind of self-criticism: the recognition that neither one's knowledge nor one's moral efforts approach the righteousness of God, the absolute normativity of the outside. In this light, he takes the lesson from *Romans*:

> It is not against faith that we are warned, but against OUR faith; not against the place that has become visible where men can stand and live, but against OUR taking up a position there and proceeding to live out our lives there; not against freedom and detachment, but against their ambiguous appearance in OUR lives, against the certainty with which WE advance in freedom and detachment. The warning is uttered against any position or manner of life or endeavor that WE think to be satisfactory and justifiable, as though WE were able in some way or other to escape the KRISIS of God.[123]

---

as it is discussed in §27, does not issue from a general account of knowledge but specifically from the hiddenness of God (*Orthodox and Modern*, 170-71). The christological and trinitarian basis of revelation, then, takes root in the conception of grace that is applied epistemologically even in the early Barth.

118. Barth, *Epistle to the Romans*, 29.
119. Barth, *Epistle to the Romans*, 29.
120. Barth, *CD* 1/2:97.
121. Barth, *CD* 1/2:102.
122. Barth, *Epistle to the Romans*, 504.
123. Barth, *Epistle to the Romans*, 504.

The judgment of the world implied in revelation applies reflexively to the one who receives it, as well: it calls into question all of the positions, social, epistemic, or otherwise, that one might take up in response to it. It is the embodiment of the "infinite qualitative distinction" of Kierkegaard, that which is totally inassimilable to the world.[124] Any attempt of ours to understand our world, our ethical obligations, or ourselves in light of revelation constitutes an instance of religion—a necessary attempt, but one that can never itself become identical with revelation.

This is the case for Barth because revelation is the self-giving of God, the self-manifestation of the Trinity. As he puts it, "revelation is God's self-offering and self-manifestation. Revelation encounters man on the presupposition and in confirmation of the fact that man's attempts to know God from his own standpoint are wholly and entirely futile."[125] The human capacity to respond to revelation—faith—labors only on the strength of this prior manifestation. "For in faith," Barth says, "man's religion as such is shown by revelation to be resistance to it."[126] The "grasping" that constitutes religion always misses the point: that God freely gives Godself, not some body of knowledge to be possessed or ethical code to be followed.[127] In this respect, revelation is precisely *not* an accurate vision of the powers, the process that makes one into a "seer" with a God's-eye view of the world. Revelation, to be truly revelation, must be the presence of the one who is infinitely categorically distinct, the exteriority become interior as subject. One cannot identify an account of religious truth with revelation; it is at best the response elicited by revelation on the side of humanity.

To say this of revelation is also to say that God is always present by grace. Barth's account of revelation is formally guided by his convictions about grace. God's grace is the "nevertheless" that contradicts every human "consequently."[128] This grace—the righteousness of God—"is righteousness from outside . . . for the Judge pronounces His verdict according to the standard of His righteousness only."[129] In that grace, "[God's] verdict is creative: He pronounces us, His enemies, to be His friends."[130] By grace alone is the relationship between God and humanity reestablished; from God's side alone is reconciliation achieved. No human knowledge or moral

---

124. Barth, *Epistle to the Romans*, 10.
125. Barth, *CD* 1/2:104.
126. Barth, *CD* 1/2:104.
127. Barth, *CD* 1/2:105.
128. Barth, *Epistle to the Romans*, 93.
129. Barth, *Epistle to the Romans*, 93.
130. Barth, *Epistle to the Romans*, 93.

effort—however true and good—can serve to make a claim on God or to call down God's presence. That presence is always the freely offered love of the divine. Indeed, Barth's understanding of the trinitarian structure of revelation—God as revealed, revealer, and revealedness—is itself an application of the principle of grace: God is present in revelation as a Trinity only in God's freedom and not on the basis of any epistemic claim we have to know God.

When applied to human knowledge, this account of grace rules out all forms of "true" religious knowledge. Rather, revelation always stands in relation to knowledge as justifying grace does to the sinner: the connection between religion and revelation should be seen as "identical with that event between God and man in which God is God, i.e., the Lord and Master of man, who Himself judges and alone justifies and sanctifies, and man is the man of God, i.e., man as he is adopted and received by God in His severity and goodness."[131] Though a connection between the two is established, that connection comes from God's prerogative and never establishes an undialectical relation of identity. Rather, a permanent asymmetry, in which religion always stands in need of "justification" from revelation (just as the sinner does before God), is instituted by this connection. When Barth speaks of "revelation as the abolition of religion," he means just this annihilating relationship: that revelation always shows itself to be categorically distinct from the religion that would grasp for it, while graciously justifying it on no account of its own. If religious knowledge is to become justified, therefore, it is justified extrinsically: by God's gracious willing that it be so. Religious knowledge is thus radically destabilized before a personal God, who stands above and against it as its judge.

Wink's idea of "revelation" or liberating vision can be seen as an instance of just this type of religious knowledge. The "vivid sense of God's counterreality" that is given to the eyes of faith is knowledge of the kingdom, knowledge of God's judgment of and intentions for the world. The reign of God—which can only be the presence of God—has already begun for those who take a stand in solidarity with God's domination-free order. For Wink, the one who, with healed vision, rightly perceives the powers as they are has appropriated revelation ("unveiling") for themselves as religious knowledge. What is unveiled in Wink's understanding of "apocalyptic" is a normative social and political order. On Barth's understanding, what is unveiled is the eternal mystery of God. While the experience of this vision can exert gravity on how we live and think politically, it stands apart from representations of it, unlike Wink's revelation.

---

131. Barth, *CD* 1/2:100.

Barth's eschatology suggests not only the renewing of social and political relationships, therefore, but also calls for constant self-criticism. Even the one whose life is determined by the revelation of God remains subject to judgment, liable to error, and condemned in himself. Since revelation never becomes identified with religion and never becomes a possession of human knowledge, one cannot conclude on the basis of revelation that one's knowledge—about God or about the world in light of God—is justified. In other words, the absolute normativity of God always remains a possession of God's and is not transferred to human activity, moral or intellectual. If this is an appropriate reading of Barth, then his account of revelation does not run afoul of Foucault's technique of reading the mutual implication of power and knowledge in the way that Wink's account does. Barth can accommodate any story that Foucault tells about the generation of knowledge by structures of power, about the self-reflexivity that challenges any claims to stable normativity for knowledge, and—especially—about the complicity that remains even when one generates an accurate account of prevailing social and political orders. Though he offers a conception of revelation, the nonidentity of revelation with its epistemic contents and religious responses means that Barth could, in principle, affirm Foucault's insights about human knowledge. Barth therefore gives us reason to believe that Christian accounts of revelation exist that do not posit intellectual exteriorities. One can hold to a systematically theological account that depends at every turn on revelation, in fact, without necessarily claiming the absolute normativity of God for oneself and, in the process, removing oneself from complicity with the world through a kind of spiritual transcendence.

VISION AND VULNERABILITY

This chapter has attempted to show that claims of intellectual exteriorities to power fail to deliver their sponsors to a position of noncomplicity. Within the tradition of reflection on the powers, such claims are exemplified by Walter Wink's argument that coming to a "healing vision" of the true character of the powers enables meaningful resistance, which is both a theological account of revelation and a representation of social critique. In both aspects, Wink's description of the powers meaningfully describes both domination and some avenues of resistance to it. But in relation to its claims about knowledge of the powers itself, a Foucauldian analysis prompts us to examine its knowingness for its implication in the powers, and a Barthian account of revelation shows how that knowingness is counterproductive as an approach to theology. If the criticisms that I have drawn from Barth and

Foucault are correct, then Wink fails to extend his insights consistently—indeed, radically—to his own position: that of the theorist.

On that basis we can posit a maxim of the spirituality of theological and political knowledge here: in light of our relationship to the powers, all criticism is simultaneously self-criticism. This is so not always by virtue of identity between criticisms—it can matter a great deal that one criticizes a dramatically different position or mode of implication in the relevant structures than one occupies oneself—but rather because the critic is also enmeshed in those structures. There can be no critical outlook on political or social life in which oneself is not also implicated, since even coming to an awareness and conscious rejection of the abuses of the powers does not suffice to disentangle one from complicity with them. That is not to say that all are identically guilty, or that the shape of responsibility remains constant across all types of complicity. Quite the contrary: one may be involved in a certain pattern or structure of power relations at a distant remove, or only in the role of the victim. Yet, one never reaches the "outside" in the sense of not being responsible at all—that is, not being involved so as to make one's actions a meaningful response to the powers. The powers are fallen, and the powers dwell within and above all of us. The very real sense in which one can simultaneously be a victim of their injustices does not change this situation. The necessary task of assigning blameworthiness in particular instances of injustice, then, to an extent swings free of the question of one's involvement or complicity in the particular dynamic of power at issue. In other words, Wink goes wrong when he argues that, because of an intellectual exteriority, one can criticize the powers in a nonrepentant mode. Demystification, when applied to the powers, may result in a vision that enables informed resistance, but that resistance should always recognize one's own complicit position.

Yet, there is still a role for critical theories of social life. Wink's "partnership society" may actually be preferable to the status quo, and a compelling vision of that society can inspire helpful criticism. Of course, it is also the case that Foucault and Barth attempt to give diagnoses of the problems of our life together that can lead to living together differently. The claim here presented is not that one is just as well off without examining the powers in a serious and critical manner (what an odd performative contradiction that would be!). Rather, the claim is that a certain understanding of such criticism—that which depends upon intellectual exteriorities in particular—itself misrecognizes our complicity with the powers. The *Times*' film critics may prefer and argue for independent films to their hearts' delight. They may develop more sensitive aesthetic and intellectual tastes in the process.

What they cannot do is sever their own relation to the industry that they criticize and thus become irresponsible, in the literal sense, for its harms.

The previous two chapters were meant to illustrate and support the claim that the scope of the powers is coextensive with human existence, and thus humans can attain to no positions of exteriority. In other words, even the best forms of resistance do not suffice to eradicate our complicity with the powers. Voluntary and nonconformed communities may offer distinct ways of responding to one's complicity with the powers, but they cannot become sites of exteriority. The church, therefore, never stands in simple opposition to the world without simultaneously remaining a part of the world. Critical and insightful social analysis may offer pathways of salutary resistance, but it cannot become a spiritual or intellectual transcendence of the powers.[132] Christian belief, therefore, ought not to be confused with the divine normativity involved in God's revelation.[133] These two lines of argument, then, ought to serve to motivate the total complicity version of the powers outlined in chapter 2. As a disciplined practice of asking questions about ourselves, we should understand the powers as totally coextensive with human life and existence—including our own, personally—and not just in their obviously social and political aspects. Claims to positions of exteriority, social locations from which one is not complicit with the powers, obscure the full scope of the influence of the powers. This means that communal forms of social distinction do not achieve "difference," and all forms of criticism are, as part of a wide-ranging social process, self-criticism.

This may lead one to despair of forms of resistance. If one cannot succeed in resisting the powers, in the sense of freeing oneself of complicity, why should one resist? Do accounts of total complicity lead to quietism and cynicism? Appropriately enough, this sentiment has motivated critiques of both Barth and Foucault, as well as arguments that take their departure from these figures. The next chapter moves through these critiques to articulate a theology on the basis of total complicity that gives a different orientation for resistance. Beyond purity, beyond innocence, there are still sites of contestation worth engaging in—and possibilities worth fighting for—as part and parcel of our love for the world.

132. Pitts phrases an analogous insight trenchantly: "Reflexive awareness of the contingent and compromised nature of theological practice should breed a deeper theological patience and humility," including a recognition of the help the theologian needs to realize this (*Principalities and Powers*, 131).

133. Though other candidate exteriorities are possible in principle, the second generation of discourse on the powers has tended toward these two. One can extrapolate the kind of theological and critical theoretical reasons that other, similar exteriorities would be rejected, on the view here advanced.

CHAPTER 5

Where There Are Powers

COMPLICITY AND THE BIAS TOWARD INACTION

To this point, this book has set up a contrast between exteriority accounts and total complicity accounts of the powers and argued in favor of the latter. On exteriority accounts of the powers, to the extent that one effectively resists the powers, one is not complicit with them. Whether or not such resistance is thoroughgoingly effective in eradicating complicity, meaningful resistance suffices to minimize complicity, since the two are inversely related. The recognition of complicity is a call to action; the responsible reaction is resistance, which fulfills that responsibility. Against this position, I have argued above that contact with the powers—the very contact that makes us historical, social persons—immediately results in complicity with them, a complicity that runs deeper than and endures despite one's attempts to resist them. That argument is, in part, recognizable as a commonplace reminder of the limits and vulnerability of human capacities: human action is not only marked by ambiguity but also situated within a complex world of forces that far exceed our control. I have used Karl Barth and Michel Foucault, however, to highlight more specific reasons for holding a total complicity account: namely, the interpenetration of human subjectivity itself by the powers, including human will, knowledge, and social life, which leaves no residual of human life outside the domain of the powers. If this vision of human life, structured by the powers through and through, represents deep entanglements of our social lives, then neither the most penetrating analysis of the present nor the most courageous action negates one's complicity with those powers in the grip of which human life exists.

Yet these views are rarely compared in abstraction from the real demands of ethical life. Indeed, any theological or metaethical account is rightly evaluated not just on the clarity and consistency of its theoretical anthropology, but also for its suitability as an ethical disposition in everyday practice. That is, a theology of the powers that cannot help us discern and act responsibly in the world is not only practically troubling but theoretically deficient. A siren song about the powers, lulling us into complacency, would seem to be another of their delusions: perhaps a carefully crafted and relatively coherent justification for acquiescing to the status quo. If exteriority accounts are particularly liable to false consciousness about their complicity, then this ineffectuality is the possibility that attends total complicity accounts. I will use "quietism" to refer to such ineffectuality in the face of a maximal vision of the powers, though it is often designated as or included in critiques of "resignation" and other dispositions blamed for short-circuiting resistance. When applied, as here, to a theology used as a guide for action, the charge of quietism implies that a view exhibits a bias toward blameworthy inaction by improperly reducing our estimation of the value of action. As a result of the apparent cynicism of total complicity accounts, so the complaint goes, the difference between resistance and nonresistance seems to have been flattened out, such that there can be no meaningful difference between action and inaction.[1] Whatever surface plausibility a total complicity account of the powers offers us, then, we may well decide that we cannot responsibly hold that view if it cannot be reconciled with our practical obligations.

This bias toward inaction, moreover, would follow not only from the dispositions likely to result from total complicity accounts, but also from the confusion they sow about power. Claims to exteriority can be the necessary byproduct of the process by which those who are perceived—perhaps rightly!—as culpable for harmful exercises of power are named and opposed: attributing complicity to some is often a way of distinguish their agency from others, and this distinction may be crucially important as a foothold for resistance. This problem is neatly illustrated by a conversation in John Steinbeck's *The Grapes of Wrath*. A nameless tenant is confronting the operator of a tractor, pleading with him not to bulldoze the farm from which the tenant has been evicted by the banks:

> "I built it with my hands. . . . It's mine. I built it. You bump it down—I'll be in the window with a rifle. You even come too close and I'll pot you like a rabbit."

---

1. Gustavo Gutiérrez offers a good example of this kind of criticism when he names "a pessimistic approach to this world which is so frequent in traditional Christian groups and which encourages escapism," in contradistinction to his "optimistic vision which seeks to reconcile faith and the world and to facilitate commitment" (*Theology of Liberation*, 101).

> "It's not me. There's nothing I can do. I'll lose my job if I don't do it. And look—suppose you kill me? They'll just hang you, but long before you're hung there'll be another guy on the tractor, and he'll bump the house down. You're not killing the right guy."
>
> "That's so," the tenant said. "Who gave you orders? I'll go after him. He's the one to kill."
>
> "You're wrong. He got his orders from the bank. The bank told him, 'Clear those people out or it's your job.'"
>
> "Well, there's a president of the bank. There's a board of directors. I'll fill up the magazine of the rifle and go into the bank."
>
> The driver said, "Fellow was telling me the bank gets orders from the East. The orders were, 'Make the land show profit or we'll close you up.'"
>
> "But where does it stop? Who can we shoot? I don't aim to starve to death before I kill the man that's starving me."
>
> "I don't know. Maybe there's nobody to shoot. Maybe the thing isn't men at all. Maybe, like you said, the property's doing it. Anyway, I told you my orders."[2]

"Who can we shoot?" is the plaintive cry of someone confronting seemingly monolithic, impersonal powers. Where, if not from the clarity of innocence over and against those who are complicit, can we get the leverage necessary to discern and to resist the great injustices of the social world, however impersonal they seem? If total complicity accounts spread power, and the responsibility for it, into utter dispersion, who is answerable for power's exercise?

You already know, reader, that this book's response to the latter question is "all of us," different as we are. Yet this is the beginning, and not the end, of an answer that must ever strive toward fullness through the dangerous anesthetic of cynical despair. If our path through an analysis of the powers is going to arrive at a political spirituality, it must face and account for the threats pointed to by those who think otherwise, because these critics are not—or need not be, anyway—enemies. At least, no spirituality predicated on the solidarity that results from our mutual implication in structures of power can assume so.

Accordingly, this chapter seeks to move through, rather than reject, some criticisms of our total complicity account. By charting a course through these criticisms, I aim to uncover an assumption that motivates many of them, and that we are better off doing without. This chapter will frame this assumption in a stark form—that complicity and resistance are annihilating

---

2. Steinbeck, *Grapes of Wrath*, 51–52.

opposites; that just insofar as one is complicit, one cannot meaningfully resist—in order to clarify how it motivates claims to exteriority. But to move through this criticism will require us to take on its concern for a dangerous leveling of complicity and the resulting bias toward inaction, a responsibility that will carry through the final chapter that follows, too.

This chapter will summarize some of the most prominent objections to total complicity in Barth and Foucault, then, in order to discern the analogous form of their complaints. Then, it will offer one perspective on how to wrestle with threats of cynicism, despair, and disaffection that run through the subterrain of this conversation. After having done so, I will offer something like a confession of faith, an account of the gospel that takes fully seriously the extent of the powers' influence and what sorts of characters we can hope to be within it, setting up the description of Christian ethics that concludes the book.

It is strange to make bedfellows of Barth and Foucault, even if it is a practice of strangeness one can learn from them. It may be stranger, still, not only to find a rhyming in how they describe complicity, but also in the ways that they are themselves criticized or dismissed. These figures are too prominent and widely published for us to cover all the possible responses to their work here, but there have been some important objections raised specifically to the route we are taking through them, and so this brief survey will help us understand better this position's argument, largely through the eyes of the detractors of its earlier versions.

DESPAIR IN THE FACE OF THE ABSOLUTE

Late in his career, Reinhold Niebuhr offers a critique of Barth that will stand in for the theological version of the charge of quietism taken up by this chapter. Niebuhr is willing to praise Barth's reintroduction of the "note of tragedy in religion" as an antidote to the spurious optimism of many of their theological contemporaries. However, Niebuhr avers that Barth's thought pays too high a moral price for this achievement.[3] He contrasts Barth's theology with others that he calls "quietistic" (which he does not here define), but charges Barth with quietism in a deeper sense: the true Christian is meant "to look upon the brutalities of history with wholesome contrition," knowing that she is a part of the world and that her sins contribute to it. "Nevertheless," Niebuhr's interpretation continues, "it is inevitable that [she] should be more concerned with the problem of [her] inner life than

---

3. Niebuhr, "Apostle of the Absolute," 144.

with the effort to protect and advance moral values in society."[4] What follows that claim is a tender and insightful, if misleading, reading of Barth's dialectical work:

> Barthian pessimism is, as all pessimism, the fruit of moral sensitiveness. It is the business of religion to create a sensitive conscience. And there is certainly more religious vitality in such pessimism than in the easy optimism of evolutionary moralism. Yet it is one of the tragedies of the religious life that it is almost impossible to create this kind of moral sensitivity without tempting the soul to despair of history and take a flight into the absolute which can neither be established upon historical grounds nor justified by any strictly rational process, but can only be assumed and dogmatically asserted because it seems morally necessary.[5]

For Niebuhr, the early Barth's dialectical theology, in which the absoluteness of the deity of God stands opposed to any claims of absoluteness on behalf of the creature, discourages the Christian person from rousing himself to energetic social action, since the differences between all possible social arrangements are infinitesimal compared to the differences between the world and the absolute. On this account, Barth's pessimism, which appears to be built into the very structure of his account of the relationship between God and creation (and is not merely the result of sin), cannot help but lead to a bias toward inaction.

Niebuhr applies the same thinking to those he considers to be in the orbit of Barth, as well. He concedes to Barthians a social sensitivity—which he again names as a relative advantage to their liberal counterparts—but complains of their lack of social vigor. In light of a concern not to confuse moral and social activity with the establishment of the kingdom of God, Barthians are critical of efforts to improve society and do not give themselves energetically to the "social task."[6] In fierce loyalty to an inaccessible

---

4. Niebuhr, "Apostle of the Absolute," 146. Since this essay first appeared in 1928, the apparent clumsiness of this interpretive claim in light of the whole of Barth's oeuvre must be excused (though, since Niebuhr claims in this essay to have read a translation of *Das Wort Gottes und die Theologie*, one wonders how he could have interpreted the 1919 Tambach Lecture in a way compatible with this conclusion). For my purposes, it is important to note that Niebuhr is inclined, from the start, to find in Barth an opposition between individual piety and social activism. The assumption that the two are in opposition (as such or perhaps merely in Barth's thought) plays an important role in these criticisms.

5. Niebuhr, "Apostle of the Absolute," 147.

6. Niebuhr, "Barthianism and the Kingdom," 148. Here Niebuhr acknowledges the connection between many of the early Barthians and socialist movements and

perfection, they are inadept at social compromise, the "nicely calculated less and more" that gets traction on contests for the good in history.[7] Though Niebuhr here moves between several idioms in describing Barth's work—as idealism that breeds pessimism, absolutism that neglects the value of relative distinctions, and others—the basic concept is the same: the totalizing claim, be it the absolute distinction between God and creation or the utter failure of human attempts at true holiness, renders one's will inert in response to conscience. The *real* problem facing the Christian, on Barth's understanding, is the infinite qualitative divide between God and creation and the necessity of appropriating the grace of God by which the divide is crossed.[8] In other words, the same theological positions that lend credence to and inform an account of total complicity cause blameworthy inaction by means of despair for human action. In removing all possibility of true sanctity from a tragic world, Barth and his followers implicitly encourage their readers to remain in their sin, that grace may abound.

Consider one final angle on Niebuhr's criticism of Barth. Barth's resistance to the regime of National Socialism drew incredible energy from his theological conviction, so much so that he writes something that seems uncharacteristic in the "Hromádka Letter" of 1938 on Czech resistance: "that now every Czech soldier will stand and fall not only for the freedom of Europe, but also for the Christian church."[9] After the Hromádka Letter came to light, Niebuhr declares victory for realists against Barthians. Barth's identification of the Czech resistance to National Socialism with the mission of the church is astonishing, "because they come from a man who has spent all his energies to prove that it is impossible to mix relative political judgments with the unconditioned demands of the gospel. Nothing discredits Barth's major theological emphasis more than his complete abandonment of his primary thesis in the hour of crisis."[10] In fact, Niebuhr agrees with

---

sympathies, but also claims that "it is not unfair to them to say that they don't work very hard at it."

7. Niebuhr, "Barthianism and the Kingdom," 149.

8. Niebuhr, "Barthianism and Political Reaction," 151. It is worthwhile to note that, in this 1934 essay, Niebuhr is still claiming that "here religious absolutism which begins by making the conscience sensitive to all human weakness ends in complacency toward social injustice," though the evidence for these claims seems to be tied up with other interpretations of dialectical theology (e.g., Gogarten's putatively "feudalistic conception of a social order," 152) and the social activities of church groups unaffiliated with Barth. While Niebuhr seems to have shifted, over the course of these six years, to a language of "appropriation" of Barthianism for the (apparently alien) ends of political reactionaries, he clearly finds fault with Barth's thought for failing to militate against this possibility.

9. Busch, *Karl Barth*, 289.

10. Niebuhr, "Karl Barth and Democracy," 164.

Barth's position, but thinks that it belies the impossibility of a rigid dialectic between Creator and creation: in the crucible of lived history, the theologian who retains a conscience cannot but take sides in conflict and, in conflict of such proportions as the Second World War, perceive the theological stakes of the outcome. The Hromádka Letter proves Barth to be insufficiently dialectical: the "no" to the exigencies of culture and politics before the letter were too unqualified, while the "yes" spoken within it is too unreserved.[11] Barthianism in its pure form, in Niebuhr's estimation, ruled political questions strictly irrelevant to the Gospel, delivering us to an arbitrary series of engagements based on attachment, passion, and interest, rather than sober moral judgment.[12] Barth can help us fight the devil "if he shows both horns and both cloven feet," but refuses to make the finer-grained judgments that detect evil where it shows "only one horn or the half of a cloven foot."[13] By displacing the moral energy of Christian theology into the negation of all creation as part of a deeper affirmation of grace, Barthian thought has rendered itself useless for the actual decisions for which most political actors in most situations are responsible.[14] Barthianism breeds exactly the wrong kind of sensitivity: rather than the necessary fruitful judgment between actual social alternatives, it trains its adherents in finding flaws with even the best available social arrangements.

In the idiom of this book, Niebuhr suggests that Barth's total complicity account is responsible for promoting quietism. Niebuhr holds that Barth's work, though it seems to promote a resistance to the powers of the

11. Niebuhr, "Karl Barth and Democracy," 165.

12. The situation was further complicated by Barth's relative silence on the Hungarian rebellion, which became the most prominent point of contention between Barth and Niebuhr. Despite the spontaneous and sympathetic character of their revolt against the Soviets, Barth refused to support the Hungarians with his considerable theological machinery. This served, again, as an instance for Niebuhr to crow that, in the Hromádka Letter, "his partisanship was probably too extreme, as his neutralism now is too undiscriminating." Barth's political judgments are haphazard, Niebuhr suggests, because his theology is "too 'eschatological' and too transcendent to offer any guidance for the discriminating choices that political responsibility challenges us to." Thus, Barth's theology traffics in absolutes that overshadow the calculated political decisions required of modern people and, therefore, relegates those political decisions to an unprincipled pragmatism ("Why Is Barth Silent on Hungary?," 184–86).

13. Niebuhr, "We Are Men and Not God," 172.

14. It is a telling and pivotal point that Niebuhr here complains of Barth's purported uselessness for the Christian *statesman*. Much was made in twentieth-century political theology about the contingency and peculiarity of the assumption that the statesman as the paradigmatic ethical actor and, consequently, the "advice to princes" genre as the central form of theological and moral writing. Suffice it to say here that Barth, among others, does not have in mind, as his primary audience, those operating the levers of political authority.

world, actually generates a bias toward inaction. In his maximal reading of the powers, which includes the best institutions and movements familiar to us, as well as the eschatological reserve Barth places over all attempts at action, Barth suppresses the impetus to attain the achievable in light of the impossibility of the perfect. As a result, Barth's total complicity account leads its holders to a blameworthy inaction and is, as a result, an irresponsible position to hold. As we turn to criticisms of Foucault's version of total complicity, the conversation shifts away from the theological terminology and impulses exchanged between Barth and Niebuhr, but the structures of the conceptual problem will meaningfully follow this pattern.

POWER AND NORMATIVITY

Because of his prominence in the world of social theory and the wide range of his work, many criticisms of Foucault have circulated over the years. But arguably the most prominent one lies squarely in the trajectory of this book. The famous quip attributed to Jean-Paul Sartre—that Foucault is the "last rampart of the bourgeoisie"[15]—anticipates a host of critics who will assert that Foucault's view of endless, undulating interiority provides cover for those who wish to preserve the status quo or seek to excuse themselves from serious political action on the grounds that there is no way out. On many topics—such as his analytical attention to neoliberalism that serves to make its "rationality intelligible"—Foucault's approach to analysis might come across as a kind of neutrality that fails to meet the moment.[16] On others, his active criticism of causes and positions—like the Marxism that would have appealed to Sartre and many other post-war continental

15. Sartre's full remark—that (in translation) "Behind the story . . . it is Marxism that is concerned. It is about creating a new ideology, the last rampart that the bourgeoisie can still muster against Marx"—is typically abbreviated and shorn of its context, which considers Marxism and structuralism. See Sartre, "Jean-Paul Sartre Répond," 88.

16. Zamora, "How Michel Foucault Got Neoliberalism." Zamora later says: "By locating resistance mainly in the relationship to the self, Foucault significantly diminished the range of his social critique. It paradoxically put out of reach precisely those economic and political structures that make up the framework within which this 'relationship to the self' can be experimented with. Questions around exploitation, the unequal division of labor (now on a global scale), or economic inequality disappear and seem completely inaccessible through these 'micro-resistances.'" The next chapter seeks to address the assumption here that the turn to the subject is a turn away from such structures. Foucault indeed does not mount a head-on assault on neoliberalism in *The Birth of Biopolitics*, but I am persuaded by David Newheiser that, given the long sweep of his argumentation that freedom is the substance on which power works, when Foucault elaborates an account of neoliberal governance, he is also rendering it vulnerable to resistances ("Foucault, Gary Becker, and the Critique," 4–5).

intellectuals—reads like a subtly reactionary way of deflating revolutionary, or even reformatory, aspirations. Many of these criticisms express a desire for normative approaches to political agency or a picture of the work of the theorist that Foucault is unwilling to provide because of how he imagines norms relate to power.

Charles Taylor, in "Foucault on Freedom and Truth,"[17] remarks that reading Foucault is disconcerting, since Foucault seems to offer insight into what modern culture has become that makes the space for critique, but simultaneously repudiates that same critique. "He dashes the hope," Taylor laments, "that there is some good we can *affirm* as a result of the understanding these analyses give us. And by the same token he seems to raise a question of whether or not there is such a thing as a way out."[18] Foucault brings evils to light and yet refuses the impulse that eradicating or reforming these evils would be an unalloyed good. Particularly, since Foucault is preoccupied with exposing the twin dynamics of power/domination and disguise/illusion, we would expect him to be committed to promoting freedom and truth. Yet, there is no truth "that can be espoused, defended, or rescued against systems of power," and "there is no escape from power into freedom, for such systems of power are coextensive with human society."[19] Taylor believes that this constitutes a normative dislocation that both marks Foucault's work as profoundly original and simultaneously leads Foucault into contradiction. Specifically, he argues that Foucault falls into inconsistency on three points: the possibility of power without a subject; power's dependence on a freedom to be exercised over and against; and the "Nietzschean relativism" into which Foucault's political epistemology delivers us. Where Foucault draws on the traditions of thought that invoke power, domination, and freedom, Taylor thinks he does so in a way that falls into contradiction with itself—illusions and masks require a "true" face; domination requires a freedom that is suppressed. The result, despite the air of possibility that surrounds Foucault's work, excludes "the possibility of a change of life form that can be understood as a move toward a greater acceptance of truth."[20] In exhorting us to seek out such relative gains, Taylor sounds much like Niebuhr: amidst perpetual social revision, "we struggle over interpretation and weightings, but we cannot shrug them off. They *define* humanity, politics for us."[21]

17. Taylor, "Foucault."
18. Taylor, "Foucault," 152.
19. Taylor, "Foucault," 152–53.
20. Taylor, "Foucault," 176–77.
21. Taylor, "Foucault," 178.

Jürgen Habermas offers a comparable critical analysis of Foucault's work on power. Like Taylor, Habermas registers Foucault's early adoption of the negative discourse about the subject, mediated to him by Claude Lévi-Strauss.[22] In Foucault's case, this takes the shape of unmasking how the human sciences and the knowledge which they take as their object participate in constituting the very subjects that they attempt to study, both by a series of exclusions (e.g., the clinical form of madness) and by creating the categories by which subjects will come to recognize themselves. The shifts in institutions and practices that Foucault studies exemplify "the intrusion of socializing," characterized by "the moment of coercive, asymmetric influence over the freedom of movement of other participants in interaction."[23] As Foucault shifts to his 1970s work on power, he seeks to interrogate the presentism in modernity's consciousness of time—related as it is narcissistically to the past and overconfidently toward the future—especially by revealing the contingent beginnings (rather than mythical origins) that make up the natural history of our forms of knowledge.[24] Thus, history in the singular is shattered into the Babel of a "plurality of irregularly emerging and disappearing islands of discourse," making Foucault's vision of power not only historicist but also empiricist, nominalist, and materialist.[25]

From this point, Habermas launches his criticisms of Foucault. He notes, first, that Foucault fails to think genealogically about his own genealogical historiography and his concept of power, though it is unclear what, exactly, Habermas thinks this would entail.[26] More to the point, Habermas thinks that Foucault cannot actually escape the philosophy of the subject, since Foucault's conception of power is itself derivative from that philosophy.[27] By merely reversing the typical relationship of subjects and power, Foucault has not resolved the aporias that he attributes to the modern philosophy of the subject; he has merely shifted them to this philosophy of power. In this way, Foucauldian genealogy is guilty of the same illusion

---

22. Habermas, *Philosophical Discourse*. This text, which appeared in German in 1985, is composed mostly of lectures given in 1983–84. I note this because Habermas attempts to "point out some themes that establish a continuity in subject matter between the earlier and the later works [of Foucault]" (242), but he cannot have had access to important instances of the later works, such as the lectures from the Collège de France. It is worth it to worry about whether Habermas's picture of continuity, as a result, takes as decisive the early works of Foucault in a way that distorts the later works.

23. Habermas, *Philosophical Discourse*, 242.

24. Habermas, *Philosophical Discourse*, 249–50.

25. Habermas, *Philosophical Discourse*, 251, 256.

26. Habermas, *Philosophical Discourse*, 269.

27. Habermas, *Philosophical Discourse*, 274.

that it attributes to the sciences its targets: it attempts to conceal its own participation in power through an apparent "reflectionless objectivity" that bears the burdens of presentism, relativism, and disavowed normativity.[28] In the attempt to erase the subject, genealogical historiography "ends up in an unholy subjectivism."[29] That is, in addition to the presentism entailed in being unable to account for one's own circumstances and the relativism that results from reducing the social world to a sea of context-dependent forms, Foucauldian analyses of power make arbitrary partisans who cannot account for their own normative presuppositions. Every counterpower vis-à-vis power—which Foucault's analyses seem to favor—is caught in an endless cycle of mutual reinscription: as counterpower, it moves within the horizon of power, while its victory would merely establish it as the new system of power, giving rise to new counterpower.[30] Silent on the question of the legitimacy or relative validity of some formations of power in comparison with others, Foucauldian genealogy attempts to bracket normative claims out of its investigation. Foucault refuses to take sides, and in so doing (on Habermas's view), raises the all-important question: "If it is just a matter of mobilizing counter-power, of strategic battles and wily confrontations," Habermas asks, "why should we muster any resistance at all against this all-pervasive power circulating in the bloodstream of the body of modern society, instead of just adapting ourselves to it?"[31] The reader is left either to take this empty-handedness at face value, which would leave Foucault's work impotent for actual political intervention consistent with its methodology, or to suspect that Foucault in fact smuggles norms into his forms of his analysis that he then coyly ignores.

Nancy Fraser gives voice to a similar set of concerns about Foucault's work. She thinks that by suppressing the question of the legitimacy of power in his genealogies, Foucault unearths truly valuable insights: the productive capacity of power, its ability to work at the lowest social levels of everyday life, and its shifting of the focus of analysis from belief to practice. At the same time, this leads to serious difficulties: it seems equally plausible that Foucault could offer: (a) a value-neutral account of modern power; (b) some normative framework that works as an alternative to modern accounts of legitimacy; or (c) a simple attempt at politically engaged critique without normativity at all. Foucault's normative suspension, then, seems to purchase

---

28. Habermas, *Philosophical Discourse*, 275–76.
29. Habermas, *Philosophical Discourse*, 276.
30. Habermas, *Philosophical Discourse*, 281.
31. Habermas, *Philosophical Discourse*, 283–84.

genuine insights into modern power at the cost of profound ambiguities.³² As she thinks through the implications of each of those explanations, Fraser finds in favor of the third option: that "it is not unreasonable to assume that the liberal framework has not been fully suspended" in Foucault's work, and Foucault is thus caught in a (perhaps unwitting) contradiction.³³ Fraser hypothesizes that Foucault contradicts himself because he assumes that the norms of modern legitimacy "can be neatly isolated and excised from the larger cultural and linguistic matrix in which they are situated," failing to perceive how normativity saturates language, interpretation, and judgment in deeper ways.³⁴ Foucault's apparent criticisms of the liberal framework as a deceptive medium for domination then depend on that framework itself, such that he implicitly hacks at the branch on which he sits. Fraser argues that Foucault is led into this contradiction because he fails to distinguish among phenomena—such as authority, force, violence, domination, and legitimation—a view of the differences of which would give him leverage for normative judgments. Because these forms are all described as "power," Foucault seems only able to reject them altogether, thus endorsing a one-sided refusal of modernity without a conception of what could replace it.³⁵

Objections to Foucault's total complicity account, though they differ in approach and apparently in estimation of the value of that work, develop according to a fairly consistent pattern. In Foucault's attempt to enfold normativity—be it epistemic or practical—within relations of power, he engages in a performative contradiction: the only hope for justifying the resistance that he valorizes lies in the kind of normativity his descriptions of resistance seem to rule out.³⁶ Without some normativity that is exempt from the cor-

---

32. Fraser, *Unruly Practices*, 18. Alongside this normative suspension, Foucault brackets what Fraser calls the "problematic of epistemic justification": attempts to discern whether the various regimes of truth Foucault studies "provide knowledge that is in any sense true or warranted or adequate or undistorted" (21). Fraser observes that, though the preponderance of textual evidence suggests that this is a substantive commitment to an epistemological cultural relativism, other texts suggest that it is heuristic and provisional. Though Fraser focuses on the effects of the normative suppression, this epistemic question seems implicated in similar issues.

33. Fraser, *Unruly Practices*, 30.

34. Fraser, *Unruly Practices*, 30–31.

35. Fraser, *Unruly Practices*, 32–33. She makes a similar case in "Michel Foucault: A 'Young Conservative'?," the next chapter in *Unruly Practices*. There she asks why we should oppose domination in the absence of a comprehensive ethics (53).

36. A similar line of complaint is directed at Judith Butler by Martha Nussbaum in "Professor of Parody." Nussbaum writes, "indeed, it is clear that Butler, like Foucault, is adamantly opposed to normative notions such as human dignity, or treating humanity as an end, on the grounds that they are inherently dictatorial" (para. 44), and argues that Butler's mere parody is not a serious mode of resistance because of its lack of normativity. This is one piece of evidence that this objection appears in response to total complicity accounts as such, and not merely to those offered by Barth and Foucault.

rosive influence of genealogy itself—since genealogy would render it arbitrary, another instance of power—there seems to be no banner in defense of which one would be motivated to employ Foucault's theories of resistance. Foucault does not actually offer this kind of normativity, and at times it is unclear if he even could do so consistently with his methodological (and frequently, substantive) positions. Yet in its absence, one might just as well seek to dominate as to resist, to revel in illusions as to endeavor to speak the truth. The absolute priority of power, and the resulting interiority of normativity *as such* to relations of power, presents a monolith, with neither weaknesses to exploit nor havens of exception. To take Foucault at his word, then, would only result in quietism: the fact of his own engagement is a biographical accident or, perhaps worse, a sign of the untenability of his thought.

These critics of Foucault react against the absolute interiority of total complicity accounts and formulate a demand for a position of exteriority. That exteriority may be intellectual, inasmuch as it offers options for committed normativity that are not themselves functions of power, or it may be voluntary, found in some practice of liberation that makes sense across systems of power and anchors a meaningful resistance. Either way, resistance seems incoherent at best and profoundly unlikely at worst in the absence of just such a position from which to resist. Though these critics typically frame their objections as naming a methodological inconsistency, their conclusions are remarkably similar to Niebuhr's moral psychological objection to Barth: the totalizing picture of our complicity discourages, even rules out, meaningful ethical activity. As a theology of resistance, then, a total complicity account, once accepted, would result in any of a range of issues. Perhaps this would be a fundamental mismatch between belief and practice, such that one's ethical practices were inhibited rather than energized as a result of one's ethical convictions. Perhaps this would mean abandoning actual ethical decisions to pragmatisms only capable of pursuing local, disorganized preferences. These critics imply, however, that a total complicity account will most likely result in a bias toward inaction: because, for one reason or another, we believe that we cannot escape the world of the powers, we will not be able to sustain our resistance, despite the good we might do through it.

POLITICS WITHOUT PURITY

"Who can we shoot?" expresses an intuitive wish for a target: a responsible party whose defeat or disempowerment will neutralize violent structures.

The finality of the bullet calls for a confidence that social evils can be localized in—or at least deflated by the puncture of—bodies that yield to its force. Even nonviolent political programs in our midst spontaneously reach for clarities, commitments held to motivate resistance to the powers that must come from a better world beyond. So prevalent is this instinct that to attempt to reconfigure political life without it raises the question, "why bother?" If there are no demons to be slain who are distinct from "us" in some final sense, or if our weapons cannot slay them, how do we fight? And if there is nothing unfailingly worth fighting for, nothing untouched by the demonic, why would we?

That narrative expression puts a mythical face on the assumption that runs through criticisms of total complicity accounts. Critics assume that a position of exteriority—a fulcrum outside the distorting influence of the powers—is necessary to get leverage for the application of force against the powers. Insofar as the agent of resistance is complicit with the powers, no such efficacious force can or will be mustered. On that assumption, if complicity is indeed total, then resistance can only embody false hope, and this belief both encourages quietism and fails to explain the common political intuition that some alternatives and forms of action are urgently better than many others. We are left with no one to shoot (even metaphorically), and therefore nothing energizing to do. The conceptual structure is the same in accounts of agency and theories of knowledge: that some position must always be judge, and never the judged, on the basis of power. To be free to resist just means to be free *from* the guilt-imparting influence of the powers. Successful resistance entails the erasure of complicity: to the extent that resistance is effective, one is no longer complicit with the power one set out to resist.

I think that those who find total complicity accounts persuasive should hear in this message a significant warning. If we are suspicious of the romance of resistance, on guard against the ways we might deliver ourselves unknowingly ever deeper into the ways of the powers, the attendant danger of that posture is inaction, a perverse confidence in infinite unmasking, endless deflation of ambitions undertaken with praiseworthy aims.[37] What is in most cases the liability proximate to the Barthian or the Foucauldian (at least, the sorts described in this book) is not thinking too highly of what

---

37. José Esteban Muñoz calls analogous positions in queer theory, "romances of the negative," attuned also to what Eve Kosofsky Sedgwick describes as paranoid forms of reading (*Cruising Utopia*, 11–12. See also Sedgwick, "Paranoid Reading.") I think that there is space in a total complicity account for the specific kind of utopianism that Muñoz hopes for, specifically as a form of horizontal transcendence, but that line of reflection will have to be explored elsewhere.

we can achieve, but setting aside what can be done for the meaner gratifications of knowingness, of superiority by finding fault, of inoculation against disappointment. It is possible, after all, to work deep falsity with true things, something we have been at pains to describe above. Critics of this position are not enemies when they remind us of the danger to which these commitments incline us. The best answer to these criticisms is likely to be, in most cases, repentant, witness-driven action rather than more discourse.

Nevertheless, it is worthwhile to make our way through one more phase of this discourse, since the prescriptions of the critics depend, I argue, on a misdiagnosis, in two distinct respects. First, there are ways of resistance that are opened specifically by understanding oneself as the medium through which the powers work; we will turn to that in chapter 6. Second, I worry that the implied suggestion of norms that we can encounter apart from our participation in the world of the powers effectively recommends an optimism—by which I mean here a kind of hopeful attachment, rather than sunny prediction—that leads down dangerous paths. In the more prevalent case, the optimism of exteriority tends to lead to a cynical disappointment, perhaps ironically enacting the worry of the critics against Barth and Foucault: while neither of these figures in fact gave up their political action and aspiration, many others in their societies and those descended from or proximate to them have. There are good reasons to think that this disaffection results from believing the critics' assumption to be true, that complicit resistance really is meaningless, in a world where exteriorities are or increasingly seem to be inaccessible. In the less prevalent, but more dangerous, case, this optimism is maintained in reaction against all that would call it to account, and to change. We sometimes call this "radicalism," as if it gets to the roots of the powers that make up the world system. In fact, it nearly inescapably reinforces that system: it makes a *particular* demand of the powers with the displaced moral force of protest against the whole, usually giving itself over to others of the powers in the process—most commonly, the power of violence. It is worthwhile, then, to consider how total complicity specifically adopted as a spiritual disposition can inoculate us against both cynical, despairing inaction and misrecognized but enthusiastic service to the powers.

Thought about political affect—the fantasies, attachments, and felt force of the structures of our social bond—has become too rich and varied for us to survey here. There is something to be gained, though, in briefly considering the prominent approach to optimism taken by Lauren Berlant. Their *Cruel Optimism* argues that a common snare in affective political life in the contemporary West takes the shape of an attachment wherein the scene or object of desire is itself "an obstacle to fulfilling the very wants that bring people to it." This particularly holds in analyzing attachment to politics, as the importance of its life-organizing activity can obscure the damage it does.[38] Berlant suggests that, especially in liberal societies, returning to political recommitment ceremonies and scenes despite widespread belief that political institutions respond mostly to elite interests gives rise to a complex and arresting tangle of attachment. The widely available modes of liberal political engagement—voting, advocacy, news consumption, dinner table conversations—confirm our attachment to the political system and the affects that bind us to it, "even if the manifest content of the binding has the negative force of cynicism or the dark attenuation of a political depression."[39] The constant demand for the repetition of attempts to repair institutions that were always meant to be broken—a demand issued with force precisely by the high stakes of those institutions' agency—wears a fatigue into the social fabric and can split optimism from tangible action.[40] One thinks here of the role of television shows like *The West Wing* as the displaced political conscience and hope of the Bush-era 2000s—or even *House of Cards* as the cynical fantasy of political efficacy and volatile hypercompetence during the frustrations of the waning years of the Obama presidency, whose earlier slogan, "Yes We Can," was arguably the most direct appeal to precisely this form of optimism.

The problem of such an optimism is not political attachment as such, as if the solution to disappointment is detachment. Such a strategy is, after all, the very logic offered by the critics of total complicity accounts described in this chapter: that in the absence of an invincible attachment, a conviction that some norm exists outside the disappointing churn, we are left only with disaffection, with arbitrary preference and prejudice. For Niebuhr, this is the despair for the world in the infinite shadow of the divine; for the critics of Foucault, it is the enactment of the belief that every norm has coordinates in relation to flows of power. In both cases, the criticism has force because it hopes to stave off disaffection by wielding some stable and stabilizing moral force. There must be some "moral values," as Niebuhr says, "to protect and advance," particularly on the basis of which our politics take shape. As Berlant says elsewhere, the assertion of something like such values can be made in a mode which closes off an object (like our role in relation to political

---

38. Berlant, *Cruel Optimism*, 227.

39. Berlant, *Cruel Optimism*, 227. By this, I take Berlant to mean at least that a kind of preoccupation with negation or criticism itself implies an optimism to the underside of the political: that the one constantly articulating a critique of the system is affectively bound to it precisely through the energies of that critique.

40. Berlant, *Cruel Optimism*, 227–28.

institutions) rather than opening it up, defending us against certain forms of self-knowledge.[41]

The problem with this form of attachment is that the optimism itself, whatever its object, cannot be metabolized within the actual vicissitudes of life among the powers: such grand commitments cannot move, adjust, or transform, and simultaneously serve as the fulcrum in exteriority that makes political commitment go.[42] Positing an exteriority—precisely if and when access to it is maintained to anchor our aspirations for challenging the powers—sets us up for a crisis. We are made insecure by the instability of the object; an object our attachment hoped would be good proves to be ambivalent, at best.[43] Because these are affective patterns, they can show up in many contexts. But in relation to the actual arrangements of political affect and commitment that we have, this disaffection usually takes the form of either disengagement from explicit political action or a turn to more reactionary politics.[44] The widely known aphorism (impossible to pin to a definitive author and phrasing)—"If you are not a liberal at 25, you have no heart. If you are not a conservative at 35, you have no brain"—charts not only the flow of financial interest or growth in practical wisdom but, arguably more deeply, the migration of optimism away from principle in response to disappointment.

The critics' worries about muddled and directionless perplexity—the unwillingness to apply consistent attention to arrive at relatively better judgments about how to act in relation to the powers—are realized every day in

41. Berlant, "Genre Flailing," 156. I also owe my understanding here, in large measure, to David Newheiser's concept of "negative political theology," described in "Why the World Needs Negative Political Theology."

42. There is an analogy here to longstanding conversations in pragmatist philosophy discussing the impossibility of suspending all of one's beliefs at once, but suggesting that each of our commitments can, in turn, be subjected to judgment on the basis of others. Kevin Hector puts something like this instinct to use to analyze claims of injustice in response to instances of social disrespect without exteriority. Hector describes how this plays out by tracing "fissures within the prevailing order," which open to a sense that the normative trajectories of our commitments outrun our actual practices (*Theology without Metaphysics*, 278–80).

43. Berlant, "Genre Flailing," 156–57.

44. As I write these words, the current object lesson in this pattern of attachment and disaffection is the movement of people who took themselves to be part of the North American political left, especially during the forms of the legitimation crisis that bubbled to the surface in 2020, to the right, along with prominent journalists and others who preceded them (see, for instance, Joyce and Sharlet, "Losing the Plot"). This is one version of a longstanding pattern, though: one can find this form of reaction to disappointment at regular intervals in the politics of the metropole: see, e.g., Lowndes, "From New Class Critique"; Packer, "Why Leftists Go Right."

the political culture that we actually have and not because political subjects are spontaneously doing genealogies of structures of power. It is, rather, the plain and prevalent sense that the contradictions of structural power become hypocrisies when the powers that be call for increased commitment in response to (indeed, to shore up their legitimacy in the face of) deteriorating conditions. Or, to switch back into the theological idiom, that we lack a spiritual practice of politics adequate to a world in which our idols are constantly smashed—including the insidious possibility of putting ultimate trust in idol-smashing—and deservingly so.

The alternative to the everyday forms of alienation from disappointing exteriorities, though, is immediately far worse: an extremism maintained as a reaction against these forms of disappointment. On these terms, extremism describes disappointed attachment that not only refuses to be metabolized, but also cannot be relinquished, breaking down the dimension of ordinary sociality that holds us to common account: for the extremist, no countervailing good to their own can be admitted, no critical perspective truly heard as a site for revealing a common vocation. This kind of optimism demands a future in continuity with the present,[45] but maintained on defensive, exclusionary terms. Because they cannot enter into a dialectical motion with other elements of the world, exteriorities held under such conditions thus become no longer political values for holders, but tyrants—no longer convictions, but idols. Through this unyielding position, the spiritual force of violence is more than willing to do its ensnaring work—a phenomenon well-documented by exactly the literature that is the precondition for this book.

The discipline of constantly reinscribing one's view of oneself and one's attachments in the working of the powers has an analogue in depressive modes of attachment, outlined by psychoanalyst Melanie Klein and further circulated, especially in queer reflections, by Eve Kosofsky Sedgwick. Attaining a depressive position is a developmental achievement, wherein one no longer categorizes objects of (potential) attachment into "good objects" and "bad objects"—inevitably leading to their fracture into parts—but rather sees complex wholes. When we succeed in attaining to this position, "it is then possible to turn to use one's own resources to assemble or 'repair' the murderous part-objects into something like a whole," with which we might identify and engage constructively.[46] Tellingly, for Sedgwick, the alternative, what she calls "paranoid readings," which are modes of knowing, maximally, "how the world works" through the use of hermeneutics of

---

45. See a convergence here in Berlant, "Critical Inquiry," 449.
46. Sedgwick, "Paranoid Reading," 128.

suspicion, place "an extraordinary stress on the efficacy of knowledge per se—knowledge in the form of exposure" (in which I hope the reader will hear once more, "vision heals").[47] A paranoid way of knowing the world urgently prioritizes the sense that "*There must be no bad surprises*," but a reparative strategy is wagered on the premise that "because there can be terrible surprises, there can also be good ones."[48] The depressive position incorporates disappointment in oneself, others, and the world, but persists in hope of knowing the other through a "guilty, empathetic view . . . as at once good, damaged, integral, and requiring and eliciting love and care."[49] What emerges is a scene replete with possibility because out from under the shadow of the demand for purity, through attention, and even love, to the whole objects we actually encounter, we can enact our commitments, seek joy and pleasure, build new things—though as Sedgwick says, this depends on the subject's movement "toward what Foucault calls 'care of the self,'" the subject of the next chapter.[50]

Analogy to this concept for our view of the powers clarifies that the positing of exteriorities—like good part-objects—and the tendency toward demonization of flesh-and-blood persons—bad part-objects—are part of a unified, if not strictly coherent, disposition toward the world. The critics of total complicity certainly know how not to be Manichean; they are worried, after all, that without some stable normative basis within the world, we will lack the means to make precisely the difficult tactical and ethical decisions that political life calls for. But in this instance, their objections mobilize serious concerns from within an assumption that our norms, or our agency, or ourselves could only make progress insofar as they are untainted by complicity. This form of mutual exclusion—between innocence and implicating participation, between freedom and power, between truth and ideology—repeats itself as a demand for a position that will sanction judgment. Once political imagination is recruited into such a form, it must always then work

---

47. Sedgwick, "Paranoid Reading," 126, 138.

48. Sedgwick, "Paranoid Reading," 130, 146; emphasis original. It is worth observing at this point that many uses of Foucault serve the paranoid impulse, as Sedgwick knows: she refers, for instance, to "the gorgeous narrative work done by the Foucauldian paranoid, transforming the simultaneous chaoses of institutions into a consecutive, drop-dead-elegant diagram of spiralling escapes and recaptures" (132) and elsewhere to the link between the paranoid reading practice and "the notion of the inevitable," which I take to be conveyed by many uses of Foucault (147). It is also possible to read Foucault differently: as emphasizing the radical contingency that is uncovered by his genealogies, for instance, or as arguing that not that everything is bad, but that everything is dangerous (Foucault, "A propos de la généalogie de l'éthique," 1205).

49. Sedgwick, "Paranoid Reading," 137.

50. Sedgwick, "Paranoid Reading," 137.

to overcome the binary logic governing it. Innocence requires a guilty party; people who know themselves to be victims, like Steinbeck's tenant farmer, must locate the perpetrators. Humans not only have intersecting identities: the very processes of social differentiation themselves flow in and out of each other,[51] change form, and operate differently under different circumstances. As a result, the political self-relation assumed by the critics is given to oscillation among enthusiasms, and between perpetrator and victim.[52] A self-relation primed to perceive and respond to complicity can name how the powers move through oneself, forming the self, what structural effects this has on a wider world, and what sorts of responses are possible, without recruiting optimisms about exteriority that are likely unsustainable.

From that depressive political position, there is, ironically, a new optimism that is possible. That, in any case, is what Foucault believes:

> If I don't ever say what must be done, it isn't because I believe that there's nothing to be done; on the contrary, it is because I think there are a thousand things to do, to invent, to forge, on the part of those who, recognizing the relations of power in which they're implicated, have decided to resist or escape them. From this point of view all of my investigations rest on a postulate of absolute optimism. I do not conduct my analyses in order to say: this is how things are, look how trapped you are. I say certain things only to the extent to which I see them as capable of permitting the transformation of reality.[53]

Foucault's optimism takes root from the fact that he thinks resistance is not, in the first case, an option for political and social actors: it is a fact about the unfolding power relations composing social life. Because nothing attains to exteriority, everything can be put in motion. Indeed, his prime indexes of domination are inflexibility, immobility. The powers structure a world weighted toward a future continuous with the present; Foucault describes a present already at odds with itself, with forces coalescing toward certain ends, but amid a contradictory morass. As an exercise of freedom, which he understands as the ontological condition of ethics,[54] it is possible to push that present toward some of its possible futures. Those futures may be remote, and our paths into them winding and indirect. Knowing this, we

---

51. See, for instance, Schneider, "What Race Is Your Sex?"

52. For more on this connection between splitting and switching back and forth between positions of guilt and innocence, especially as a response to trauma, see Cooper-White, *Psychology of Christian Nationalism*, 97.

53. Foucault and Trombadori, *Remarks on Marx*, 174.

54. Foucault, "L'éthique du souci de soi comme pratique de la liberté," 1531.

may assume, as one of his interviewers did, Foucault thinks that this means we just have to wait: that because history does not change as if we are the subjects guiding it, we are only passive before it. Here Foucault interjects: "No, not wait—do, practice! Rising up must be practiced, by which I mean one must practice rejecting the subject status in which one finds oneself, the rejection of one's identity, the rejection of one's own permanence, the rejection of what one is. It's the first condition of rejecting the world."[55] If these claims about freedom and truth seem modest in comparison to hopes of getting "outside," they are no less ambitious and potent relative to the world we actually have.

In the hearing of many, this activity does not rise to the level of critique because it either does not have or cannot account for the normative basis of its preferences.[56] Foucault seems to delight in aggravating this worry occasionally: he does years of work with the Group d'Information sur les Prisons (GIP) and steadfastly refuses to transmute that experience into "activist" credibility for his theorizing. When asked directly, he expresses a preference specifically not to make the connection between his work on carcerality and his advocacy, finally expressing palpable frustration: "If I occupy myself with the GIP, it is only because I prefer efficacious work to university chatter and book doodling. [To write a sequel to *The History of Madness*] is devoid of interest for me. On the other hand, a concrete political action on the side of prisoners seems to me charged with meaning."[57] He nevertheless does more book scribbling after that, of course, but he constantly refuses to be frozen into exemplarity, to become the alter-ego and alibi of the political partisan.[58] We can take this as a provocation to think of the theorist as a pilgrim, or as an exile: one who does not contend to host every conversation, but who rather travels to the sites of the world wherein their presence may be welcome.[59] By refusing, in modes that often invoke the prophetic, to "be a prophet" by way of issuing edicts and proclamations, Foucault might help the liberal democrat ask questions about actually existing in democracy, or might prompt those who trust in their liberated sexuality to strive for deeper freedoms still.[60] Foucauldian techniques have had some enduring

55. Foucault, "Political Spirituality," 133.
56. See, e.g., Hector, *Theology without Metaphysics*, 274–78.
57. Foucault, "Le grand enfermement," 1169 (Jacques Chavy translated the German into French for the volume; my French translation appears here). He publishes *Discipline and Punish* three years after this, which is remarkably reticent about his own experience and knowledge of contemporary French prisons.
58. See Foucault and Trombadori, *Remarks on Marx*, 158.
59. I owe this metaphor of "hosting" to my colleague Lucila Crena.
60. See especially the last two pages of Christina Hendricks's very helpful paper, "Foucault's Prophecy."

appeal arguably because they can intensify or rewrite our relationship to and understanding of many such normative regimes.

Like Foucault, Barth does not believe that the tenor and extent of his criticism will lead to inaction: resistance to the powers is not only commanded by God, as if it were an ad hoc addition to normal human activity, but represents the very shape of human life before God and neighbor.[61] Indeed, as Barth thinks seriously about demonic structures, the figure of the neighbor remains present with him (and not only as a figure: in the later years in which he is writing *The Christian Life* fragment, for instance, visiting inmates at Basel Penitentiary twenty-seven times to preach, discuss, and offer pastoral care).[62] It is easy to take this as a Christian commonplace (as it is), but we could remember here that many alternative figurations for the neighbor are available to Barth, and to us—the other, or the one who may be friend or enemy—and that, when pressed to choose a load-bearing representation in our political imagination, choosing "neighbor" recalls our vocation to love and solidarity. That spirit can infuse even the encounter with the enemy, as a young Barth knew when he wrote that "thou and the enemy smitten by God are one. His evil is thy evil; his suffering thy suffering; his justification thy justification."[63] So, too, did he argue in this spirit years later, reminding his audiences that on the basis of what God has shown in history, "we have to think of *every* human being, even the oddest, most villainous or miserable, as one to whom Jesus Christ is brother and God is Father, and we have to deal with him on this assumption."[64] Barth, at what I judge to be his best, knows that there are genuine antagonisms in history, and in his

---

61. It behooves anyone who draws on Barth's theology as a resource for contemporary political action to take into account Barth's manifest failures on certain social questions. Though Barth, read today, appears sensitively thoughtful from the beginning of his career on certain issues—such as class and state violence—he falls badly flat in, e.g., his sexism and antisemitism. I take it as a given that many of Barth's actual positions and the potentially emancipatory political witness of his thought are in tension and that both forces in this tension draw on basic elements of his thought. Many scholars of Barth have attempted to do justice to his failings while pushing his thought toward its more equitable implications. These include Gorringe, *Karl Barth*; Fiddes, "Status of Women" (especially his conclusion that Barth's argument against role-sharing is overpowered by the "neutralising of sex altogether"); Sonderegger, *That Jesus Christ Was Born a Jew*; Busch, "Indissoluble Unity," as well as many others. Arguably, Foucault and those inspired by him bring perceptive analysis to some of these questions where Barth's witness to a liberating gospel fails.

62. See, e.g., Schwarz, *Karl Barth in der Strafanstalt*. I am grateful to Dr. Joseph Longarino and the Center for Barth Studies at Princeton Theological Seminary for pointing me toward this text.

63. Barth, *Epistle to the Romans*, 475.

64. Barth, "Humanity of God," 53.

analysis of those antagonisms inhabits the spirit of the author of Ephesians, who sees our common subjection to them as releasing us from the instinct to hold that those who are our enemies in the truest sense have flesh and blood.[65] From this position, wherein we are returned to the neighbor in an ethical relation and freed by the grace of God, we are bound to perceive the neighbor in all the ambivalence and complexity that we ourselves bear. The optimism Barth holds, and his basis for recommending action in the world that corresponds to grace, is the possibility of truly human relationship, including political and social relationship.

It makes a difference when we shift ethical optimism away from exteriority—away from purity—and toward the unfolding possibilities of the world actually before us. Out from under the demand for noncomplicity, there is space for creative, free living that allows us to approach life in a world of powers, which is our world, differently, including as we seek to resist what the powers work. Consider this in two aspects.

First, letting go of exteriorities allows us to proceed in our attempts to map our world, but without heroes, idealized figures whose attempts at truth we must defend endlessly. This book has thought alongside and built upon two major figures, and so we are here in danger of performative contradiction. Yet the reflexive negativity called for by our total complicity account can think in such accompaniment, just not in the instinctual deference and endless attention imagined owed to a "master." It may well be the case that we cannot do without some structures of imitation that help us to internalize the spirit of those who have gone before. It makes a difference, then, to invite formative encounters, insofar as one can, with figures who discourage this form of tutelage: figures who would not have themselves for heroes. Barth invoked Paul "against Paulinism," knowing as Paul did that we cannot identify those whose investigations serve as the preconditions for our thought with the truth itself.[66] So, too, did Foucault seek loyalty-by-disloyalty to his great teacher at a distance, Nietzsche: "The only valid tribute to thought such as Nietzsche's is precisely to use it, to deform it, to make it groan and protest. And if commentators then say that I am being faithful or unfaithful to Nietzsche, that is of absolutely no interest."[67] There is and will be something important in preserving our archives and to striving to read

---

65. As described above, it is often the case that history is made in part by those persons who have given themselves over to the powers, so identifying with them that we do not err in thinking of them also as "enemies." What thought like Barth's opens for us is the possibility of denying the impulse to essentialize or ontologize the position of enemy, rather including it in the dialectic that binds all things together.

66. Barth, *Epistle to the Romans*, 504.

67. Foucault, "Prison Talk," 54.

our sources as well as we can. The practices of receiving intellectual sources that we have, though, can far outrun these genuine goods, rhapsodizing our mighty dead as the ones who bore an esoteric truth. Seeing them, too, as complicit in the world—and these two figures are abundantly so, often worthy of the critical attention directed at them—empowers us to engage their thought constructively as fruit picked by neighbors, not deliverances from on high. The best loyalty to such figures is loyalty to the forms of truth and life that their own hopes orbited, a loyalty that will be ambivalent on our part, too.

Second, doing without exteriorities means doing without certainties. As distinct from "confidence," which entails trust, certitude *knows*, which all too often means that it is invested in particular forms of *not* knowing. Instead, one who holds a depressive account rooted in total complicity carries along all its resources, hoping when called upon to have the discernment to take contextually appropriate action that meets a moment. We need not fetishize perplexity to know the provisional character of our work and witness and the unpredictability of their faithfulness. Even Barth, confident though he almost always sounds, encourages the one engaged in Christian ethics to the "persistent asking of questions and steady refusal to provide answers to these questions," since Christian ethics can only bear witness to an answer beyond itself.[68] Arguably, the point is not to maintain a preference for the grammatical form of the question—many moments require answers from us—but rather to see in all of our doings the shape of the question, the venturing of a self that does not include self-justification, in all its senses. In this project, Foucault might help, since his own aim was to frame problems with the greatest possible rigor, "with the maximum complexity and difficulty so that a solution does not arise all at once because of the thought of some reformer or even in the brain of a political party."[69] A spirit of conviction that knows its own entanglement in the world can hold both commitment and revision, both partisanship for particular causes in the world and an ecumenical sense of accountability to broader goods than one's own. The driver of quietism is not an engaged, attentive view that our agency is unavoidably complex and contradictory, but rather the presumption that bold action requires certitude, which is too brittle to support a living collective faith.

Resistance involves using freedom in creative ways in order to transform power's working through oneself and others. To use the theological vocabulary, the powers seek invisibility; resistance attempts to name them. The powers seek acquiescence; resistance discerns points at which

---

68. Barth, *Epistle to the Romans*, 466.
69. Foucault and Trombadori, *Remarks on Marx*, 158.

noncooperation might have crucial effects. The powers seek to constrain our imagination of what could be and cede that imaginative territory to them; resistance works for a more expansive range of possibilities. Complicity and resistance are not annihilating opposites because the range of possibilities for resistance is far larger than attempts to "escape." The implicit claim that we must either find positions of exteriority or find ourselves empty-handed when it comes to a responsible posture toward the powers is a false dilemma. A total complicity view of the powers does entail relinquishing certain species of hopes and attachments one might hold. We might not turn out to be the actors on the historical stage we thought we were. We may not be able to navigate fully around the powers that attempt to make our path. We may inadvertently do more harm than good, even by our own lights. We may not live to see how these questions are resolved, if at all. In that relinquishment, there can be loss. But it can also be an occasion for gain: a returning to a world replete with occasions for resistance and transformation, including transformation of oneself.

A CONFESSION FOR CAPTIVE HOPE

Discourse about the powers pulls us into a narrative presentation of the gospel—or, better, prompts us to read history, including histories of the present, through the lens of the gospel. Many of the figures analyzed in this book take responsibility for presenting their own understanding of theological history in outline, and so it seems important to do the same, not least since the final chapter will suggest tactics for being a character who resists the powers within that history. But doing so risks the suggestion of finality or false closure which would be strictly at odds with the analysis this book has already pursued. And so—genuinely doubting that I alone am up to this task and in an attempt to point beyond this text itself—I cite others while doing so, which seems to be the best way to embody that political theology must be the work of many hands and also to avoid the safety of a critical position that hides its own constructive account.

Though systematic and constructive theologies have been guiding lights so far, this confession abstains from any attempt to be comprehensive or to exhaust these topics, addressing itself to the questions that have animated us and raising many others, leaving them unanswered. I offer it instead in the spirit of a song (though admittedly a prosaic one), meant to accompany those in whom it strikes a chord through the tumult of public life.

- God created a world in order to share the gift of living love that God just is.[70] Through the wisdom of God, that world is not just potency, but life; through the power of God, that world is not just structure, but dynamism. Creatures are empowered to act in ways that participate in the unfolding of that world's history in a communion of interdependence with cosmic consequences.[71]

- There was one human creature, Jesus of Nazareth, in whose person and witness creation was revealed to itself anew.[72] In the light present in Christ, the very structuring forces of the world were exposed to have betrayed their vocations. Hiding beneath those aspects of the mission given to them by God to endow the world with joyful complexity, they violated the communion of all creation, setting enmity between creatures and enviously seeking glory for themselves, all the while holding all creation in humiliating captivity.[73] In the crucifixion of Christ—who, despite entering the world those powers compose and thereby becoming sin for us, resisted their betrayals at every turn—their indenture to death is exposed.[74] In the resurrection, the lie that the power of death is ultimate is refuted, for the sting of death is its threat that it will have the last, determining word on our lives.

- Those powers are heterogeneous: some animate nameable institutions or collectives, while others are known in inference from the patterned trail they leave behind in history. Some continue to bear the weight of functions necessary for human life; others seem at best a parody, or a cruel echo, of dimensions of our social existence.[75] They act as rivals as often as they collaborate.

70. Tanner, *Christ the Key*, viii.

71. Thus Townes, *Womanist Ethics*: "We need each other to help us understand the worlds we have created and are creating. This assumes a positive value for interdependence and dialogue. This invitation to growth, as it were, admits that we are a complex of historical interactions on a cosmic playing field" (114).

72. Adorno, *Minima Moralia*: "The only philosophy which can be responsibly practiced in the face of despair is the attempt to contemplate things as they would present themselves from the standpoint of redemption. Knowledge has no light but that shed on the world by redemption; all else is reconstruction, mere technique" (247). It is particularly important for me to highlight my own choice to turn to Christology in light of Adorno as an expression of my own conviction, which differs from his.

73. From Ruti, *Singularity of Being*: "That we are frequently humiliated by the very structures of power that sustain our existence is, in many ways, the foundational tragedy of life" (45).

74. Stringfellow, *Ethic for Christians*, 81.

75. I think something like this distinction is necessary to convey my sense that some of the powers—like capitalism—embody necessary functions such as human

- In the history that we experience, the powers are our own collective capacities, alienated from our conscious control: they reproduce themselves in and through our agency. They are also the forms that make us the people we are: in the social bond of which they are the force, we come to speak our own names and the names of others.[76] They cannot live without us, nor we without them, but the intensity of our captivity is redoubled in stagnation and despair when we fail to perceive how they—and we—could be different.

- From within this history—as these words are—our thoughts, including our thoughts about God, breathe also with the whispers of the powers—and sometimes, of course, they simply shout in our voices.[77] Our actions, though they be infused with desire and disciplined into habit, are nevertheless underdetermined by our conviction: we may know not fully what we do, or the ground may shift beneath our feet, or we may simply be enacting whims we little understand.[78]

- Whatever else God's salvation entails, it sets in motion an energy, often felt as hopeful desire—especially among those most fiercely ravaged by the powers' domination, extraction, and neglect—for the transformation of the necessary intimacy of all life.[79] When we act on this desire,

---

production and consumption, while others—like race or the nation-state—do not have a function that is given with creation.

76. From Gramsci, *Prison Notebooks*: "The starting-point of critical elaboration is the consciousness of what one really is, and is 'knowing thyself' as a product of the historical processes to date, which has deposited in you an infinity of traces, without leaving an inventory" (324).

77. "This is High Theology: an imperial enterprise, the art of the android epistemologies but not of humans, and this is one of the factors which allows theology to perpetuate itself (resurrect)," even through appropriations of liberation-oriented theologies, as Marcella Althaus-Reid describes (*Indecent Theology*, 91). A basic assumption of this book has been that T-theology is the (Christian iteration of the) religious logic of the powers and that working across Christian theology to invite something different is the challenge of the person of living faith.

78. Thus James Baldwin, commenting on *The Exorcist* near the end of *The Devil Finds Work*: "For, I have seen the devil, by day and by night, and have seen him in you and in me: in the eyes of the cop and the sheriff and the deputy, the landlord, the housewife, the football player: in the eyes of some presidents, governors, wardens, in the eyes of some orphans, and in the eyes of my father, and in my mirror. It is that moment when no other human being is real for you, nor are you real for yourself. The devil has no need of any dogma—though he can use them all—nor does he need any historical justification, history being so largely his invention. He does not levitate beds, or fool around with little girls: *we do*" (571).

79. Compare with Foucault, "Masked Philosopher": "I can't help but dream of a kind of criticism . . . that would light fires, watch the grass grow, listen to the wind, and catch the sea foam in the breeze and scatter it. It would multiply not judgments but

God may act with and through us, as the source and sustainer of all that we do.[80] It is simultaneously possible that our highest aspirations are warped by the distortions that curve our world around the power of death: we are most in danger of doing harm on its behalf when we (and others) take ourselves to do service to the reign of God. We may have trusted teachers, a compendium of lives, a store of wisdom, skills of analysis, any number of resources at our disposal to make our lives correspond more closely to the grace we have been given, to present a more compelling parable of the world we desire. But in the absence of the elaboration of God's judgment within history, this is and will always be a wager of faith: a venturing of the self in love, a disposition toward the marvelous.[81]

- The original difference between God and creation is refracted in the multiplicities among creation, from which emerges strength and life. In the world differentiated and (dis)ordered by the powers as we know them, though, difference is figured as antagonism and reified through hierarchy, exploitation, and violence. What is division categorically is a horrifying regime of proximity in history: the communion meant for life has wrapped around it an undead machine for transmuting life into "value" for others. No one deeply grasped by the gospel can ignore the death-dealing of the powers and how it flows along axes that bear the names of the identities that they create for us. And yet, there is force in insisting on the third-person plural, "we," on the far side of this accounting, as an expression of our common, differentiating subjection to this world and therefore the mutuality of our fate, and a commitment to undoing all that chokes out life. It is as likely a site of revelation as anything else not to give up on each other by insisting on conversation, contestation, prayer, demand, apology, and the whole inventory at our disposal of living together and learning from each other.[82]

---

signs of existence; it would summon them, drag them from their sleep. . . . It'd be like a criticism of scintillating leaps of the imagination. It would not be sovereign or dressed in red. It would bear the lightning of possible storms" (323).

80. See Tanner, *Jesus, Humanity, and the Trinity*, 2–3.

81. I got this framing from Suzanne Césaire's idea of surrealism as the "permanent readiness for the Marvelous," cited in Kelley, "Poetics of Anticolonialism," 15.

82. From Césaire, "Letter to Maurice Thorez": "I am not burying myself in a narrow particularism. But neither do I want to lose myself in an emaciated universalism. There are two ways to lose oneself: walled segregation in the particular or dilution in the universal. My conception of the universal is that of a universal that is enriched by all that is particular, a universal enriched by every particular: the deepening and coexisting of all particulars" (152).

The story of the economy of grace goes broader and deeper still: the thing itself simply is not grasped by our best representations of it. But the inflections present in those moments of the story as they imagine our agency and character represent the interventions that this book has attempted to make in theologies of the powers, the making explicit of which can set us up for the final step to come.

The burden of this chapter has been to show that exteriority accounts of the powers have at their heart an assumption worth rigorous questioning: that complicity and resistance are annihilating opposites. Gone unexamined, this assumption leads theorists behind exteriority accounts to assume that total complicity accounts can only nullify the possibility of resistance, both analytically and as a disposition toward practice. This is evident in the frequent charge of quietism applied to the total complicity accounts here in question, namely, those of Barth and Foucault. Neither Barth nor Foucault thought of their work on power as a justification for resignation. In fact, both had cause to believe that their maximal accounts would conduce toward a hyperactivity, a preponderance of possibilities for resistance. This chapter has suggested that there is good reason to think that a total complicity account can encourage an approach to resistance through forms of life that avoid some of the dangers of attachment to exteriority. To be clear: it is possible that one could interpret a total complicity theory so as to authorize indifference or resignation in the face of the powers. It is the particular task of the theorist of total complicity to give reasons and motivations for refusing to do so.

It is appropriate to ask, at this point, how to embody the theology presented so far in practical judgment and action in the world. To the extent that those practices make sense of the simultaneous possibility of complicity and resistance, their description serves to strengthen the argument of this chapter. But more importantly, they illuminate specifically the possibilities for meaningful resistance that are prompted by the political spirituality we have been building. Appropriately enough, that spirituality has needed to dwell in reflection with the world that precedes and conditions us first, but it also calls for practices of self-relation and self-transformation that can be undertaken as a sign and symbol of a world differently composed. To that we now turn.

CHAPTER 6

A Spirituality of Resistance

SPIRITUALITY AND MACHINERY

This book has presented itself as outlining a political spirituality, but has given over much of its attention to political and theological description. This is not a mistake—or at least, it is an intentional one.

The reader is likely familiar with a textbook criticism of (especially, but not exclusively, white) Protestantism: that its historical mainstream has ceaselessly repeated the separations made by its founding generations between spirituality and politics, private and public, inner and outer self, the economy of salvation and the domain of the world. This is true, and insofar as the aging machine of Christendom has visited expropriation and violence on so much of the world, its truth reverberates into our contemporary world. Yet the criticism bears even more truth than appears to be widely appreciated in Christian thought and practice.

The image of the machine has haunted many of these pages: the gears and weapons of war that shocked a young Barth; the mechanisms traced by Foucault—not only his famous reading of the panopticon, but the techniques of appropriation and transmutation of agency that often invoke the image of the overwhelming apparatus. And of course the powers themselves, the often-anonymizing structures that both enable and constrict life, frequently at an industrial—or digital—scale. A great temptation here, especially with the invocation of "spirituality," is to hope for a re-enchantment of the world, an assertion of higher and deeper things against the impersonal forces that have made the world doubly mundane, from which position we might criticize those powers "out there."[1] Instead of battening down the hatches in actually

---

1. I owe much of my understanding of these themes to Rose, "Machines of Loving Grace."

existing Christian communities—for the powers are there, too—this book has wagered that a greater gain in self-encounter comes, as Adorno warned, neither from immediacy as uncritical inwardness nor from retrenchment in "tradition," but rather from an encounter with what is impersonal, what is alienating: the world in oneself, or how what one thinks of as oneself just is a mode of the presence of the world. Spirituality, then, is not in the first instance what is produced by a regimen of prayer or a discipline of fasting, but rather what is recollected of the self when one journeys openly into the not-so-far country of our public life—and how one determines to live in light of it.

Such a shift in the practice of spirituality would require a different index of exemplary lives, and a different form of exemplarity itself. Saidiya Hartman's *Wayward Lives, Beautiful Experiments: Intimate Histories of Riotous Black Girls, Troublesome Women, and Queer Radicals* helps here in its elaborating "an archive of the exorbitant, a dream book for existing otherwise."[2] The powers, specifically in determinate forms as the afterlives of slavery,[3] often work forcefully and in exposure toward these women, whose lives are violently patterned by racial minoritization and gendered expectations derived from the lives of upper-class white women. One place Hartman finds these women is the prison in Bedford Hills, New York. The prison was (and is) not only the paradigmatic social machine—for making and making visible, and then perhaps expurgating, guilt—but also a site of civil death: "The number assigned replaced [each woman's] name, possessed the body and indexed the state's dominion. . . . The numbers impose an identity and produce an account of her, severed from family and friends, sequestered from the world, held in the body of the state, and vulnerable to gratuitous violence."[4] Such a person no longer has meaningful agency or preferences, but is "now a statistical aggregate, a member of an abstract social category; she is an inmate, a prisoner."[5] Outside the prison walls, though, where there is meant to be civil life, many of the same structures attempt to govern intimacy and affiliation. Harlem nightclub owner Lloyd Thomas ventured a multifariously creative and bohemian life, enjoying the

---

2. Hartman, *Wayward Lives*, xv. The preface, "A Note on Method," includes reflections on how the historical archive itself sets limits on what can be known, calling for this kind of elaboration.

3. Hartman, *Lose Your Mother*, 6.

4. Hartman, *Wayward Lives*, 264. Hartman positions this after her discussion of Eva Perkins and policing after the 1905 San Juan Hill riot as a picture of what she likely would have experienced in almost two years there (258, 267).

5. Hartman, *Wayward Lives*, 264. Compare with Foucault's "About the Concept of the 'Dangerous Individual.'"

company of cultural types "whose desires were not fixed by the coordinates of identity," but nevertheless falls into possessive, patriarchal, and jealous forms of intimacy that worked to consume his wife, Edna, until she herself found "something electric" in the arms of an unidentified "colored leading lady" of the stage.[6] Over and over again, Hartman tells us of lives lived through such playful resistance, alternating between attempts at visibility on unpredictable terms and concealment as a refusal of being figured simply in conformity with power's dictates, affiliation with those whom life has presented one, all against a backdrop of the structures who claim history as their own story. Such creative lives refuse—and reveal—the bland reproduction that the powers seek: they do (especially gendered) parody where the powers reify through repetition without difference. As Hartman finds in the example of Mabel Hampton—whose gendered performances raised questions that could only be answered by a claim that she felt like herself—life among the powers, especially when they reveal themselves as distributing exposure to and thereby doing the service of death, occasions embodied gestures of resistance. Hartman recalls the horrors of how the regime of lynching was enforced specifically against women and, citing Mabel's everyday acts of refusal, asks: "In the face of all of this what could one do, but refuse the categories?"[7] That gesture of refusal declines to repeat the categories wielded by the powers and resists the names they wish to give us.

When Mabel dresses in clothing typically associated with men, or when Edna leaves a husband full of secrets kept from her and finds a relationship with a woman that is itself the exhilarating secret, they know that they have not escaped the machinery of racialized sexuality into a place apart. And if they were tempted to believe that, the world would violently reassert itself in turn. Their lives, as well as others Hartman offers glimpses of, are ventured on the possibility that life can be reconstructed, that the materials with which the powers make history are subject to transformations within biography.[8] The beauty of the black ordinary, for Hartman, is "the beauty that resides in and animates the determination to live differently, the beauty that propels the experiments in living otherwise," which is a means of "creating possibility in the space of enclosure, a radical art of subsistence, an embrace of our terribleness, a transfiguration of the given."[9] Our descriptive work so far in this book has been intended to put us in

6. Hartman, *Wayward Lives*, 209–12.

7. Hartman, *Wayward Lives*, 338–39.

8. This thematic reflection is most explicit in the speculative account of what an Oscar Micheaux film documenting La Bentley, a drag performer in Harlem, might have been like, especially in Hartman, *Wayward Lives*, 197.

9. Hartman, *Wayward Lives*, 33.

A SPIRITUALITY OF RESISTANCE 169

a position to say now that this is not a gesture of aestheticizing politics, or a reduction of properly structural phenomena to individual, expressive preferences. The powers reproduce themselves in and through our action, including minutely in how we relate to ourselves and embody that relationship in practices that may be deemed "cultural," but are no less structural, no less political for it. If machinery and personality are mutually exclusive, if other and self crowd each other out, then this is bleak news indeed, but the burden of this book so far has been to argue for a more complex dialectic at just this point. Most of Hartman's figures may not have had easy access or high regard for the canon that includes figures like Adorno and Kierkegaard—the latter of whom invites us to consider spirit as a relation of the self to itself, folded back on itself again as a third element, aware of itself.[10] But in her rendering they show how that relation to a relation, the stewardship of oneself as a spiritual task, is infused with the micropolitics of our social fabric: the affects, the loves, the practices, the understandings of oneself and the world that each of us must mobilize, even if implicitly, to make our best attempt to claim the possibilities we want.

Hartman names among the desires embodied in her archive "waywardness," the "avid longing for a world not ruled by master, man or the police . . . the social poesis that sustains the dispossessed."[11] Waywardness on this account is a practice of freedom specifically befitting, to switch into our theological idiom, creatures: those who cannot account for their own existence, who do not set its terms, whose agency is first and foremost a response. A response to the surprising source of that existence most deeply, but always also a response to the particular historical forces and circumstances that make up the world to which one belongs. Hartman characterizes this practice as unrepentant to highlight its refusal of shame as a mode of self-governance on behalf of authority. Beyond devoting oneself to doing the work of the powers that be, "waywardness is an ongoing exploration of *what might be*; it is an improvisation with the terms of social existence, when the terms have already been dictated, when there is little room to breathe, when you have been sentenced to a life of servitude, when the house of bondage looms in whatever direction you move."[12] Waywardness knows the power of death and all its friends, and knows that it does not arrive at a domain of purity, or self-creation *ex nihilo*. It names, rather, the possibility

10. Kierkegaard, *Sickness unto Death*, 43. One is always in danger of mistaking "Kierkegaard" for the voice of the text, hence this construction. Most of Hartman's figures lived most of their lives before Adorno himself started publishing in the early 1930s, of course.

11. Hartman, *Wayward Lives*, 227.

12. Hartman, *Wayward Lives*, 228.

made actual, under some of the most trying circumstances, of resistance without exteriority.

In Christian communities, practices of resistance often look different, and one may indeed find an aversion therein to celebrations of waywardness. But if the reflections of previous chapters hold, we should not be surprised to find some kinship between the forms of creative living that Hartman describes and practices that can take inspiration from Christian conviction. Liberation theologies of all sorts have recommended a reorientation of the paradigmatic human subject to those whose lives are choked by domination, since in and to those lives the God who loves and emancipates the oppressed is revealed most directly. We can echo something of that procedure, in a different voice, here. The portraits painted by Hartman show persons as only ever being the persons they are while subjected to structural powers, a subjection enacted on these lives by a violent clarity that dispels confusions engendered by illusory comforts and meager privileges, and that calls for meaningful resistance. These experiences at the intersections of the powers are deeply particular and historically determined, not to be reduced to theological anthropology in abstraction. They simultaneously disclose something of the truth, often less clear in and to other lives, of our common subjection to those same powers, and the occasion presented to us by that fact. That disclosure always could have been the social basis for Christian spiritual practice, among other things, and at its best, the church has stewarded resources for the transformation of that life and its world-making structures.

This chapter describes how the argument of this book so far opens toward a political spirituality that rests on a particular understanding of ethics, as well as the types of practices that flow within these forms. In relation to the critics of total complicity accounts, the ethical position elaborated here bears the responsibility to establish that one can resist the powers despite one's ineradicable complicity or without attaining to a position of exteriority.[13] This chapter thus attempts to buttress the case for a total complicity account of the powers by casting doubt on the assumption outlined above: that complicity and resistance are annihilating opposites. However, it is also an attempt to outline a mode of relating to the self that can serve as an ethical account of resistance, expanding the range of possible responses to the world. In this respect, we can hope to notice the expansive domain of

---

13. As mentioned above, I do not presume that the appropriate response to the powers is always and everywhere to resist their activity; they are fallen—not purely evil—creatures, after all. However, I do assume that resistance is the more ethically complex case since it requires intentional action on the part of the one seeking to resist.

ethically relevant responses to the powers and to mark occasions for finding more life among the powers.

THE SELF AND THE POWERS

In a world of fallen powers that know no difference of kind between our interior life and our action in the world, an expansive, creative faith requires a range of available spiritual dispositions, forms of relation to the self that occur under particular signs, that pull forward certain habits, expectations, and modes of readiness for action. In the corner of the world most likely reached by this book, the political disposition that prevails is the protest of powerful others, which almost always involves a gesture of distinction between the self lodging the protest and those figured as responsible. As a spiritual disposition, disappointment in the other, freely expressed, is often politically necessary and represents a protest on the part of a self whose access to wholeness may be blocked by social conditions. I take it that the particular contours such protest can take is documented well enough that I do not need to rehearse them here. Contemporary people also need other political spiritual dispositions at our disposal. We need to be able not only to avow, but to inhabit and act upon various possible forms of relation to the social whole, relation to particular instances of power, and to ourselves, from moment to moment. Let us stipulate that every person spontaneously does all these things already, since they are some of the ways that we must cope with how our lives just are political. The object of many traditions of Christian spiritual reflection, though, is to make explicit one's commitments and practices of being a self, to try to develop more muscles than might already draw strength from regular use, to find ways to let fiercer life in.

Keeping with our established pattern, we should feel the failure of any such project, including the elusive failure written into its success, ever at hand. In particular, even the most politically sharp and self-aware projects of self-fashioning are dangerously close to repeating the pattern of the liberal subject, the subject of (human) capital. Lauren Berlant frames this necessary proviso incisively: sometimes what is called for is not more self-control, but rather self-suspension, or "sites of episodic intermission from personality, of inhabiting agency differently in small vacations from the will itself, which is so often spent from the pressures of coordinating one's pacing with the pace of the working day."[14] There are gratifications that

---

14. Berlant, "Slow Death," 779. One could fruitfully read Berlant as offering a way of approaching the suffocating consciousness of being an embodied image at the disposal of the gaze of others through a kind of sabbath.

work precisely in the interruption of one's striving for consciousness and efficacy, which interruption reasserts forceful embodied impulses over and against imposed regimens of the will. This is a helpful reminder not only of the somatic machinery that may (rightly!) protest attempts at the forceful governance of personality—many Christian traditions have preserved the insight that "spirit" is not intrinsically more trustworthy than the intuitions of the body—but also that agency and personhood themselves only irregularly embody visible, linear progress, or unambiguous lifelong projects of accumulation and fashioning.[15] The reader may already have interpreted this as a statement about the need for grace; indeed it is. It is also the failure that must be not only acknowledged as a passing possibility, but built into our sense of what political spirituality is and what it might offer. Our attempts at resistance will not only fail to deliver us "outside"; they will also be marked by all the complexity and ambivalence that compose our ordinary, messy lives.

Our central figures can once again provide resources here. For both Barth and Foucault, a political spirituality that takes the self as the ethical substance emerges from thinking of the powers as the frame for human agency. The character of human life—especially in its constitutive vulnerability to influence from the powers—gives occasion for and body to the ethical task. Tracing how they both connect their accounts of the powers to the relationship to oneself will give us an occasion to describe what total complicity means and enables for contemporary life.

For several years near the peak of his career, Foucault famously published no new books, but taught yearly seminars at the Collège de France where he works out over time the connection between his analysis of power and his thinking about practices of the self. Over the course of his 1977–78 lectures, *Security, Territory, Population*, Foucault works the notion of biopower he had previously outlined into a more expansive concept that he calls "governmentality." Foucault here makes an important distinction: one does not govern a state, a territory, or a political structure, since these are abstractions. Instead, one governs people.[16] Governmentality as a set of phenomena thus depends on instances of conduct as negotiated between people. Foucault chooses "conduct" especially for its two-sided application: it can be simultaneously the way that one conducts others and oneself.[17] In

---

15. Berlant, "Slow Death," 758. Berlant here makes the crucial point that it is possible in projects like this one to repeat the "moral science of biopolitics, which links the political administration of life to a melodrama of the care of the monadic self." We will have to name and avoid this possibility, insofar as we can, below.

16. Foucault, *Security, Territory, Population*, 121–22.

17. Foucault, *Security, Territory, Population*, 193.

each action there is an element of response to informing influences—being conducted, as toward a particular end—and an element of directing one's own behavior—"conducting oneself" in a certain manner. However—as is evident in ancient and medieval Christian forms of pastoral power—conduction arises in order to incorporate and attempt to transform opposition and disorder. As a result, there is an "immediate and founding correlation" between conduct and counter-conduct, "revolts of conduct" that attempt to change how one is conducted.[18] Such counter-conduct typically draws on "border-elements" to push back against predominant modes of government: in the case of the medieval Christian history that Foucault here considers, these include mysticism, eschatology, asceticism, and direct appeals to Scripture (Luther is a paradigmatic practitioner of counter-conduct). The struggle against the imperative to conduct oneself in one way, therefore, is not "conducted in the form of absolute exteriority," but rather in tactics that resist being governed straightforwardly for the ends of another.[19] What his earlier work had developed by way of political resources becomes ethical in framing how people might conduct themselves as well as be conducted.[20] Foucault's analysis thus shifts from building the theoretical resources to represent power to outlining possible ethical responses, here understood as conduct and counter-conduct.

Foucault's lecture series from 1981–82—entitled *The Hermeneutics of the Subject*—describes in even richer detail the connection between power and subjectivity. He invokes the traditional view of the Delphic injunction—"know thyself"—and unearths its complement—"care for yourself."[21] The former charge is a species of the latter: within a larger task of care of the self, one must know the truth of oneself. In performing this larger task, one: (a) takes on a particular attitude toward self, others, and world; (b) converts one's gaze towards oneself;[22] and (c) undertakes actions exercised on oneself

18. Foucault, *Security, Territory, Population*, 196. Foucault considers several possible alternative labels for this phenomenon—disobedience, insubordination, dissidence—but settles on "counter-conduct" since it communicates the struggle "against the processes implemented for conducting others" (201).

19. Foucault, *Security, Territory, Population*, 214–15.

20. As Arnold Davidson explains, "the notion of counter-conduct adds an explicitly ethical component to the notion of resistance," while it also "allows one to move easily between the ethical and the political, letting us see their many points of contact and intersection" ("Introduction," in Foucault, *Security, Territory, Population*, xxi).

21. Foucault, *Hermeneutics of the Subject*, 3.

22. It is importantly telling (and one of the benefits of receiving this text through transcription of the spoken word) that Foucault here feels tempted to say that one converts one's gaze from the "outside" to the "inside" but immediately rejects that notion: self and other do not line up cleanly against the distinction of inside and outside because of Foucault's account of subjectivity amidst the powers.

"by which one takes responsibility for oneself and by which one changes, purifies, transforms, and transfigures oneself."[23] At a pivotal moment, however, trends in modern philosophy (Foucault tentatively refers to these as "Cartesian") break apart this original unity of knowledge of and care for the self by redefining self-knowledge and discrediting self-care as a philosophical task. As a result, the modern world receives a distinction between philosophy—"the form of thought that asks what it is that enables the subject to have access to the truth and which attempts to determine the conditions and limits of the subject's access to the truth"—and spirituality—"the search, practice, and experience through which the subject carries out the necessary transformations on himself in order to have access to the truth."[24] Foucault attempts, in light of this, to ask questions about the distinction between thought and spirituality that will recuperate some approaches to the self, but under distinctly modern forms of government.

Foucault intends three interventions on behalf of re-esteeming spirituality as a practice of truth. First, practices of spirituality assume that the subject does not have access to the truth by right: that one may not be capable of receiving the truth without undertaking deliberate action to become a different subject. The truth is "only given to the subject at a price that brings the subject's being into play," a price paid for by intentional work on oneself in order to become able to perceive the truth.[25] Second, it follows that the subject cannot access the truth without conversion, transformation, and change. This conversion requires a double movement that serves to cross the distance between the subject and the truth: *askēsis*, the responsible work of the self on itself, and *eros*, the drive that displaces one from her default position in dynamic motion toward the truth. Finally, Foucault believes that spiritual practices possess "rebound effects" on the truth of the subject. The truth is not simply esoteric information communicated to a worthy subject. It is transfiguration: the truth enlightens, beatifies, gives tranquility.[26] From this position, the subject can intimate not only where she was, but the new place where she stands. Only the one who has undergone such a conversion, then, can truly know her previous condition.

But, crucially, these dynamics of spirituality result from the ways that subjectivity is implicated in power. The object is not to create a new (old) spiritual elite, but to observe that if the powers are genuinely having a deforming effect on us, our techniques of truth, inflected as they are by desire,

---

23. Foucault, *Hermeneutics of the Subject*, 10–11.
24. Foucault, *Hermeneutics of the Subject*, 14–15.
25. Foucault, *Hermeneutics of the Subject*, 15.
26. Foucault, *Hermeneutics of the Subject*, 16.

A SPIRITUALITY OF RESISTANCE

habit, and convenience, are not reliable by default. This goes for "self-care," too: as Foucault considers the possibility of an ethics of the self for contemporary life, he worries that it is too easily conflated with the emptiness of our familiar expressions—getting back to oneself, freeing oneself, being authentic, and the like[27]—none of which are likely to include the necessary *askēsis* of transformation.[28] Consequently, Foucault laments that we may find it impossible to use an ethic of the self today, "even though it may be an urgent, fundamental, and politically indispensable task, if it is true after all that *there is no first or final point of resistance to political power other than in the relationship one has to oneself*."[29] Thus—and in perhaps the best account of how Foucault thinks we should move from thinking about power in the world to subjectivity within fields of power—Foucault clarifies what is at stake:

> In other words, what I mean is this: if we take the question of power, of political power, situating it in the more general question of governmentality understood as a strategic field of power relations in the broadest and not merely political sense of the term, if we understand by governmentality a strategic field of power relations in their mobility, transformability, and reversibility, then I do not think that reflection on this notion of governmentality can avoid passing through, theoretically and practically, the element of a subject defined by the relationship of self to self. . . . Quite simply, this means that in the type of analysis I have been trying to advance for some time you can see that power relations, governmentality, the government of the self and others, and the relationships of self to self constitute a chain, a thread, and I think it is around these notions that we should be able to connect together the question of politics and the question of ethics.[30]

The genealogical account of relations of power that Foucault has been developing since the early 1970s fills in aspects of the picture of subjectivity that Foucault has said all along was his true interest.[31] The celebrated maxim—

---

27. Also see, for instance, his remarks on the "Californian cult of the self," which he says is diametrically opposed to the ancient culture of the self ("A propos de la généalogie de l'éthique," 1221–22).

28. Foucault, *Hermeneutics of the Subject*, 251.

29. Foucault, *Hermeneutics of the Subject*, 252; emphasis mine.

30. Foucault, *Hermeneutics of the Subject*, 252.

31. As he says, "sex is boring" ("A propos de la généalogie de l'éthique," 1202); what Foucault was always concerned with was the problem of subjectivity and truth ("L'étique du souci de soi," 1527). We can accept the point, I think, even as we decline to take the first claim at face value.

"where there is power, there is resistance"—is specified here as a claim about the subject. The claim that the subject is a latecomer relative to the relations of power that give rise to it, and therefore cannot escape complicity with the activity of that power, has a flip side: power has no medium for its transmission other than the subjectivity of persons, who are free to respond on the terms of an ethics of the self. An ethics of spiritual self-formation is simultaneously a politics of resistance. The maximal reading of the powers that closes off the possibility of exteriority at once opens the powers to vulnerability.

This is the kind of freedom that Foucault believes we cannot fail to exercise. No person has control, in an unconditioned sense, over the conditions of her life or the range of actions within which she will be forced to choose. But through attention to oneself, each person can participate in how they are formed as the moral subject of their own actions.[32] "What is ethics," he asks, "but the practice of freedom, the reflective practice of freedom?"[33] As such, ethics and freedom are mutually implicated: freedom is the ontological condition of ethics, and ethics is freedom in its reflective form.[34] When Foucault translates the Socratic injunction to care for oneself as the imperative, "root yourself in freedom, through the mastery of yourself," he is gesturing toward the possibility of standing behind one's own desires, habits, dispositions, and actions such that they flow from the self willingly—or at least comparatively so, relative to the alternatives.[35] Though these forms of affect and action are and always will be received—learned, inherited, formed, and otherwise conditioned by one's environing circumstances—they are not necessarily selected for one in advance: there exists a range of possible responses in every fact, the decision for one of which is a practice of freedom.

Whatever self-relation we have exists within the field of power relations and not in exteriority: it is not a theoretical back-door through which Foucault smuggles a notion of freedom as pure indeterminacy or unconditioned choice. Rather, it is the action of a self-conscious person to use some of the materials of life to shape others, to identify with some habits

---

32. Foucault, "A propos de la généalogie de l'éthique," 1212–13. Yin-An Chen puts this very succinctly: one ought to look for freedom "within power relationships, rather than a power-free zone of liberation, because it is impossible to find a place without any involvement of power. Political resistance is based on the practice of the self in which individuals reject being incorporated into the task of reproducing and consolidating social structures" (*Toward a Micro-Political Theology*, 7).

33. Foucault, "L'étique du souci de soi," 1530.

34. Foucault, "L'étique du souci de soi," 1530–31.

35. Foucault, "L'étique du souci de soi," 1548.

and desires and attempt to promote them over their opposites, and so forth. This is ethical agency within total complicity: to pattern one's own participation in power after a model of subjectivity with which one identifies.[36] Foucault transitions from analysis of the powers—detailing the kind of freedom we cannot have, namely exteriority—to an ethics of the self that builds resources for imagining the use of the freedom we cannot *but* use in our negotiations with the powers.

In Barth's case, the connection between an analysis of the powers and an ethics of the self may be less explicit, but it can still be made clear.[37] Just as Barth's treatment of creation leads to a theological ethics in *Church Dogmatics* III/4, the doctrine of reconciliation leads back to a reconsideration of ethics in the *Christian Life* fragments. Theological ethics can only be understood within a larger dogmatic frame since it must exist within "the critical science of true church proclamation."[38] Ethics, that is, exists in light of the unity of the divine and the human in Christ, responsive to the goodness of God revealed therein. As a result, Barth's general ethics holds that "the human action is good which is commanded by God in his Word and is obedient to him," familiar in itself as a form of divine command ethics.[39] However, this is complicated in the *Christian Life* fragment. Where general ethics situates the divine command within a theology of the goodness of God, special ethics treats the goodness of the particular person, located within historical and cultural contexts, who acts in particular ways.[40] The evaluation involved in such special ethics still concerns the divine command but layers in new considerations about the biographical and historical elements of the ethical subject, the dynamic situation for "the ever-new event of [one's] encounter with the living God."[41] The continuity of human being, attitude, and action opens ethics to the fact that the event of encountering the commanding God takes place in a historical encounter of God with the human person and the human person in community.[42] The concrete and

---

36. Of course, that identification, also, can be seen as a relationship to the powers—we relate also to the modes of relation that we are. This means, among other things, that the identification is never strictly final.

37. A similar account of Barth's moral anthropology in its theological context can be found in chapter 7 of Webster, *Barth's Ethics of Reconciliation*. There, Webster describes Barth's "moral ontology" with reference to the "situated freedom" described in the *Christian Life* fragment, among other places (227).

38. Barth, *Christian Life*, 3.
39. Barth, *Christian Life*, 3.
40. Barth, *Christian Life*, 4.
41. Barth, *Christian Life*, 5.
42. Barth, *Christian Life*, 5.

dynamic command of the living God elicits a response in a concrete human history, this time in the newly-understood milieu of life shaped by powers.

Barth intends for us to hear this shift toward "specific" ethics in his subsequent theological call for a specific uprising.[43] The revolt against disorder—that is, against the powers that struggle against God's creative and redemptive purposes—responds, in light of the doctrine of reconciliation, to the divine command. This revolt can be undertaken, as Kathryn Tanner says, not because an already-replete God needs anything from us, but because the world does, especially insofar as our agency hinders the world's reception of God's gifts.[44] A threatening possibility can call one both to a rejection of the state of the powers and to a constructive ethical response, following the dialectical pattern of a localized negation in favor of a larger, free affirmation.[45] Indeed, there is a general imperative to engage in just such specific forms of resistance. However, Barth also identifies another form of specificity: namely, the distinctive conflict that Christian discipleship engages with the disorder of the world. As outlined in chapter 2, this conflict is not directed against any group of people, but rather toward the plight generated collectively by all, and for which all are responsible.[46] In view of what Barth has outlined in the doctrine of reconciliation, the divine command has been specified as conflict with the disorder that "both inwardly and outwardly controls and penetrates and poisons and disrupts all human relations and interconnections."[47] That disorder consists of nothing other than the system of lordless powers as dynamic actors in the world. World history is not just the history of humanity in the abstract, but the unfolding story of human lives determined by them.[48] Where Barth's divine command ethics elsewhere descends from a systematic understanding of creation, here that ethics ascends from the individual encounter with that command in the concrete person, which encounter must happen in a history that can only be told fully as a history of the powers.

Looking back to his early work, however, one can see that Barth often knits together his understanding of the powers and the process of discerning the ethical demands on the historical person. Of course, this sort of connection shows up when he says that the doctrine of original sin is not merely one among many, but *the* doctrine that emerges from a study

---

43. Barth, *Christian Life*, 207.
44. Tanner, *Jesus, Humanity, and the Trinity*, 68–69.
45. Barth, *Christian Life*, 207.
46. Barth, *Christian Life*, 210–11.
47. Barth, *Christian Life*, 211.
48. Barth, *Christian Life*, 216.

A SPIRITUALITY OF RESISTANCE

of history.[49] The divine command is not met by an empty subject, but one determined in large measure by a narrative history of alienation from God's creative purposes. In parallel, the call of grace—itself "the indicative which carries with it a categorical imperative"—bids one to "take up arms against the world of men and against the men of the world," calling for a resistance with specific reference to the sphere of the powers.[50] Lest this be misunderstood, however, as the kind of partisanship that he later explicitly seeks to avoid, Barth continues: "The object which I, as the subject, am bidden to attack is—myself."[51] In the last analysis, the ethical imperative addresses us within the reality that our active lives bear the form of this world, and that form is ineradicable.[52] Something like an ethics of the self takes its character from our participation in a world shaped by the powers. Even though the identification of the powers with sin and the world is often left implicit, that identification exists in a mutually determinative relationship with the ethical demands on the human person.

In a meaningful way, then, Barth and Foucault make a parallel transition to an ethics of the self from their total complicity accounts of the powers. That this is so might cast further doubt on the charge that their total complicity accounts lead to quietism. It does, however, matter that here we touch on something that both figures addressed as a matter of revision over the course of their careers. For Barth, it was essential to arrange the resounding "no" of his earlier work not just in a critical relation to the powers, but in relation to the "yes" revealed in God's humanity; for Foucault, the account of power elaborated in the '70s, eventually "worn and hackneyed" on its own terms, calls for a specification of government through the subject.[53] Both of these revisions call for a reframing of the human not around clarities, purities, or exteriorities, but what is exalted by grace in the tangle, what is possibly beautiful amidst the absurdity. In short, the analysis of power, to be spirituality useful, must not only find what is hidden and rewrite itself into the story; it must find some humane form as an impulse for everyday living. In this spirit, I think, Barth and Foucault come to see their work on the powers as opening to a specific kind of ethical response: if the powers have invaded the most intimate corners of personal existence, resistance is newly possible on a human scale. These forms of resistance would not erase

49. Barth, *Epistle to the Romans*, 85–86.
50. Barth, *Epistle to the Romans*, 207–8.
51. Barth, *Epistle to the Romans*, 208.
52. Barth, *Epistle to the Romans*, 434.
53. For Barth's account of this, see "The Humanity of God," cited above. For Foucault, see Lorenzini, *Force of Truth*, 28, 33. Lorenzini takes this quotation from Foucault's lecture series, *Government of the Living*.

our complicity with the powers. Nevertheless, meaningful action could push for significant changes in their particular shape—rendering them more humane, or more just, or better able to support an authentic life—and that effort may be a responsible form of resisting their effects.

Surveying how Barth and Foucault tie description of the powers to the spiritual and ethical task of life in the world does not nearly give us all the spiritual dispositions we need. My hope here is that they recommend, in different vernaculars, a crucially important movement in the relation to oneself that can spawn several dispositions that are vital accompaniments to the spirit of protest against an other. We can describe that spiritual movement as critical attention to the self precisely as a site of the reproduction of what is received, where "critical" does not indicate disparagement, necessarily, but only a sign of open inquiry. Self-examination is not new, particularly in the compendia of practices available to religious communities. But having taken this route through description of the structures of the world, arriving at this point now allows us to draw unusual energies for it as a spiritual disposition. Here, self-attention is not recommended as retreat from the world, or as a "responsibilizing" shift of social burdens to individuals, but rather as a step within an approach of the world's urgent demands. With the distinction between public and private intentionally blurred—in the final analysis, because the distinction itself is likely unsustainable—self-attention is the inclusion of the eye that perceives the world, the rewriting of the will that seeks to act upon it, within its picture. That spiritual movement gives a different tenor to certain dispositions that can reemerge without deadening repetition that avoids the vocation of transforming the world. One of those dispositions seeks the contradictions of the world in one's own agency and character, naming its conditions of possibility and the resistances intrinsic to our own best aspirations. Another is an incitement found precisely in our protest and resistance of fallen powers, and not as a qualification on them—for sometimes our protest and resistance must be unqualified—to a fierce solidarity with the neighbor, even the one whom the powers seek to differentiate from oneself. Yet another is being returned to a position where one can meaningfully ask how to take next steps to become the kind of person who can live in a world of transformed powers. A spirituality that is arrived at specifically after traversing theological and theoretical attention to the structures of secular life might do these things nimbly, and remain open to more. It may not yet have fully earned the name, "political spirituality," but it may proceed in hope, even in its failures, against that horizon.

This book is not a manual of spiritual practices, first and foremost, because of the limitations of its author. But as our sources show, for self-attention to be a technique of political spirituality also just requires the kind of specific, contextual discernment that cannot be legislated in advance, only nourished and encouraged by the sorts of reflection available in books. There are, nevertheless, means of deliberately undertaking and enacting the responsibility to live as though the forms of this world are passing away, practices of the self that might open one to receive or prefigure or repeat in new scenes the grace in which one trusts. With the remainder of this chapter, I will outline "self-attentive asceticism" as an ethical approach undertaken as part and parcel of the form of relation to oneself, here cast as our political spirituality. This will involve a brief set of comparisons with other prevalent ethical hermeneutics, then an accounting for how self-attentive asceticism is present in our figures, including with some examples of practices and convictions they offer. This will leave some questions unanswered and forms of practice underdetermined, no doubt, but my hope is that it reframes the task of political spirituality in a way that invites the reader to live the parable of transformed life within the world.

SELF-ATTENTIVE ASCETICISM AS A SPIRITUAL PRACTICE OF FREEDOM

Ethical theories abound, and yet we need a rearticulation of the ethical life if we want to take the theological anthropology offered here seriously as a framing for human agency. If this book attempts to name an emerging theory—or a rearranged formulation of elements from existing theories—it does so because of the peculiar demands of its own motion toward a political spirituality and not because of some imagined deficiency on the part of other ethical reflection. Nevertheless, it will be helpful to consider self-attentive asceticism's relationship to the predominant ethical theories in order to clarify its disposition toward the moral life. Though space here allows for only the most basic forms of comparison, even the broad outlines of these ethical theories can illuminate what makes self-attentive asceticism both continuous with and distinct from these other accounts.

Self-attentive asceticism makes use of the description of subjectivity among the powers detailed above. It involves self-attention inasmuch as it perceives the powers' activity happening in and through oneself: the refusal to reify the powers in a way that leaves one in a position of exteriority entails, on this account, that one's own self is a conduit for the powers and therefore site for possible ethical activity. On this reading of subjectivity, the Delphic injunction—"know thyself"—becomes also a call to know the powers that live and move within oneself, to perceive how social structures are repeated within even the apparently private recesses of one's own personality. That care of the self is rightly described as "ascetical," but the asceticism here recommended involves far more than self-denial: it is instead a form of spiritual exercise, undertaken upon oneself with a larger picture of the world in view. This asceticism aims to put one in a different relationship to one's own character and actions by enabling considered choices among the elements of oneself that are visible on this account of the powers. Yin-An Chen usefully describes this type of asceticism as a practice of constant detachment from relations of power, rather than mere renunciation of self, where I would argue that "detachment" is usefully understood (as Chen's whole argument suggests) not as exteriority but as finding the intervals, finding the gaps within power that allow us to act and desire differently.[54] Rather than attempt to eradicate complicity, then, self-attentive asceticism would encourage us to reshape our participation in the activity of the powers—indeed, to recognize that such participation is always being reshaped due to their dynamic character—and insofar as we can, to become agents within the process of the formation of our selves.

Like Kantian ethics, self-attentive asceticism acts on a certain inexorable responsibility for self, other, and world that may be experienced as a kind of duty. In disposition, therefore, it can be seen as a kind of responsibility ethics. However, this responsibility is not oriented primarily toward the execution of (Kant's understanding of) the moral law. Insofar as Kant's vision of that law is founded on a metaphysics of morals "completely isolated, not mixed with any anthropology, theology, physics, or hyperphysics,"[55] it relies on an account of pure (practical) reason that is substantially called into question by the vision of the powers here presented. Self-attentive asceticism attempts responsibly to ask a basically different question than Kantian ethics: if Kant's ethics asks of the agent, "what must anyone do who is similarly situated?," self-attentive asceticism asks, "who will I become if I undertake this action and what bearing will that person have on the world?" Self-attentive asceticism in its Christian form would place, rather than moments of divine command, something like Romans 12:1–2—the call to present one's body as a "living sacrifice" in order not to be "conformed to this world" but in hopes of renewal—near the center of responsibility ethics. Within such a larger frame, conforming one's behavior to forms of law may sometimes be among our obligations, but that lawlikeness of behavior would be an element of one's activity in constituting a relation to oneself.

Like virtue ethics, self-attentive asceticism is concerned with forms of work on oneself that lead to the development of capacities. These forms of

---

54. Chen, *Toward a Micro-Political Theology*, 14.
55. Kant, *Metaphysics of Morals*, 34.

work are required since, as Aristotle argues, virtues do not arise spontaneously, but rather require habituation.[56] Where Aristotle discusses the natural capacity of humans to acquire virtues, we can here qualify "nature" not just as the potencies and liabilities of human persons, but also the situatedness of human life within the powers. Thus, to read Aristotle's assertion that "the virtues arise in us neither by nature nor against nature"[57] in this light is to perceive that the powers will not inculcate habits that we can consider virtuous within us apart from our intentional effort: they will form in one certain capacities and dispositions, to be sure, but in a state of acquiescence alone, one cannot fully recognize those capacities and dispositions as one's own and as cohering with an expression of one's vision of the good life.[58] In its particular accent, though, self-attentive asceticism seeks to push this personal development toward a living witness to different signs of life as a form of resistance, and not merely to structure an individual good life.[59] Virtues and practices must take note of and orient themselves toward reform of the constellation of powers that bears upon us, lest they become solipsistic.

There is a way that self-attentive asceticism evokes Spinoza's ethics, as well. Rather than unconditioned will, the true "freedom of the spirit" for Spinoza consists in exercising the highest power of mind: to perceive things in their essence, as attributes of the eternal God.[60] The personal conatus—or highest expression of self that seeks to assert itself in and through persistent being[61]—is a kind of affirmation of the forces that shape one's own life, and an attempt to find those forces within oneself. The care of the self, for Spinoza as for self-attentive asceticism, involves not creating oneself *ex nihilo* but rightly perceiving and navigating one's life specifically as received. Identifying and standing behind certain parts of oneself over and against others (for Spinoza, the maelstrom of emotions that disturb us by raging against the order of things) is the deliberative moment of the ethical task.[62]

56. Aristotle, *Nicomachean Ethics*, 18 (1103a19).

57. Aristotle, *Nichomachean Ethics*, 18 (1103a24–26).

58. Aristotle would call such actions involuntary (or some mixture of voluntary and involuntary), not because they are coerced but instead because they lack a principle within the agent herself (*Nichomachean Ethics*, 30, 1110a16). This picture of voluntariness, with some qualification, is an element of the understanding of self-constitution presented in self-attentive asceticism.

59. One useful study in developing virtue ethics in this direction is Tessman, *Burdened Virtues*.

60. Spinoza, *Ethics*, 214. For an explanation of the three types of knowledge, see p. 91.

61. Spinoza, *Ethics*, 108.

62. In many respects this account of freedom bears a resemblance to Harry Frankfurt's work on volition and love. Frankfurt argues that, if a person is performing an

Yet Spinoza's picture of human life is deterministically one-directional: persons are strictly subject to, and unclearly influencers of, the world or God. On this account of total complicity, we may say that God's direct agency lies within the activity of the powers, but that this does not come at the expense of creaturely integrity. From our perspective, the character and career of the powers is marked by at least some contingency, and thus they—and we—are free to be otherwise, if not free in an unconditioned sense. Indeed, one reason for reading especially Foucault in connection with this argument—rather than the many other figures from social theory who could provide an analogous account of subjectivity and power—is precisely how his stories of how power develops move at the impulse of accident, discontinuity, opportunities seized and lost, surprises, mistakes. The horizontal transcendence occasioned by this sort of contingency matters for the form of self-attentive asceticism's ethics.

To elaborate on self-attentive asceticism less contrastively, we can draw upon a form of moral perfectionism, recently articulated by Stanley Cavell. The moral perfectionism that Cavell assembles from Emerson, Nietzsche, Mill, and others shifts the aim of moral reasoning to the task of making oneself intelligible to oneself. Thus, it recognizes that many difficulties in the moral life "arise not from an ignorance of your duties, or a conflict of duties, but from a confusion over your desires," broadly construed.[63] The moral perfectionist works from such a moment of crisis through conversation in friendship with one who has moral standing with her.[64] Moral confrontation or challenge comes not from an abstract moral law or from an impulse toward utility-maximizing but from the demand to become worthy of oneself or one's potential, embodied in the presence of an interlocutor who perceives that potential and makes appeals on its behalf.[65] As a result, the self is "drawn on a journey of ascent to a further state of itself, where the higher is determined not by natural talent but by seeking to know what you are made of and cultivating the thing you are meant to do, or to be."[66] Like

---

action that he wants to perform (including its motivation), such that "neither the action nor the desire that motivates it is imposed on him against his will or without his acceptance," such a person is "enjoying as much freedom as it is reasonable for us to desire" (*Reasons of Love*, 20). The mind is healthy insofar as it is wholehearted: settled in its desires and commitments and willing to stand behind its "volitional configurations" (95).

63. Cavell, *Cities of Words*, 42.

64. This mention of friendship as an encouragement in self-improvement brings us in close proximity as well to Tyra Lennie's helpful piece, "Self-Improvement in Astellian Friendship."

65. Cavell, *Cities of Words*, 12, 42–43.

66. Cavell, *Cities of Words*, 446.

this moral perfectionism, self-attentive asceticism takes the development of the self, especially the self as participant in a culture often worthy of rebuke, as a (perhaps *the*) morally urgent task. As will be discussed below, the material practices for such asceticism additionally require the participation of others as interlocutors and sharers in the moral task. At the same time, self-attentive asceticism would amplify Cavell's attempts to mitigate the apparent elitism of moral perfectionism by directing one's vision to one's own implication in, rather than distinction from, the surrounding culture. Though Cavell's parsing of moral perfectionism gestures toward the public witness of the lives it recommends, self-attentive asceticism invests more attention in how the personal stakes of public phenomena are immediately apparent and difficult to ignore.

Finally, self-attentive asceticism shares much in common with other recent work in theological ethics using *askēsis* or related categories to approach political life. Charles Mathewes, in *A Theology of Public Life*, employs an interpretation of Augustine in the service of a political asceticism available to Christians as a practice of political life. This asceticism focuses on endurance, training us to suffer in the right way, including "a habituated receptivity, an alert waiting" within the Christian understanding of eschatological time.[67] Thus, faithful, hopeful, and charitable citizenship—practices themselves based on an anthropology in which the self is vulnerable to, even displaced by, human and divine others—become exercises that take place in public life while simultaneously forming the person in anticipation of the publicity of the kingdom of God. In similar fashion, Jennifer McBride's book, *The Church for the World: A Theology of Public Witness*, offers a nontriumphal witness to Christ and a hope that the church could communicate redemption to the world through confession unto repentance.[68] Drawing on Bonhoeffer, McBride finds the resources for a Protestant ecclesiology in which the church's role is to proclaim its own participation in structures of sin and enact repentance through practices contributing to the common good. Through such communal practices—McBride explores the Eleuthero community in Maine and the Southeast White House in Washington, DC—Christians can reflect and act on their own complicity with the powers in a movement of humility and solidarity with the world.[69] The version of ethics recommended here draws gratefully on these and other studies of the political dimensions of asceticism, but differs from these accounts in at least two particulars. First, it speaks with the accent(s) and emerges from within the

---

67. Mathewes, *Theology of Public Life*, 11.
68. McBride, *Church for the World*, 119.
69. McBride, *Church for the World*, 141.

worlds of its central figures rather than the alternatives offered by Mathewes and McBride. As a result, this position takes its form within an account of subject that puts structural powers first and foremost not only as the ethical problem, but as the source of ethical matter that the subject engages in the encounter with the self.

It bears repeating that self-attentive asceticism, as imagined here, is not strictly a new ethical theory but a way of reading certain ethical practices into and across one another with a position on (in this case) the powers in mind. While the ethical practices and dispositions detailed below may be available irrespective of the credibility of this more general theory, my purpose in outlining it has been to suggest one possible account of their coherence and situation within the moral life. In what follows, I will use self-attentive asceticism as a means of understanding the ethical thought of both Barth and Foucault insofar as their views of ethics calls for a response to the powers. Like so many ethical theories—including those named here—it works largely as a hermeneutic on the moral life, a method of interpretation that pulls some concerns and tasks to the fore and encourages in us a certain set of questions and understanding of our resources.[70] Its particular strength, we may hope, is that it will provide the kind of exercises that will empower us for the creative living that our political spirituality calls for.

This book has aired worries about dangerous optimisms above, and that form of worry should accompany us here too. Attempts to intensify one's own agency bear a tendency toward a kind of harmful mastery and control—of self and, likely, others. The political ascetic working from this book's portrait of the powers ought to take special care to avoid some particular forms of contradiction that can arise especially from tacit investment in the hope that one is simply praiseworthy because one has exercised freedom in an intentional manner and in connection with one's convictions.[71] This is so not least because of the way it disposes oneself to evade and misrecognize one's own complicity, the difficulties of agency that we have been at pains to outline above. There is a genuine species of courage required to take on a project of self-fashioning, one that will inevitably be marked by ambivalence and failure, in a world like ours. And nevertheless, gains can be won. The self will never be master of its own house, as Freud averred, but one need not remain a lifelong guest, either: it could be useful to know (and possibly

---

70. I owe this way of reading ethical theories to a longstanding conversation with Emanuelle Burton.

71. This mode of paying compliments to oneself on the basis of the use of freedom has an inverse side, too: as Adam Kotsko describes, "modern freedom remains an apparatus for generating blameworthiness," functioning as the responsibility-imparting precondition for the collective state of the world (*Prince of This World*, 200).

to address) the gaps through which a draft enters, or the purposes of those who designed its layout, or how to reset a tripped circuit breaker, or the histories of the land on which it sits. That form of optimism is still vulnerable to the ways subjects are subjected to a world, but it names possible concrete achievements of resistance, and even repair, amid a world of powers.

TAKING THE SELF AS ETHICAL SUBSTANCE

Foucault engages ancient Greek and Roman practices of the self in order to make visible certain dimensions of ethics that modern ethics may obscure. This is decidedly not a program of nostalgia. When asked if ancient practices offer an alternative that would relieve the theoretical pressures of modern ethics, Foucault rejects the idea of a simple return to an old ethical system: "one cannot find the solution to one problem in the solution of another problem, posed in another epoch by different people."[72] Instead of borrowing preexisting solutions, he seeks a genealogy of problems, the ways in which ethical life is thematized and, within that thematization, the tasks given to the individual as concrete ethical challenges. To recall ancient practices of the self, then, is for Foucault to highlight the many dimensions of subjectivity that are susceptible to self-work. Some of those practices may be adapted and adopted for contemporary use, but there is no refuge from the demands of life today in the forms of subjectivity preserved by historical memory.

Foucault outlines an aspect of ethics that he calls the "mode of subjectivation," the manner in which persons are compelled to experience themselves as moral subjects. Taking inspiration from narrative theologies and ethics, many political theologians would reach here for metaphors that invoke a story that we find ourselves placed in and the sorts of characters within it that we are summoned to be. Foucault does not offer a fully elaborated story, but he does think that there are genres of ethical experience that cue us to become more intensely the subjects of our own actions, especially in expressing the self-relation that we are. The ethical "I" arises in response to, for example, revealed divine command, perceiving natural law or cosmological order, realizing that life is governed by universal rationality, or seeking after an aesthetics of existence.[73] Self and world collaborate as figures in the ethical imagination that, even if left implicit, makes sense of who we seek to become. In a moment of ethical awakening, one finds oneself living in a concrete moral situation that calls oneself to moral subjectivity, and

---

72. Foucault, "A propos de la généalogie de l'éthique," 1205.
73. Foucault, "A propos de la généalogie de l'éthique," 1214.

the peculiar character of that situation becomes the mode of subjectivation. From there, how we act on ourselves—asceticism in a broad sense—is the means by which one changes oneself in order to rise to meet this challenge, intensifying the relationship to oneself as an ethical subject. The practices that follow have various homes in normative story: as discussed above, Foucault generally tries to take an inventory of what is possible rather than prescribe a content-rich sense of what his readers ought to do. Their common goal is not a universal telos of ethical life, but a set of techniques that prompt the practitioner to ask if they stand behind the subject they are becoming in light of how humanity is governed by contemporary powers.

The first practice to consider is what Foucault calls "self-writing." Citing Athanasius's *Vita Antonii*, Foucault sees in ancient practices of spiritual writing a standing-in for "the eyes of our fellow ascetics," so that the recluse (who does not have immediate access to such relationships) pays attention to himself to help bring the body in line with one's convictions.[74] Generally speaking, such writing does something common to many ascetical forms: "render discourses received and recognized as true into reasons for action."[75] The contemporary reader might think here about the figure common in the middle classes of the Anglophone word, the "political junkie," who consumes news in part as a form of entertainment. Such a news consumer receives a high volume of discourse (perhaps even about structural power) and likely has strong opinions about what is true or good within it. But there are additional steps that translate discourse taken to be true into actions that meaningfully write us as agents into the political scene; having opinions and using occasions to vote on their basis vastly underdetermines what sorts of political subjects we are. Self-writing serves the purpose of making explicit the relations between our discourse and our actions, prompting the practitioner of a political spirituality to think of their concrete actions in relation to a world.[76] Writing thus serves an "ethopoietic" function: it trans-

---

74. Foucault, "L'ecriture de soi," 1235. Clearly, some of this language sits somewhat uncomfortably with Foucault's larger anxiety about the internalization of disciplinary power. Foucault intends here to draw out some themes about self-writing that coalesce near the beginning of the medieval period, even if he thinks that their Christianization tends to distort them in fundamentally anti-ascetical ways (1235–36). More interestingly, however, whereas readers of Foucault typically assume that "the gaze of the other" is simply violent—an expression of disciplinary and normalizing regimes of power—he also uses the figure of the gaze more constructively in his ethical phase, as described below.

75. Foucault, "L'ecriture de soi," 1237.

76. Some Christians may wonder here if this practice is anything more than journaling or other practices that are already widespread, or at least widely-known. Let's say that what Foucault describes is identical in form with these forms of "spiritual

forms truth into *ethos*, translating judgments about ethical substance into exercises incorporated into daily life.[77]

In the ancient world, this category of self-writing took two specific forms: *hypomnēmata*, gathered, disparate maxims and aphorisms (e.g., in a notebook) used as fortification for the continuous project of self-mastery, and correspondence, written dialogue with another that serves both as an exercise in self-manifestation and as a rehearsal for challenges that one is likely to face in the course of a day.[78] The collection of *hypomnēmata* buttresses the effects on oneself of the mode of subjectivation. In contrast to the personal journals or recitations of spiritual experience that Foucault thinks characterize medieval Christian writing, these "notebooks" do not seek to reveal or discover the hidden truth of oneself.[79] Rather, they assemble quotations, passages from books, exemplary figures and actions, and other fragments that create scaffolding around the designed and desired good life.[80] After one is introduced into an ethical discursive field and awakened by it to a particular domain of moral experience, this scaffolding helps internalize the norms of that field. Ready access to such norms as a result of *hypomnēmata* allows one to respond to ethical demands when necessary: they must therefore be contemplated so as to become a part of ourselves: "the soul makes them not only its own, but itself."[81] This type of self-work in writing reflects, in a sense, the ambivalence of the self's entanglement with others through power. On the one hand, *hypomnēmata* are deployed against the pressures experienced in daily life that can cause the scattering and dispersal of one's ascetic efforts: spiritual agitation, distraction, fluctuation in opinion and will, and lack of resolve in response to ethical challenges.[82] Though they are themselves heterogeneous elements, *hypomnēmata*

---

discipline": the object within the sweep of this argument would be to write one's discourse about structural racism or the immiseration of the poor or the constraints of heteronormativity with a particular and concrete focus on how these things are working through one's own action, inaction, evasions, and habits, and looking for opportunities for personal transformation and the expression of solidarity, as a regular practice. If the reader thinks this is already sufficiently widespread among the Christian communities likely to receive this book, then consider this a grateful endorsement of that practice and a recommendation that it continue.

77. Foucault, "L'ecriture de soi," 1237.
78. Foucault, "L'ecriture de soi," 1237–38.
79. Foucault, "L'ecriture de soi," 1237–38.
80. Foucault, "L'ecriture de soi," 1237.
81. Foucault, "L'ecriture de soi," 1238. One needs not only to have a vague sense of familiarity with something and the ability to Google it; one may need to know it with a confidence that allows it to become an actual guide to concrete action.
82. Foucault, "L'ecriture de soi," 1239.

repeat one's decision to identify with certain currents within the manifold of our experience of power, rather than to be left passively subjected to its ebb and flow. On the other hand, *hypomnēmata* show the extent of our situatedness within traditions that are partially constituted by power. In a deft summation of his thoughts on personal identity, Foucault tells us that it is one's very soul that is constituted in what one writes, "but, as a man bears on his face his natural resemblance to his ancestors, it is equally good for one to perceive in what he writes the filiation of thoughts that are engraved on his soul."[83] *Hypomnēmata* thus reflect back to one the elements from which one has composed (or received) an intelligible vision of the ethical life and, in so doing, facilitate the repeated affirmation or the adjustment of that life.

The type of correspondence that Foucault considers under this rubric serves at least two ethical purposes, both of which depend on its written form of address to another. Such letters, written within a relationship of mutual ethical support and consisting of advice, exhortation, admonishment, and the like, are an occasion to exercise oneself.[84] First, this correspondence represents a kind of training, "a little like soldiers in times of peace practicing the handling of arms."[85] That is, entering the imaginative space of an ethical dilemma or engaging in a thoughtful interpretation of an ethical moment has value for both the addresser and the addressee. For both parties, the written conversation serves as a reactivation or recitation, a recommitment to shared convictions and a rehearsal of ethical subjectivity in preparation for future events.[86] Correspondence therefore represents an opportunity for a kind of premeditation, as "the writing that aids the recipient arms the writer."[87] Second, the letter poses an occasion for self-manifestation, making oneself present to the other, that intensifies and refines self-reflection. To write is to try to show oneself, and this means that the letter is simultaneously a gaze aimed at the addressee and an exposure of the writer himself to that gaze.[88] Within this type of relationship, the "gaze" is not necessarily normalizing; rather, one "puts the correspondent in the place of the inner god," placing a check on the deliverances of one's own

---

83. Foucault, "L'ecriture de soi," 1242.
84. Foucault, "L'ecriture de soi," 1243.
85. Foucault, "L'ecriture de soi," 1243.
86. Foucault, "L'ecriture de soi," 1243.
87. Foucault, "L'ecriture de soi," 1243.
88. Foucault, "L'ecriture de soi," 1244. Foucault also mentions this type of correspondence in "Technologies of the Self," highlighting especially (in the case of Marcus Aurelius's use of the technique) the extreme level of detail used to represent the self fully to someone else.

conscience.[89] Correspondence, then, can serve as a meditative conversation that reorients one with respect to one's norms and normative community. Within the economy of self-formation, it can play an ascetic role, helping one to constitute oneself according to a particular ethical model. And while it is nowhere near foolproof, its dialogical character enacts the truth that our attempts at straightforward self-control are likely ambivalent at best: writing oneself for another is not only mutual accountability, but a performance of the receptivity and mutuality that make us who we are.

The thematic use of repetitive exercise in ethical training continues in Foucault's 1982 seminar at the University of Vermont, published under the title, *Technologies of the Self*. Here focusing especially on roots in (but not limited to) Stoicism, Foucault identifies the process of *paraskeuazo*, "to prepare oneself."[90] In order to prepare oneself, one undertakes ascetic practices "to acquire and assimilate the truth, and to transform it into a permanent principle of action"—in an intensification of subjectivity, "*alēthia* [truth] becomes an *ēthos* [way of life]."[91] Thus, ascetic practices serve as a kind of test, probing a personal response to an imagined likely event. Through iteration one gains the knowledge of where one stands in relation to one's own ethical commitments: whether they are more avowed than embodied or truly internalized as an ethos or somewhere in between. Foucault finds that this preparatory labor tends to have two poles: forms of meditation and disciplines of training exercise.[92] Like practices conducted by correspondence, meditation of this kind entails inhabitation of possible ethical events in order to conjecture about how one would react. Such meditation harnesses the imagination in order to place oneself within a challenging situation, to feel its contours and its stakes, and then attempts to work out—and importantly, to memorize—one's best available response. Consequently, just as a jazz musician may have reliable riffs and themes ready to use in a larger improvisational context, when the ethical subject is called upon to improvise a response to a particular event, she will have available certain well-practiced and "premeditated," in the literal sense, ethical dispositions.[93] *Gymnasia* work similarly within real situations, presumably artificially constructed, such as periods of sexual abstinence, fasting, and other forms of privation. Foucault here cites Plutarch's *On the Daemon of Socrates*, in which one, for example, tempts oneself by placing in front of oneself very

89. Foucault, "L'ecriture de soi," 1245.
90. Foucault, "Les techniques de soi," 1619.
91. Foucault, "Les techniques de soi," 1619.
92. Foucault, "Les techniques de soi," 1619–20.
93. Foucault, "Les techniques de soi," 1619.

appetizing dishes and then renouncing them, as well as a letter of Seneca in which he prepares for a festival through the mortification of the flesh "in order to convince himself that poverty is not an evil and that he is capable of bearing it."[94] These mental and physical repetitions help to produce both ethical self-knowledge and the habits of mind and spirit on which one will depend in a moment of trial. Even here, then, the object of *askēsis* is not simple renunciation[95] but self-formation: giving oneself the means by which to enact an ethos under future conditions of difficulty.

Foucault also examines two ancient Christian ethical practices in light of what he has unearthed from classical alternatives.[96] Like other schools of thought, Christianity requires practitioners to know themselves through awareness of their desires, temptations, and faults. Christianity adds to this, however, an imperative to reveal these facets of oneself—and therefore to "bear witness against oneself"—either to God or to one's community or both, often in a set of prescribed steps toward reconciliation.[97] Foucault claims that such discourse naming one's place within an authoritative discourse, called *exomologēsis*[98] even by Latin patristic sources, typically involved (in its ancient practice) a dramatic performance of penance and recommitment to the community. The core of the practice, Foucault believes, is ritually to enact one's acceptance of the obligation to reveal oneself: what was private for the Stoics (at least in the sense of occurring only within intimate relationships) becomes public for Christians.[99] At the same time, the ancient Christian practice of *exagoreusis*[100] bears a closer resemblance to its Stoic and other counterparts. This species of self-examination involves

---

94. Foucault, "Les techniques de soi," 1620–21.

95. Foucault revisits this theme constantly, especially clearly in the third volume of the *History of Sexuality*: the purpose of ascetic disciplines (at least for the Stoics) was not renunciation for its own sake but rather "to make one capable of going without superfluous things by establishing over oneself a sovereignty that does not depend at all on their presence or absence" (*Le souci de soi*, 81–82).

96. It bears mentioning again here that Foucault's own observations about Christian traditions tend to be hasty and overgeneralized, even if he puts them to interesting use within his genealogy of confessional power.

97. Foucault, "Les techniques de soi," 1624.

98. It is reasonable to assume that Foucault translates this as "recognition of fact," rather than the more common "confession," in order to guarantee that his reader perceives its doxological or self-identifying aspects, and not exclusively its penitential use.

99. Foucault, "Les techniques de soi," 1625–26.

100. Foucault uses "self-examination" here, the implication being that it is broader than penitent confession. One might closely associate this also with forms of spiritual direction, especially since he thinks it necessarily involves obedience and a relationship of direction from another.

A SPIRITUALITY OF RESISTANCE

making a continuous (for a time, at least) and complete account of oneself within a relationship to a teacher or spiritual director. For Foucault, ancient Christian self-examination demands not only vigorous attention and sustained contemplation of God, but also obedience to another within a hierarchy. In this, as in practices of confession, Foucault sees what he takes to be a common Christian anthropological position: self-revelation cannot be conceived without renunciation.[101] However widespread it may be, I venture that it is not theologically necessary as a way of making sense of the gospel. What an understanding of the powers makes possible for us is moving beyond the blackmail of "renunciation," of either self-affirmation or self-abandonment as a comprehensive spiritual disposition, and opening ways of disidentifying with (and attempting to move beyond) some of the elements of who one has been made.[102] Doing this "in public" by allowing oneself and one's self-reports to be known in community holds potency for confronting contradictions we may have a hard time perceiving ourselves. This does not strictly require hierarchy, but it can only function if we take the judgments and insights of the community around us at least as seriously as our own.

Perhaps the practice that Foucault most emphasizes in his ethical phase is *parrhēsia*, or frankness of speech. The parrhesiast does not hide anything, but rather "opens his heart and mind completely to other people through discourse."[103] Having undertaken the spiritual exercise necessary to give one access to the truth, one thus speaks from a privileged position: Foucault reads the ancient sources as claiming that in the parrhesiast, belief and truth are perfectly coextensive. Foucault readily admits that such an untroubled coincidence is not plausible on modern epistemology generally or his political epistemology in particular, but finds a parallel form of "proof" of *parrhēsia* in the courage required to perform it.[104] One is only practicing *parrhēsia* insofar as that one takes a real risk in doing so, either by speaking the truth to (usually political) authorities, or opposing a popular opinion in a way likely to cost one social capital, or by endangering a personal relationship

---

101. Foucault, "Les techniques de soi," 1631.

102. Foucault is simply not engaged in a project of theological reconstruction, and I do not mean to imply that he ought to strain to perceive or create better versions of Christian faith and practice. I only observe that his characterizations of Christian practice do not bear obligations for Christian persons.

103. Foucault, *Fearless Speech*, 12 (These lectures were originally given in English at Berkeley in the fall of 1983). Within this initial and broad definition, Foucault accounts for the relatively rare occurrences of *parrhēsia* in ancient texts that seem derogatory (e.g., on one occasion in Plato's *Republic* and occasionally in Christian literature, contrasted with spiritual disciplines of silence).

104. Foucault, *Fearless Speech*, 14–15.

with a serious rebuke. The choice to engage in *parrhēsia*, consequently, is a rejection of the options of silence or engaging in "rhetoric"—here narrowly construed to include only dissimulation or strategic speech meant to protect one from the consequences of the truth. Finally, *parrhēsia* necessarily entails an element of criticism, most frequently of the interlocutor(s), but also occasionally of oneself in cases where the interlocutor is in a position to enact consequences in response to such a confession.[105] The parrhesiast, then, consciously chooses a certain kind of relationship to himself: to be a truth-teller rather than "a living being who is false to himself."[106] To practice *parrhēsia* is to identify with a truth and wager one's life on it, at risk of one's own self-interest. It is a discipline of resistance: especially since the threat behind all the activity of the powers is death, to refuse moral apathy or cowardice and instead venture the truth is a witness to their penultimacy.

Foucault's treatment of the specifically Socratic practice of *parrhēsia* draws into even closer contact with an ethics of resistance of the powers. In addition to the aspects bearing on public speech, the literary figure of Socrates presents *parrhēsia* as a cultivation of *bios*: the life on which care of the self works.[107] In a parrhesiastic relationship, one can probe the interlocutor in order to discern her relationship to the truth. In many cases, this will take the form of a call to conversion, from ignorance about oneself (remembering the famous Delphic oracular pronouncement to Socrates himself) to a concern for the care of oneself. This form of *parrhēsia* aims not only at self-knowledge, but also creating the conditions under which the interlocutor can progress in her relation to the truth as such, helping her toward not only self-government but also participating in the government of others.[108] Fittingly, Foucault uses Socratic *parrhēsia* to push the practice toward dispersal: it still pertains to political activity, but does so in and through the call to self-care that is performed outside the *agora* or the monarch's court. Even though it may mitigate the factors of risk in these circumstances, the use of *parrhēsia* can become a spur to consciousness of one's complicity with the powers and a call to reinvent one's relationship to them.

105. Foucault, *Fearless Speech*, 17. Summarizing *parrhēsia* in early 1984 during his lectures at the Collége de France, Foucault included three aspects which the translators represent as truth, commitment, and risk (*Courage of Truth*, 11–13). His description here is largely similar, but it also highlights the role of the interlocutor, who may show courage "in agreeing to accept the hurtful truth that he hears" (13).

106. Foucault, *Fearless Speech*, 17.

107. Foucault, *Fearless Speech*, 101. This is the Socrates especially of the *Laches* and *Alcibiades*.

108. Foucault, *Fearless Speech*, 107. Foucault also discusses the urgency of the care of the self, and *parrhēsia* as a provocation to it, in forming those capable of governing the city at large during the *Hermeneutics of the Subject* lectures (e.g., on p. 44).

A SPIRITUALITY OF RESISTANCE

These are just some of the ancient and contemporary practices that Foucault represents in his ethical phase.[109] Again, they are not commands for twenty-first century people, but possibilities that illuminate the aspects of the self that can be worked upon with an eye to resistance. Foucault thinks of these as embodied critique in response to the efforts to govern oneself and one's conduct. The impulse toward resisting the powers can be phrased as a series of questions: "how not to be governed *like that*, by that, in the name of those principles, with such and such an objective in mind and by means of such procedures, not like that, not for that, not by them."[110] The critical attitude toward power takes up an art of not being governed "like that and at that cost," the art of "not being governed quite so much."[111] Arriving at this critical attitude requires work of the kind that Foucault has detailed through his ethics:

> I will say that critique is the movement by which the subject gives himself the right to question truth on its effects of power and question power on its discourses of truth. Well, then!: critique will be the art of voluntary insubordination, that of reflected intractability. Critique would essentially insure the desubjugation of the subject in the context of what we could call, in a word, the politics of truth.[112]

This politics of truth depends on the ethical standing of the individual with respect to herself: the right (and ability) to question both truth and power as they flow through the subject. Through ethical practices of the self, one finds means of asserting oneself within the powers to challenge their working. The freedom that results does not lead to exteriority; rather, it gives us some self-conscious agency over the regimes of truth and power in which we live. We can resist the powers not by escaping them but by reforming and reorienting them, especially in and through our agency as subjects.

ENERGETIC REPENTANCE AND THE RESISTANCE OF LOVING FREEDOM

Karl Barth's ethics are not frequently associated with the strands of thought with which we are weaving self-attentive asceticism. Yet, undercurrents

---

109. Others that I judge to be less useful here are documented in volumes two and three of the *History of Sexuality* series, *L'usage des plaisirs* and *Le souci de soi*.
110. Foucault, "What Is Critique?," 44.
111. Foucault, "What Is Critique?," 45.
112. Foucault, "What Is Critique?," 47.

within his ethics, especially when amplified by the tight connection between his account of the lordless powers and the ethical demands on the historical subject, make this identification possible without distorting Barth's thought. In fact, using self-attentive asceticism to understand Barth's ethical practices not only highlights his surprising affinity with Foucault on these topics but also serves as a rejoinder to complaints that his full theological account of life before God leads to quietism. More importantly for our purposes, though, it clears some theological ground for taking up the sorts of spiritual practices described by Foucault within Christian practice, giving a sense of the ends to which they may be put and the themes that they may invoke.

Self-attentive asceticism is an ethical outlook in which one examines oneself with the intent of understanding how the powers are working in and through one's own action, and through which one undertakes spiritual exercises in order to reform oneself, and thereby the powers. In Barth's idiom (especially in the *Römerbrief*), when undertaken in light of the God revealed in Christ, this is a fair approximation of repentance.[113] The view of the world that underlies Barth's total complicity account shades his ethics as well—"Our whole behaviour," he writes in a striking meditation on Romans 12, "always and to the world's end, bears stamped upon it the *form* of this world."[114] That is, even the very best actions of which we are capable involve using the resources we draw from a fallen world and therefore cannot escape implication within the situation of that world. From within this situation, however, one can still fashion oneself according to the transformation, rather than the present form, of this world.[115] Such self-fashioning does not remove oneself from the world: instead, it arranges the elements of one's life to testify against the sufficiency, the holiness, the indispensability of oneself.[116] In doing so, human activity can become nearly transparent to a light that comes from beyond its reach—"a parable, a token, of the action of God."[117] Such parabolic activity itself has a tendency toward protest against

---

113. In line with how we have distinguished "complicity" from "blameworthiness" above, I want to suggest that repentance here does not directly imply that one has committed particular sins or is strictly "at fault" for the state of world. Instead, we will be discussing repentance as the way of living befitting a hope for transformation of the world and one's part in it, however complex.

114. Barth, *Epistle to the Romans*, 434.

115. Barth, *Epistle to the Romans*, 434.

116. As Gerald McKenny notes, "the good is not an object of human moral striving assisted by divine grace; rather it is as already accomplished in the humanity of Jesus Christ that the good confronts us with its demand that we affirm it in our active existence" (*Analogy of Grace*, 14).

117. Barth, *Epistle to the Romans*, 435.

the world, as it expresses an enmity against the drives that organizes it.[118] For Barth, the word for this parabolic activity is repentance: the affirmation of the ambiguity of human existence, that foundational ethical activity on which all particular activity rests.[119] Repentance involves a rethinking of one's ethical standing before God and the world, even if this thinking itself is conducted within the sphere of relativity.[120] Repentance, then, means reconstituting one's ethical action on the basis of one's complicity with the world, the sphere of the powers, especially in opening one's action to transformations that parabolically bespeak new possibilities for the world. Barth has hesitations about *askēsis* as an orienting ethical practice, but it seems nevertheless available as one way of describing how to locate oneself in the world and act accordingly.

The stance of repentance is further clarified by Barth's examination of the "great negative possibility"—political revolution—in his treatment of Romans 13. In Barth's view, the challenge of Romans 13, and its injunction to "let every person be subject to the governing authorities" (13:1), is to find "the One in the other," in this case in the powers which govern human affairs.[121] Discovering God within their activity, however, cannot be achieved through simple identification of God with the powers, nor by a straightforward assent to their authority. Such "legitimism" would deceive itself into subscribing to the pseudo-transcendence that powers claim for themselves, thereby making their deceptions that much more powerful.[122] Especially with its subtexts of protest against the imperial and bellicose drives of early twentieth-century Europe, the *Römerbrief* here moves quickly past mere legitimation as an option, and considers the more dangerous (because more plausible) alternative of violent revolution. No one could be swayed, Barth believes, toward acquiescence to the present order by a reading of the epistle and by extension in reading Barth's commentary on it; the "revolutionary Titan is far more godless, far more dangerous, than his reactionary counterpart—because he is so much nearer to the truth."[123]

The revolutionary judges the existing order correctly in rejecting its false transcendence. One gathers here—especially from the occasional mentions of the Bolsheviks[124]—that Barth, known in his early career as the "Red

---

118. Barth, *Epistle to the Romans*, 451.
119. Barth, *Epistle to the Romans*, 436.
120. Barth, *Epistle to the Romans*, 436.
121. Barth, *Epistle to the Romans*, 476.
122. Barth, *Epistle to the Romans*, 479.
123. Barth, *Epistle to the Romans*, 478.
124. For example, in a key moment in Barth, *Epistle to the Romans*, 480.

Pastor of Safenwil," sympathizes with the criticism of political economy made by Marxist movements but cannot give himself over to their prescriptive responses. Revolutionary movements seek "to remove the existing ordinances, in order that [they] may erect in their place the new right."[125] On its own, such action is intelligible to Barth, and one in which we might very well take part: the theological commitment here does not involve a prior preference for the powers we have over those we might have. Barth does not see, though, how the revolutionary can avoid allowing himself to be "overcome of evil," forgetting that he is not "the subject of the freedom which he so earnestly desires," the freedom to overturn the system of powers.[126] In making this mistake, the revolutionary "aims at the Revolution by which the true Order is to be inaugurated; but he launches another revolution which is, in fact, reaction."[127] This species of revolution, then, ironically reasserts what already exists: it justifies and confirms the specious reign of the powers through violence or partisanship or nationality. In other words, the revolutionary sees the established order of the world correctly but fails to see himself as inescapably part of that order, thus forgetting that repentance is the cornerstone for ethical and political action that does not merely repeat the pattern of the object of its protest. In this respect, the possibility of "no-revolution" represents no more security or value than revolution before the judgment of God on the world, and perhaps the equality of these options in a fundamental respect leaves open space for a repentant revolutionary. In either case, the character of our complicity, woven as it is into our very selves, calls for an ethic of repentance to distribute ethical value among the options for personal and political action.

We should pause to observe how self-attention, as a spiritual disposition, pivots around this understanding of repentance. Repentance is not intrinsically self-renunciation, as Foucault finds in the archive, or acquiescence to the shame that resubmits oneself to the powers, which Hartman's figures reject. Repentance can be understood as something more like reflexivity, a gesture of including oneself as implicated in one's critical energy. If the forms of this world are passing away, so too do the forms of the self derived from the world slide and fade. Repentant self-attention, then, is precisely not paying attention to the self rather than what is outside; it is a form of recollection by which one moves between internalization and externalization in order to break the habitual link between the spontaneous impulses or habits of the self and a life that is genuinely new. In that gap

---

125. Barth, *Epistle to the Romans*, 480.
126. Barth, *Epistle to the Romans*, 480.
127. Barth, *Epistle to the Romans*, 481.

perhaps opened by repentance, itself a disposition of dispossession, new possibilities might become ours.

If repentance is the primary ethical activity available in response to the powers, then love, as the "great positive possibility," is the affirmation for which it clears the way. Repentance shows a conscious self-criticism; love "ought to be undertaken as the protest against the course of this world, and it ought to continue without interruption."[128] Love, rather than rejection, is the true denial of the existing order, since love alone establishes a relationship with the neighbor grounded within the knowledge of God and responsive to them in their otherness. Yet, this familiar rhetoric of love takes on a particular character within Barth's total complicity account. In the world, love can only be defined in negative terms—"love does *not*," as 1 Corinthians 13 rhythmically repeats.[129] Love in the truest sense is a human religious impossibility, the impossible possibility of God toward which all of our actions can only gesture as their presupposition.[130] If love ever happens as an event in the world, it does so as the secret of revelation borne in regular action or of eternity hidden away in time.[131] Once we know that the eternal "Moment" does not enter into the sphere of the powers, "we should then become aware of the dignity and importance of each single concrete temporal moment, and apprehend its qualification and its ethical demand."[132] Human actions can therefore take shape "as though it were already day": demonstrating the temporary character of competition and conflict among people and acting out, parabolically, the coming communion.[133] An ethics of repentance recognizes the position of complicity one inhabits; the command to love enjoins one to arrange that complicity in ways that foretell a deeper communion and solidarity with others. This requires the labor of coming to see God in others, including the enemy, of perceiving one's drives and resisting their dominion over oneself. Barth's dialectic of repentance and love, therefore, gives a clearer Christian vocabulary to use in order to situate self-attentive asceticism. Where Foucault offered more clarity on the nature of ethical work required for such an ethics of the self, Barth relates a Christian ethical telos, *agape*, to the texture of human complicity and addresses both to the situation of the worldly person. Self-attention as a spiritual disposition is a way of asking oneself where there are new opportunities

---

128. Barth, *Epistle to the Romans*, 492.
129. Barth, *Epistle to the Romans*, 496.
130. Barth, *Epistle to the Romans*, 493–94.
131. Barth, *Epistle to the Romans*, 497.
132. Barth, *Epistle to the Romans*, 501.
133. Barth, *Epistle to the Romans*, 501.

for solidarity, communion, and delight; ascetical practices might ease anxieties or habits in us that deflect our attention away from them, or help build in us the capacity to inhabit them more whole-heartedly.

Barth's ethics, specifically because it is an ethic of repentance, is also oriented toward freedom. The repentant person knows how deeply the world marks himself and all others, and consequently disbelieves in the idols that he could be tempted to worship (in this case, by attributing purity or divinity to them). "Having freed himself of all idolatry," therefore, "he does not need to engage himself in endless protestations against idols," because he perceives "that the shadow of the judgment of God which spreads itself over them all is the shadow of righteousness."[134] In light of this, the "endeavours which men make to purify themselves have real importance as parables and as witnesses; for, inasmuch as the powers that be do . . . put a check upon human caprice, they do something to remind men of the sacrifice of their bodies that is demanded of them."[135] The relative good that human ethical possibilities represent is not to be disparaged, and the one whose life is characterized by repentance "examines [those possibilities] and participates in them. As routine exercises and representations, they must not be neglected."[136] Though no one is ever simply safe from the threat of misrecognizing oneself, the standpoint of repentance lifts—or, better, names and thereby lifts the deception of—the shadow of idolatry, freeing one to make determinate and relative choices for the good. Barth continues to consider this theme under the heading of "the *Krisis* of human freedom and detachment." Such detachment bespeaks an ethical attitude that moves toward activism but simultaneously remembers that it coexists among other possibilities, possible only on an understanding in which certain forms of resistance do not have the categorical superiority bestowed by an exteriority. The repentant person practicing free detachment "has discovered that he is his own worst enemy long before he has experienced the hostility of others," and can therefore remain in fellowship with others despite the presence of other ethical possibilities within that fellowship.[137] In contrast to the pathos of moral indignation indulged in by a "Total Abstainer, a really religious Socialist, a Churchman, or a Pacifist," the one who lives in free detachment differentiates herself by refusing to take such differentiations with final seriousness.[138] Freedom in this context, then, means freedom

134. Barth, *Epistle to the Romans*, 488.
135. Barth, *Epistle to the Romans*, 488.
136. Barth, *Epistle to the Romans*, 488.
137. Barth, *Epistle to the Romans*, 506.
138. Barth, *Epistle to the Romans*, 509.

A SPIRITUALITY OF RESISTANCE

from the constraining imperatives bestowed by claims to exteriority, and the resulting freedom to undertake acts of resistance without justifying those acts in terms of exteriority.

When Barth thinks of free detachment, he considers the example of Jesus's life, as is particularly clear when Barth discusses the Christology of the "royal man." Barth thinks that in Jesus's thought and action, "there is a correspondence, a parallel in the creaturely world, to the plan and purpose and work and attitude of God."[139] Though Jesus uniquely incarnates the divine life—and this represents a real sense in which he has access to a position of exteriority that all other humans do not—the translation of that life into human habit and action gives a model, the imitation of which would be itself a kind of repentant response to the powers. In relation, then, to the orders of life and value current in the world around him, Jesus's "pronouncedly revolutionary" witness consists in just the sort of free detachment that Barth had previously described in the *Römerbrief*.[140] Jesus so unsettled the authorities of his day "simply because He enjoyed and displayed, in relation to all the orders positively or negatively contested around Him, a remarkable freedom which again we can only describe as royal."[141] He had neither any need to acknowledge the absolute authority of those powers, nor felt any requirement only and ever to challenge, overthrow, or replace them (though he often did).[142] Instead,

> He simply revealed the limit and frontier of all these things—the freedom of the kingdom of God. He simply existed in this freedom and summoned to it. He simply made use of this freedom to cut right across all these systems both in His own case and in that of His disciples, interpreting and accepting them in His own way and in His own sense, in the light shed upon them all from that frontier. It was just that He Himself was the light which was shed upon all these orders from that frontier.[143]

Jesus acted in freedom by making of his participation in the powers what he would; he needed neither to be defined by them nor to be defined in negation of them. Of course, this includes resistance: Jesus "clashed with these orders in the interpretation commonly placed on them in the world in which He lived."[144] By showing their provisional and relative character—

---

139. Barth, *CD* 4/2:168.
140. Barth, *CD* 4/2:173.
141. Barth, *CD* 4/2:173.
142. Barth, *CD* 4/2:173.
143. Barth, *CD* 4/2:174.
144. Barth, *CD* 4/2:174.

and therefore the falsity of their claims to absolute value—he threatens the powers with the freedom to witness to another order. In Christ, God sheds an "alien light" on the powers "as on that which He has limited," and calls for a creative response to their predominant forms.[145]

Without access to the same exteriority—this light is, again, shed uniquely through Christ—human persons can repeat in their exercise of freedom what Jesus accomplished in terms of resistance in his.[146] Barth names the orders of the family, economics, religion, and politics specifically as those realms about which Jesus felt no compulsion to become a partisan and within which he used the freedom to rearrange prevailing social patterns. He thus attacked the old order of the world by ignoring its claims on him and instead being the presence of another order within it.[147] In doing so, many of the patterns that he inaugurated—Barth names the "dangerous alternatives" of remaining unmarried and not taking part in the acquisition or holding of possessions[148]—remain open to creative reappropriation to his followers. These material actions are not required of them, per se, but represent a shaking of the foundations available for imitation that would take as its criterion for faithfulness a similar "questioning of the very presuppositions [of these orders] which is all the more powerful in its lack of any direct aggressiveness."[149] That is, once we see ourselves as out from under the burden of seeking exteriorities, but also liberated from the demands of the powers to conform to their current shape, we have a space of freedom to attempt to rearrange our lives for the better, however finite and fallible that judgment must be.[150] In terms of resistance, the traditional concept of the

---

145. Barth, CD 4/2:174.

146. Though one may be tempted to see a shadow cast on the imitation of Christ by Barth's high Christology, Barth is also clear that part of Christ's work is to enable further human action. See, e.g., Webster's claim that alongside the vicarious humanity of Christ, "there is a complementary account of Christ's relationship to humanity as *generative* and *exemplary*" (*Barth's Ethics of Reconciliation*, 185).

147. Barth, CD 4/2:179.

148. Barth, CD 4/2:179.

149. Barth, CD 4/2:180. Again, reading these passages in Barth through some others on the ethical demands of unique situations, "direct aggressiveness" may not be categorically ruled out as a form of resistance. The criterion here is positive rather than negative: there are forms of resistance that, despite not being apparently "revolutionary" in seeking to overthrow the powers, question them to their core by signaling a kind of freedom from their dictates.

150. Compare this with the—very different!—argument pursued by José Esteban Muñoz in *Disidentifications*. Muñoz chronicles forms of performance and self-making that employ utopian impulses to "use the stuff of the 'real world' to remake collective sense of 'worldness' through spectacles, performances, and willful enactments of the self for others. The minoritarian subject employs disidentification as a crucial practice

imitatio Christi becomes a call to use what freedom we do have to renegotiate our relationship with the powers as they are. Within this total complicity account, then, to say that Christ was made sin for our sake (2 Cor 5:21) is to claim that he willingly subjected himself to the powers, entering fully into the sphere of the world, in order to show how "the righteousness of God" could be acted out under the conditions of dependence on them (even while maintaining a certain independence from them). The attitude of free detachment gives a certain color to self-attentive asceticism: one is invited to repeat in a new context Jesus's free self-determination amidst the powers, since it is established that both acquiescence and non-participation with the powers are ruled out.

Within the orbit of Barth's depiction of the powers, then, an ethic of repentance emerges that calls to an imitation of Christ in love for the neighbor, a parabolic representation of an order yet to come. Self-attentive asceticism becomes here a practice of reconfiguring one's life and action such that one's being signifies: though only in Christ does that life perfectly embody a new world, all of our historical actions can approach such signification by degrees of likeness.[151] In another of Barth's idioms, we can say that Christians "are claimed for action in the effort and struggle for human righteousness."[152] The sharp distinction between divine and human righteousness in no way authorizes indifference toward the condition of the world; humans still have responsibility for that specifically human righteousness, "even at best, an imperfect, fragile, and highly problematical righteousness."[153] Indeed, Barth explicitly rejects as absurd any ethical response that would regard human effort as worthless because it is imperfect,[154] instead pointing out that the distinction between these forms of righteousness "absolve[s one] from wasting time and energy sighing over the impassable limits of their sphere of action and thus missing the opportunities that present themselves in this sphere."[155] Those opportunities direct one to a view of others, in address to others, and with the aim of helping others. The true object of ethical attention—and that which should structure one's "thought, speech, and

---

contesting social subordination through the project of worldmaking.... Our charge as spectators and actors is to continue disidentifying with this world until we achieve new ones" (200). However different Barth's discursive situation is, his description of free detachment has a close analogue here.

151. Barth, *Christian Life*, 249–50.
152. Barth, *Christian Life*, 264.
153. Barth, *Christian Life*, 265.
154. Barth, *Christian Life*, 265.
155. Barth, *Christian Life*, 265.

action"—can only be the human other.[156] The labor of structuring one's forms of relationship to the powers in order to facilitate this can fairly be called a kind of asceticism, given Barth's call for self-awareness amidst human moral ambiguity. Yet, even that ambiguity calls for a response of attention and action toward the world, made no less urgent because it stands in the shadow of a higher and unattainable righteousness.

Barth's ethical work in relation to the powers, then, specifies the dispositions, orientation, and ends that Christian persons and communities could apply to the ethical outlook of self-attentive asceticism. When given the normative frame of Christian conviction, self-attentive asceticism is translated into an ethics of repentance, calling for self-examination of one's complicity with the powers and action to rearrange that complicity. In light of the limitations of human ability, particularly with respect to the powers, Barth recommends that we channel efforts away from some options and toward others, namely, those that embody the communal love foreshadowed by Christ's free disobedience of the powers.[157] We therefore have ethical criteria drawn from within Barth's total complicity account that do not depend on exteriority but still give an imperative to resistance, as well as a theological picture that makes sense of that resistance and what it can achieve. Insofar as this dimension of Barth's ethics works on our theological self-understanding at the level of disposition and orientation, it requires additional work to be translated into practices (though Barth does, of course, treat the paradigmatic cases of forgiveness of enemies, mutual acceptance in community, and others). Nevertheless, it is evident that Barth's ethical stance toward the world of the powers seeks to work against a bias toward inaction by encouraging a repentant engagement that can and must be applied by those who seek to appropriate it.

The political spirituality recommended by this book, then, can be recapitulated anew on the other side of detailed description of life among the powers. In the final analysis, we wish to say that public theology can encourage love, freedom, and transformation of self and world, which everyone already knows. The object has been to think solidarity and mutual implication responsive to love's demands at the fraught intersection of the intimate and the public that comes with life in a world of powers. Becoming the subject of one's own acts, becoming the self one is called to be: these are extraordinarily elusive and complex tasks, even before we take on particular

---

156. Barth, *Christian Life*, 266–67.

157. As McKenny shows, Barth seeks to navigate between pure voluntarism and the usurpation of God's office as lawgiver and judge (*Analogy of Grace*, 264). One of the assets of my interpretation and extension of Barth's ethics, I believe, is that it preserves this impulse and gives it shape within Barth's political theological context.

vocation to love for enemies or building peace in a violent world. Because we are formed as political creatures in our deepest recesses, all of life brings us occasions for this set of tasks. The occasions we take and what we make of them—including those we systemically neglect or disavow—will make us who we are. By paying the right kind of attention, those who are grasped by the power of love may find, by grace, that they tell its story anew, amid the noise.

SEARCHING FOR WHO WE MAY YET BE

These thinkers represent important moments of articulating a total complicity account of the powers, and they outline in their own ways an ethics—one that can be faithfully expressed as self-attentive asceticism—that offers avenues for meaningful resistance under conditions of persistent complicity. Though their critics often assume that their total complicity accounts lead to an irresponsible bias toward inaction, both Barth and Foucault take themselves to have shown how the powers' penetration into the personal recesses of daily life actually widen the ethical field and set before us abundant opportunities for resistance. To do so requires a deliberate application of what we have called a political spirituality, namely a form of self-attention that seeks opportunities to grow in the expression of commitments that resist the powers that be.

Saidiya Hartman does not describe many of the practices of her subjects as "spiritual," but they live the truth of fractured freedom in a world of powers. In the crucible of social dispossession, they attempt to live something beautiful, seeking pleasures unforbidden and uncommanded—at least by any authority they recognize—and building a community around the displaced truth of the social real. Hartman's figures knew that they had to claim their own lives, to shape the selves they wanted to be, in an immediate sense: the world was not made for them, and the subordinate forms of personhood readily on offer to them represented no life worthy of the name. Those of us who live in the same harsh world with gentler lives, with more social privileges and life chances, may have a more difficult time facing this task with their abandon and commitment. It is especially in those venues, to those people, that our complicity with a world that does structural violence daily must be rehearsed, not as the deepest or only truth about who any of us are, but as the occasion for us to receive ourselves differently, as a task. What I have described as self-attentive asceticism writes our agency differently into the story, inhabiting the political spirituality made possible by our description of the powers. We may yet be different people, newly free, newly in love with the world that can be.

As an ethical practice, self-attentive asceticism might do some justice to the complex dynamics of contemporary life in their own right. We have named some of the world-remaking challenges along the way—structural racism, the degradations of the anthropocene, constricting regimes of gender and sexuality, political economics that expropriate and immiserate the masses—and the reader knows those many more that plague us all according to who we are made by the world. With Barth and Foucault, I contend that none of these challenges admit of "great refusals," points of ethical leverage that would allow us simply to overturn their effects on our world and ourselves by heroic action. However, self-attentive asceticism reminds us just how much power we *do* possess: that these phenomena exist necessarily in and through our action, that we have created them just as much as they form us, and that the forms of our world can look quite different. By arranging power, complicity, and resistance as it does, self-attentive asceticism removes the distraction of posited exteriorities so that the full range of possibilities for creative living can come into view. Through the identification of our very selves with our social world, it invites us to work meaningfully—in ways large and small—toward a better set of social arrangements. Thus, in Barth's words, not exteriority but love is the "great positive possibility"—"because in [love] there is brought to light the revolutionary aspect of all ethical behavior, and because it is veritably concerned with the denial and breaking up of the existing order."[158] As we live along and within the fractures of that order, such a love is always available to us and will always be a sign of the true revolution: a coming reign.

---

158. Barth, *Epistle to the Romans*, 493.

Bibliography

Adorno, Theodor. *Minima Moralia: Reflections on a Damaged Life.* Translated by E. F. N. Jephcott. Radical Thinkers Series. London: Verso, 2005.

——— . "Resignation." In *The Culture Industry: Selected Essays on Mass Culture*, edited by J. M. Bernstein, 198–204. London: Routledge, 1991.

Ahmed, Sara. "Declarations of Whiteness: The Non-Performativity of Anti-Racism." *Borderlands* 3 (2004). https://rbb85.wordpress.com/2014/08/24/declarations-of-whiteness/.

——— . "The Nonperformativity of Antiracism." *Meridians* 7 (2006) 104–26.

Alexander, Michelle. *The New Jim Crow: Mass Incarceration in the Age of Colorblindness.* New York: New, 2010.

Althaus-Reid, Marcella. "Gustavo Gutiérrez Goes to Disneyland: Theme Park Theologies and the Diaspora of the Discourse of the Popular Theologian in Liberation Theology." In *From Feminist Theology to Indecent Theology: Readings on Poverty, Sexual Identity, and God*, by Marcella Althaus-Reid, 124–42. Norwich, UK: Hymns Ancient & Modern, 2004.

——— . *Indecent Theology: Theological Perversions in Sex, Gender, and Politics.* London: Routledge, 2000.

Aristotle, *Nichomachean Ethics.* Translated by Terence Irwin. Indianapolis: Hackett, 1999.

Aulén, Gustaf. *Christus Victor: An Historical Study of the Three Main Types of the Idea of Atonement.* Translated by A. G. Herbert. Eugene, OR: Wipf and Stock, 2003.

Baldwin, James. "The Devil Finds Work." In *James Baldwin: Collected Essays*, edited by Toni Morrison, 477–572. New York: Library of America, 1998.

Barth, Karl. *Anselm: Fides Quarens Intellectum: Anselm's Proof of the Existence of God in the Context of His Theological Scheme.* Edited by Dikran Y. Hadidian. Eugene, OR: Pickwick, 1975.

——— . "The Christian in Society, 1919." In *The Word of God and Theology*, translated by Amy Marga, 31–70. London: T. & T. Clark, 2011.

——— . *The Christian Life: Church Dogmatics.* Vol. IV/4, *Lecture Fragments.* Translated by Geoffrey W. Bromiley. Grand Rapids: Eerdmans, 1981.

——— . *Church Dogmatics.* 1/1: *The Doctrine of the Word of God.* Translated by G. W. Bromiley, G. T., Thomson, and Harold Knight. Edited by G. W. Bromiley and T. F. Torrance. London: T. & T. Clark, 2010.

——— . *Church Dogmatics.* 1/2: *The Doctrine of the Word of God.* Translated by G. W. Bromiley, G. T., Thomson, and Harold Knight. Edited by G. W. Bromiley and T. F. Torrance. London: T. & T. Clark, 2010.

―――. *Church Dogmatics. 4/1: The Doctrine of Reconciliation*. Translated by G. W. Bromiley. Edited by G. W. Bromiley and T. F. Torrance. London: T. & T. Clark, 2010.

―――. *Church Dogmatics. 4/2: The Doctrine of Reconciliation*. Translated by G. W. Bromiley. Edited by G. W. Bromiley and T. F. Torrance. London: T. & T. Clark, 2010.

―――. *Church Dogmatics. 4/3: The Doctrine of Reconciliation*. Translated by G. W. Bromiley. Edited by G. W. Bromiley and T. F. Torrance. London: T. & T. Clark, 2010.

―――. *Church Dogmatics. 4/3.2: The Doctrine of Reconciliation*. Translated by G. W. Bromiley. Edited by G. W. Bromiley and T. F. Torrance. London: T. & T. Clark, 2010.

―――. *Church Dogmatics. 4/4: The Doctrine of Reconciliation*. Translated by G. W. Bromiley. Edited by G. W. Bromiley and T. F. Torrance. London: T. & T. Clark, 2010.

―――. *The Epistle to the Romans*. Translated by Edwyn C. Hoskyns. London: Oxford University Press, 1933.

―――. "The Humanity of God." In *The Humanity of God*, translated by Thomas Wieser, 37–68. Louisville: Westminster John Knox, 1960.

Berkhof, Hendrikus. *Christ and the Powers*. Translated by John Howard Yoder. Scottdale, PA: Herald, 1977.

Berlant, Lauren. "Critical Inquiry, Affirmative Culture." *Critical Inquiry* 30 (2004) 445–51.

―――. *Cruel Optimism*. Durham: Duke University Press, 2011.

―――. "Genre Flailing." *Capacious: Journal for Emerging Affect Theory* 1 (2018) 156–62.

―――. "A Properly Political Concept of Love: Three Approaches in Ten Pages." *Cultural Anthropology* 26 (2011) 683–91.

―――. "Slow Death (Sovereignty, Obesity, Lateral Agency)." *Critical Inquiry* 33 (2007) 75–80.

Betz, Hans Dieter. "Dynamis." In *Dictionary of Deities and Demons in the Bible*, edited by Karel van der Toorn et al., 267–70. Leiden: Brill, 1995.

Blum, Peter C. "Foucault, Genealogy, Anabaptism: Confessions of an Errant Postmodernist." In *The New Yoder*, edited by Peter Dula and Chris K. Huebner, 90–105. Eugene, OR: Cascade, 2010.

Bonhoeffer, Dietrich. "After Ten Years." In *Letters and Papers from Prison*, translated and edited by Eberhard Bethge, 3–20. New York: SCM, 1953.

Bonilla-Silva, Eduardo. *Racism without Racists: Color-Blind Racism and Racial Inequality in Contemporary America*. 3rd ed. Lanham, MD: Rowman and Littlefield, 2010.

Bourne, Richard. "Governmentality, Witness, and the State: Christian Social Criticism with and beyond Yoder and Foucault." In *Power and Practices: Engaging the Work of John Howard Yoder*, edited by Jeremy M. Bergen and Anthony G. Siegrist, 99–115. Scottdale, PA: Herald, 2009.

Breton, André. *Manifestoes of Surrealism*. Translated by Richard Seaver and Helen R. Lane. Ann Arbor: University of Michigan Press, 1969.

Brown, Wendy. *Politics Outside of History*. Princeton: Princeton University Press, 2001.

Busch, Eberhard. "Indissoluble Unity: Barth's Position on the Jews during the Hitler Era." In *For the Sake of the World: Karl Barth and the Future of Ecclesial Theology*, edited by George Hunsinger, 53–79. Grand Rapids: Eerdmans, 2004.

———. *Karl Barth: His Life from Letters and Autobiographical Texts*. Translated by John Bowden. Philadelphia: Fortress, 1976.

Caird, G. B. *Principalities and Powers: A Study in Pauline Theology*. Eugene, OR: Wipf and Stock, 1956.

Carrette, Jeremy. *Foucault and Religion: Spirituality Corporality and Political Spirituality*. London: Routledge, 2000.

Cavell, Stanley. *Cities of Words: Pedagogical Letters on a Register of the Moral Life*. Cambridge, MA: Belknap, 2004.

Césaire, Aimé. "Letter to Maurice Thorez." Translated by Chike Jeffers. *Social Text* 28 (2010) 145–52.

Chen, Yin-An. *Toward a Micro-Political Theology: A Dialogue between Michel Foucault and Liberation Theologies*. Eugene, OR: Pickwick, 2022.

Chomsky, Noam. "The Responsibility of Intellectuals." *New York Review of Books*, February 23, 1967. https://www.nybooks.com/articles/1967/02/23/a-special-supplement-the-responsibility-of-intelle/.

Cohen, Adam, and Elizabeth Taylor. *American Pharaoh: Mayor Richard J. Daley: His Battle for Chicago and the Nation*. Boston: Little, Brown, and Company, 2000.

Collins Winn, Christian T. *"Jesus Is Victor!": The Significance of the Blumhardts for the Theology of Karl Barth*. Eugene, OR: Pickwick, 2009.

Cone, James. *A Black Theology of Liberation*. Twentieth Anniversary ed. Maryknoll, NY: Orbis, 1990.

Cooper-White, Pamela. *The Psychology of Christian Nationalism: Why People Are Drawn In and How to Talk Across the Divide*. Minneapolis: Fortress, 2022.

Cramer, David, et al. "Theology and Misconduct: The Case of John Howard Yoder." *Christian Century*, August 20, 2014. https://www.christiancentury.org/article/2014-07/theology-and-misconduct.

Cremonisi, Laura, et al. *Foucault and the Making of Subjects*. New Politics of Anatomy 3. London: Rowman & Littlefield, 2016.

Cullmann, Oscar. *Christ and Time: The Primitive Christian Conception of Time and History*. Translated by Floyd V. Filson. Philadelphia: Westminster, 1950.

Cyril of Alexandria. *On the Unity of Christ*. Translated by John Anthony McGuckin. Crestwood, NY: St. Vladimir's Seminary Press, 1995.

Dargis, Manohla, and A. O. Scott. "In Defense of the Slow and Boring." *New York Times*, June 3, 2011. https://www.nytimes.com/2011/06/05/movies/films-in-defense-of-slow-and-boring.html?_r=1.

Dawn, Marva J. "The Biblical Concept of 'the Principalities and Powers': John Howard Yoder Points to Jacques Ellul." In *The Wisdom of the Cross: Essays in Honor of John Howard Yoder*, edited by Stanley Hauerwas et al., 168–88. Grand Rapids: Eerdmans, 1999.

Deleuze, Giles. *Foucault*. Translated by Seán Hand. Minneapolis: University of Minnesota Press, 1988.

Dreyfus, Hubert L., and Paul Rabinow. *Michel Foucault: Beyond Structuralism and Hermeneutics*. 2nd ed. Chicago: University of Chicago Press, 1983.

Fiddes, Paul. "The Status of Women in the Thought of Karl Barth." In *After Eve: Women, Theology, and the Christian Tradition*, edited by Janet Martin Soskice, 138–55. London: Pickering, 1990.

Fields, Sabrina. "Decolonizing the Map: Creating the Indigenous Mapping Collective." *PBS Teachers' Lounge*, April 1, 2021. https://www.pbs.org/education/blog/decolonizing-the-map-creating-the-indigenous-mapping-collective.

Fisher, Marc, et al. "Pizzagate: From Rumor, to HashTag, to Gunfire in D.C." *Washington Post*, December 6, 2016. https://www.washingtonpost.com/local/pizzagate-from-rumor-to-hashtag-to-gunfire-in-dc/2016/12/06/4c7def50-bbd4-11e6-94ac-3d324840106c_story.html.

Forbes, Chris. "Pauline Demonology and/or Cosmology? Principalities, Powers, and Elements of the World in their Hellenistic Context." *Journal for the Study of the New Testament* 24 (2002) 51–73.

———. "Paul's Principalities and Powers: Demythologizing Apocalyptic?" *Journal for the Study of the New Testament* 23 (2001) 61–88.

Foucault, Michel. "About the Concept of the 'Dangerous Individual' in Nineteenth-Century Legal Psychiatry." In *Power*, translated by Robert Hurley, edited by James D. Faubion, 176–200. The Essential Works of Michel Foucault 1954–1984, vol. 3. New York: New, 2001.

———. "A propos de la généalogie de l'éthique: un aperçu du travail en cours." In *Dits et Écrits II: 1976–1988*, edited by Daniel Defert and François Ewald, 1202–31. Paris: Gallimard, 2001.

———. *The Birth of Biopolitics: Lectures at the Collège de France, 1978–1979*. Translated by Graham Burchell. Edited by Michel Senellart. New York: Picador, 2008.

———. "Body/Power." In *Power/Knowledge: Selected Interviews and Other Writings, 1972–1977*, translated and edited by Colin Gordon, 55–62. New York: Pantheon, 1980.

———. "The Confession of the Flesh." In *Power/Knowledge: Selected Interviews and Other Writings, 1972–1977*, translated and edited by Colin Gordon, 194–228. New York: Pantheon, 1980.

———. *The Courage of Truth: The Government of Self and Others II: Lectures at the Collège de France, 1983–1984*. Translated by Graham Burchell. Edited by Frédéric Gros. New York: Picador, 2011.

———. *Discipline and Punish: The Birth of the Prison*. Translated by Alan Sheridan. 2nd ed. New York: Vintage, 1995.

———. "L'écriture de soi." In *Dits et Écrits II: 1976–1988*, edited by Daniel Defert and François Ewald, 1234–49. Paris: Gallimard, 2001.

———. "L'éthique du souci de soi comme pratique de la liberté." In *Dits et Écrits II: 1976–1988*, edited by Daniel Defert and François Ewald, 1527–48. Paris: Gallimard, 2001.

———. *Fearless Speech*. Edited by Joseph Pearson. Los Angeles: Semiotext(e), 2001.

———. "Le grand enfermement." Interview with Niklaus Meienberg, March 25, 1972. In *Dits et écrits I, 1954–1975*, edited by Daniel Defert and François Ewald, 1164–74. Paris: Quarto Gallimard, 2001.

———. *The Hermeneutics of the Subject: Lectures at the Collège de France, 1981–1982*. Translated by Graham Burchell. Edited by Frédéric Gros. New York: Picador, 2005.

———. *Histoire de la Sexualité*. Vol. 1, *La volonté de savoir*. Paris: Gallimard, 1976.

———. *Histoire de la Sexualité*. Vol. 2, *L'usage des plaisirs*. Paris: Gallimard, 1984.

———. *Histoire de la Sexualité.* Vol. 3, *Le souci de soi.* Paris: Gallimard, 1984.
———. *The History of Sexuality.* Vol. 1, *An Introduction.* Translated by Robert Hurley. New York: Vintage, 1978.
———. "The Masked Philosopher." In *Ethics: Subjectivity and Truth,* translated by Robert Hurley et al., edited by Paul Rabinow, 321–28. The Essential Works of Michel Foucault, 1954–1984, vol. 1. New York: New, 1997.
———. "Of Other Spaces: Utopias and Heterotopias." Translated by Jay Miskowiec. *Diacritics* 16 (1986) 22–27.
———. "Political Spirituality as the Will for Alterity: An Interview with the *Nouvel Observateur.*" Translated by Sabina Vaccarino Bremner. *Critical Inquiry* 47 (2020) 121–34.
———. "Pouvoirs et stratégies." In *Dits et Écrits II: 1976–1988,* edited by Daniel Defert and François Ewald, 418–28. Paris: Gallimard, 2001.
———. "Prison Talk." In *Power/Knowledge: Selected Interviews and Other Writings, 1972–1977,* translated and edited by Colin Gordon, 37–54. New York: Pantheon, 1980.
———. "Questions on Geography." In *Power/Knowledge: Selected Interviews and Other Writings, 1972–1977,* translated and edited by Colin Gordon, 63–77. New York: Pantheon, 1980.
———. *Security, Territory, Population: Lectures at the Collège de France.* Translated by Graham Burchell. Edited by Michel Senellart. New York: Picador, 2007.
———. "Le sujet et le pouvoir." In *Dits et Écrits II: 1976–1988,* edited by Daniel Defert and François Ewald, 1041–62. Paris: Gallimard, 2001.
———. "Les techniques de soi." In *Dits et Écrits II: 1976–1988,* edited by Daniel Defert and François Ewald, 1602–32. Paris: Gallimard, 2001.
———. *This Is Not a Pipe.* Translated and edited by James Harkness. Berkeley: University of California Press, 1983.
———. "Truth and Power." In *Power/Knowledge: Selected Interviews and Other Writings, 1972–1977,* translated and edited by Colin Gordon, 109–33. New York: Pantheon, 1980.
———. "What Is Critique?" In *The Politics of Truth,* translated by Lysa Hochroth and Catherine Porter, edited by Sylvère Lotringer, 41–82. Los Angeles: Semiotext(e), 2007.
Foucault, Michel, and Duccio Trombadori. *Remarks on Marx: Conversations with Duccio Trombadori.* Translated by R. James Goldstein and James Cascaito. New York: Semiotext(e), 1991.
Frankfurt, Harry. *The Reasons of Love.* Princeton: Princeton University Press, 2004.
Fraser, Nancy. *Unruly Practices: Power, Discourse, and Gender in Contemporary Social Theory.* Minneapolis: University of Minnesota Press, 1989.
Gerwig, Greta, dir. *Barbie.* Warner Brothers, 2023.
Goossen, Rachel Waltner. "'Defanging the Beast': Mennonite Responses to John Howard Yoder's Sexual Abuse." *Mennonite Quarterly Review* 89 (2015) 7–80.
Gorringe, Timothy J. *Karl Barth: Against Hegemony.* Oxford: Oxford University Press, 1999.
Gramsci, Antonio. *Selections from the Prison Notebooks of Antonio Gramsci.* Tranlsated and edited by Quintin Hoare and Geoffrey Nowell Smith. New York: International, 1989.

"Graves Sink, Fisheries Shrink as Climate Change Hits Fiji." *Al-Jazeera*, January 15, 2023. https://www.aljazeera.com/gallery/2023/1/15/graves-sink-fisheries-shrink-as-climate-change-hits-fiji.

Gregory of Nyssa. "On the Soul and Resurrection." In *Saint Gregory of Nyssa: Ascetical Works*, translated by Virginia Woods Callahan, 195–276. The Fathers of the Church 58. Washington, DC: Catholic University of America Press, 1999.

Guth, Karen V. "Doing Justice to the Complex Legacy of John Howard Yoder: Restorative Justice Resources in Witness and Feminist Ethics." *Journal of the Society of Christian Ethics* 35 (2015) 119–39.

Gutiérrez, Gustavo. *A Theology of Liberation*. Translated and edited by Caridad Inda and John Eagleson. Maryknoll, NY: Orbis, 1998.

Habermas, Jürgen. *The Philosophical Discourse of Modernity: Twelve Lectures*. Translated by Frederick Lawrence. Cambridge: MIT Press, 1987.

Haddorff, David. *Christian Ethics as Witness: Barth's Ethics for a World at Risk*. Eugene, OR: Cascade, 2010.

Hart, David Bentley. *The Beauty of the Infinite: The Aesthetics of Christian Truth*. Grand Rapids: Eerdmans, 2003.

Hartman, Saidiya. *Lose Your Mother: A Journey along the Atlantic Slave Trade*. New York: Farrar, Straus, and Giroux, 2007.

———. *Wayward Lives, Beautiful Experiments: Intimate Histories of Riotous Black Girls, Troublesome Women, and Queer Radicals*. New York: Norton, 2019.

Hauerwas, Stanley. "The Christian Difference, or Surviving Postmodernism." In *The Blackwell Companion to Postmodern Theology*, edited by Graham Ward, 144–61. Oxford: Blackwell, 2001.

Healy, Nicholas M. "The Logic of Karl Barth's Ecclesiology: Analysis, Assessment, and Proposed Modifications." *Modern Theology* 10 (1994) 253–70.

Hector, Kevin. *Theology without Metaphysics*. Cambridge: Cambridge University Press, 2011.

Hendricks, Christina. "Foucault's Prophecy: The Intellectual as Exile." Presented at a meeting of the International Association for Philosophy and Literature, Stony Brook, New York, May 2000.

Hess, Cynthia. *Sites of Violence, Sites of Grace: Christian Nonviolence and the Traumatized Self*. Lanham, MD: Lexington, 2009.

Horkheimer, Max, and Theodor Adorno. *Dialectic of Enlightenment: Philosophical Fragments*. Translated by Edmund Jephcott. Edited by Gunzelin Schmid Noerr. Cultural Memory in the Present. Stanford: Stanford University Press, 2002.

Hütter, Reinhard. "The Church: Midwife of History or Witness of the Eschaton?" *Journal of Religious Ethics* 18 (1990) 27–54.

Jackson, Lauren Michele. "What Is an Anti-Racist Reading List For?" *New York Magazine*, June 8, 2020. https://www.vulture.com/2020/06/anti-racist-reading-lists-what-are-they-for.html.

Johnson, Keith L. "A Reappraisal of Karl Barth's Theological Development and His Dialogue with Catholicism." *International Journal of Systematic Theology* 14 (2012) 3–25.

Jordan, Mark D. *Convulsing Bodies: Religion and Resistance in Foucault*. Stanford: Stanford University Press, 2015.

———. *Telling Truths in Church: Scandal, Flesh, and Christian Speech*. Boston: Beacon, 2003.

Joseph, Miranda. *Against the Romance of Community*. Minneapolis: University of Minnesota Press, 2002.

Joyce, Kathryn, and Jeff Sharlet. "Losing the Plot: The 'Leftists' Who Turn Right." *In These Times*, December 12, 2023. https://inthesetimes.com/article/former-left-right-fascism-capitalism-horseshoe-theory.

Kant, Immanuel. *Fundamental Principles of the Metaphysics of Morals*. Translated by Thomas K. Abbott. Upper Saddle River, NJ: Prentice-Hall, 1949.

Käsemann, Ernst. *Jesus Means Freedom*. Translated by Frank Clarke. Minneapolis: Fortress, 2007.

Kelley, Robin D. G. "A Poetics of Anticolonialism." In *Discourse on Colonialism*, by Aimé Césaire, 7–28. New York: Monthly Review, 2000.

Kierkegaard, Søren. *The Sickness unto Death: A Christian Psychological Exposition for Edification and Awakening by Anti-Climacus*. Translated by Alastair Hannay. London: Penguin, 1989.

Kois, Dan. "Eating Your Cultural Vegetables." *New York Times*, April 29, 2011. https://www.nytimes.com/2011/05/01/magazine/mag-01Riff-t.html.

Kotsko, Adam. *Neoliberalism's Demons: On the Political Theology of Late Capital*. Stanford: Stanford University Press, 2018.

———. *The Prince of This World*. Stanford: Stanford University Press, 2017.

Lennie, Tyra. "Self-Improvement in Astellian Friendship." *Feminist Philosophy Quarterly* 19 (2023) 1–24.

Levi, Primo. *The Drowned and the Saved*. Translated by Raymond Rosenthal. New York: Simon & Schuster, 2017.

Lloyd, Vincent. *Black Natural Law*. Oxford: Oxford University Press, 2016.

Lorenzini, Daniele. *The Force of Truth: Critique, Genealogy, and Truth-Telling in Foucault*. Chicago: University of Chicago Press, 2023.

Lowndes, Joseph. "From New Class Critique to White Nationalism: *Telos*, the Alt Right, and the Origins of Trumpism." *Konturen* 9 (2017) 8–14.

Mandela, Nelson. *Long Walk to Freedom: The Autobiography of Nelson Mandela*. New York: Little, Brown, and Company, 1994.

Martens, Paul. *The Heterodox Yoder*. Eugene, OR: Cascade, 2012.

Mathewes, Charles. *A Theology of Public Life*. Cambridge Studies in Christian Doctrine 17. Cambridge: Cambridge University Press, 2007.

McBride, Jennifer M. *The Church for the World: A Theology of Public Witness*. Oxford: Oxford University Press, 2012.

McCormack, Bruce L. *Orthodox and Modern: Studies in the Theology of Karl Barth*. Grand Rapids: Baker Academic, 2008.

McKenny, Gerald. *The Analogy of Grace: Karl Barth's Moral Theology*. Oxford: Oxford University Press, 2010.

Milkman, Ruth. "Introduction: Toward a New Labor Movement? Organizing New York City's Precariat." In *New Labor in New York: Precarious Workers and the Future of the Labor Movement*, edited by Ruth Milkman and Ed Ott, 1–24. Ithaca, NY: Cornell University Press, 2014.

Miller, Vincent J. *Consuming Religion: Christian Faith and Practice in a Consumer Culture*. New York: Continuum, 2004.

Muñoz, José Esteban. *Cruising Utopia: The Then and There of Queer Futurity*. New York: NYU Press, 2009.

———. *Disidentifications: Queers of Color and the Politics of Performance*. Minneapolis: University of Minnesota Press, 1999.

Munro, Kirstin. *The Production of Everyday Life in Eco-Conscious Households: Compromise, Conflict, Complicity*. Bristol: Bristol University Press, 2023.

Nation, Mark Theissen. *John Howard Yoder: Mennonite Patience, Evangelical Witness, Catholic Convictions*. Grand Rapids: Eerdmans, 2006.

Newheiser, David. "Foucault, Gary Becker, and the Critique of Neoliberalism." *Theory, Culture, & Society* 33 (2016) 3–21.

———. *Hope in a Secular Age*. Oxford: Oxford University Press, 2019.

———. "Why the World Needs Negative Political Theology." *Modern Theology* 36 (2020) 5–12.

Niebuhr, Reinhold. "Barth—Apostle of the Absolute." In *Essays in Applied Christianity*, edited by D. B. Robertson, 141–46. New York: Meridian, 1959.

———. "Barthianism and Political Reaction." In *Essays in Applied Christianity*, edited by D. B. Robertson, 150–55. New York: Meridian, 1959.

———. "Barthianism and the Kingdom." In *Essays in Applied Christianity*, edited by D. B. Robertson, 147–49. New York: Meridian, 1959.

———. "Karl Barth and Democracy." In *Essays in Applied Christianity*, edited by D. B. Robertson, 163–64. New York: Meridian, 1959.

———. "We Are Men and Not God." In *Essays in Applied Christianity*, edited by D. B. Robertson, 168–74. New York: Meridian, 1959.

———. "Why Is Barth Silent on Hungary?" In *Essays in Applied Christianity*, edited by D. B. Robertson, 183–89. New York: Meridian, 1959.

Nussbaum, Martha. "The Professor of Parody." *New Republic*, February 22, 1999. https://newrepublic.com/article/150687/professor-parody.

Oberman, Heiko A. *The Dawn of the Reformation: Essays in Late Medieval and Early Reformation Thought*. Grand Rapids: Eerdmans, 1992.

O'Farrell, Clare. "Power and Culture." In *Michel Foucault*, by Clare O'Farrell, 96–108. London: SAGE, 2005.

Packer, George. "Why Leftists Go Right." *New Yorker*, February 14, 2016. https://www.newyorker.com/magazine/2016/02/22/why-leftists-go-right.

Park, Joon-Sik. *Missional Ecclesiologies in Creative Tension: H. Richard Niebuhr and John Howard Yoder*. New York: Lang, 2007.

Pitts, Jamie. *Principalities and Powers: Revising John Howard Yoder's Sociological Theology*. Eugene, OR: Pickwick, 2013.

Poisson, Jayme. "The Outcry." *Toronto Star*, May 29, 2011.

———. "Parents Keep Child's Gender Secret." *Toronto Star*, May 21, 2011. https://www.thestar.com/life/parents-keep-childs-gender-secret/article_03418142-70e8-561e-9cdf-0a04c8df3b79.html.

Prather, Scott. *Christ, Power, and Mammon: Karl Barth and John Howard Yoder in Dialogue*. London: Bloomsbury, 2013.

Rose, Marika. "Machines of Loving Grace: Angels, Cyborgs, and Postsecular Labor." *Journal for Cultural and Religious Theory* 16 (2017) 240–59.

Rossi, Andrea. *The Labour of Subjectivity: Foucault on Biopolitics, Economy, Critique*. Futures of the Archive. London: Rowman & Littlefield, 2016.

Rothberg, Michael. *The Implicated Subject: Beyond Victims and Perpetrators*. Cultural Memory in the Present Series. Stanford: Stanford University Press, 2019.

BIBLIOGRAPHY

Ruti, Mari. *The Singularity of Being: Lacan and the Immortal Within*. New York: Fordham University Press, 2012.
Sartre, Jean-Paul. "Jean-Paul Sartre Répond." *L'Arc* 30 (1966) 87–96.
Schirato, Tony, et al. *Understanding Foucault: A Critical Introduction*. 2nd ed. London: SAGE, 2012.
Schlier, Heinrich. *Principalities and Powers in the New Testament*. New York: Herder and Herder, 1961.
Schneider, Laurel. "What Race Is Your Sex?" In vol. 2 of *Queer Religion: LGBT Movements and Queering Religion*, edited by Donald L. Boisvert and Jay Emerson Johnson, 125–42. Santa Barbera, CA: Praeger, 2012.
Schwartz, Martin. *Karl Barth in der Strafanstalt*. Basel, 1968.
Sedgwick, Eve Kosofsky. "Paranoid Reading and Reparative Reading, or, You're So Paranoid, You Probably Think This Essay Is About You." In *Touching Feeling: Affect, Pedagogy, Performativity*, by Eve Kosofsky Sedgwick, 123–52. Series Q. Durham: Duke University Press, 2003.
Shao, Elena. "What This Year's 'Astonishing' Ocean Heat Means for the Planet." *New York Times*, August 3, 2023. https://www.nytimes.com/interactive/2023/08/03/climate/ocean-temperatures-heat-earth.html.
Shotwell, Alexis. *Against Purity: Living Ethically in Compromised Times*. Minneapolis: University of Minnesota Press, 2016.
Sider, J. Alexander. "'Who Durst Defy the Omnipotent to Arms?': The Nonviolent Atonement and a Non-Competitive Doctrine of God." In *The Work of Jesus Christ in Anabaptist Perspective: Essays in Honor of J. Denny Weaver*, edited by Alain Epp Weaver and Gerald J. Mast, 246–62. Scottsdale, PA: Cascadia, 2008.
Simon, David. "An Interview with David Simon." Interview by Nick Hornby. *The Believer*, August 1, 2007. https://www.thebeliever.net/an-interview-with-david-simon/.
Smith, Mychal Denzel. "Paved with Good Intentions." Interview by Brooke Gladstone. *On the Media*, April 6, 2018. https://www.wnycstudios.org/podcasts/otm/episodes/on-the-media-2018-04-06?tab=summary.
Sonderegger, Katherine. *That Jesus Christ Was Born a Jew: Karl Barth's Doctrine of Israel*. University Park: Pennsylvania State University Press, 1992.
Spinoza, Baruch. *The Ethics*. Translated by Samuel Shirley. Edited by Seymour Feldman. Indianapolis: Hackett, 1992.
Standing, Guy. *The Precariat: The New Dangerous Class*. Rev. ed. London: Bloomsbury Academic, 2014.
Steinbeck, John. *The Grapes of Wrath*. New York: Viking, 1939.
Stevenson, Bryan. *Just Mercy: A Story of Justice and Redemption*. New York: Spiegel & Grau, 2014.
Stewart-Kroeker, Sarah. "'What Do We Do with the Art of Monstrous Men?': Betrayal and the Feminist Ethics of Aesthetic Involvement." *De Ethica* 6 (2020) 51–74.
Stringfellow, William. *An Ethic for Christians and Other Aliens in a Strange Land*. Eugene, OR: Wipf and Stock, 1973.
———. *Free in Obedience*. Eugene, OR: Wipf and Stock, 1964.
———. *A Private and Public Faith*. Eugene, OR: Wipf and Stock, 1962.
Táíwò, Olúfémi O. *Elite Capture: How the Powerful Took Over Identity Politics (and Everything Else)*. Chicago: Haymarket, 2022.

Tanner, Kathryn. *Christ the Key*. Current Issues in Theology 7. Cambridge: Cambridge University Press, 2010.

———. *Jesus, Humanity, and the Trinity: A Brief Systematic Theology*. Minneapolis: Fortress, 2001.

Taylor, Charles. "Foucault on Freedom and Truth." *Political Theory* 12 (1984) 152–83.

Tessman, Lisa. *Burdened Virtues: Virtue Ethics for Liberatory Struggles*. New York: Oxford University Press, 2005.

Tonstad, Linn. "Debt Time Is Straight Time." *Political Theology* 17 (2016) 434–48.

Townes, Emilie. *Womanist Ethics and the Cultural Production of Evil*. Black Religion/Womanist Thought/Social Justice Series. New York: Palgrave MacMillan, 2006.

Tran, Jonathan. *Foucault and Theology*. Philosophy and Theology Series. London: T. & T. Clark, 2011.

Tsing, Anna Lowenhaupt. *Friction: An Ethnography of Global Connection*. Princeton: Princeton University Press, 2005.

Walker, David. "Walker's Appeal, in Four Articles; Together with a Preamble to the Coloured Citizens of the World, but in Particular, and Very Expressly, to Those of the United States of America." Written in Boston, Massachusetts, September 28, 1829. Documenting the American South, University of North Carolina, 2001. https://docsouth.unc.edu/nc/walker/walker.html.

Webster, John. *Barth's Ethics of Reconciliation*. Cambridge: Cambridge University Press, 1995.

Wendland, Ernst. "Contextualising the Potentates, Principalities, and Powers in the Epistle to the Ephesians." *Neotestamentica* 33 (1999) 199–223.

West, Cornel. "Introduction: The Radical King We Don't Know." In *The Radical King*, edited by Cornel West, ix–xvi. Boston: Beacon, 2016.

Winant, Gabriel. "The Social Question." Interview by Daniel Denvir. *The Dig*, January 3, 2021. https://thedigradio.com/podcast/the-social-question-with-gabriel-winant/

Wink, Walter. *Engaging the Powers: Discernment and Resistance in a World of Domination*. Minneapolis: Fortress, 1992.

———. *Naming the Powers: The Language of Power in the New Testament*. Philadelphia: Fortress, 1984.

———. *Unmasking the Powers: The Invisible Forces that Determine Human Existence*. Philadelphia: Fortress, 1986.

Wollen, Audrey. "Looking at Pictures of Marilyn Monroe Reading." *Affadavit*, February 25, 2019. https://www.affidavit.art/articles/marilyn-monroe.

Yoder, John Howard. *Body Politics: Five Practices of the Christian Community Before the Watching World*. Scottdale, PA: Herald, 2001.

———. "The Otherness of the Church." In *The Royal Priesthood: Essays Ecclesiastical and Ecumenical*, edited by Michael G. Cartwright, 53–64. Scottdale, PA: Herald, 1998.

———. "'Patience' as Method in Moral Reasoning: Is an Ethic of Discipleship 'Absolute'?" In *The Wisdom of the Cross: Essays in Honor of John Howard Yoder*, edited by Stanley Hauerwas et al., 24–42. Grand Rapids: Eerdmans, 1999.

———. "A People in the World." In *The Royal Priesthood: Essays Ecclesiastical and Ecumenical*, edited by Michael G. Cartwright, 65–101. Scottdale, PA: Herald, 1998.

———. *The Politics of Jesus: Vicit Agnus Noster*. 2nd ed. Grand Rapids: Eerdmans, 1994.

———. "To Serve Our God and to Rule the World." In *The Royal Priesthood: Essays Ecclesiastical and Ecumenical,* edited by Michael G. Cartwright, 127–42. Scottdale, PA: Herald, 1998.

Zamora, Daniel. "How Michel Foucault Got Neoliberalism So Wrong." Interview by Kévin Boucaud-Victoire. Translated by Seth Ackerman. *Jacbobin,* September 6, 2019. https://jacobin.com/2019/09/michel-foucault-neoliberalism-friedrich-hayek-milton-friedman-gary-becker-minoritarian-governments.

Index

Adorno, Theodor, 66, 100, 162n72
agency, limits of, 2–3, 23–24, 48–49, 59–60, 67–68, 91–96, 97–98, 137
Ahmed, Sara, 104–5
Alexander, Michelle, 7–13
Allen, Richard, 13
Althaus-Reid, Marcella, 163n77
Aristotle, 183
askēsis, viii, 174–75, 185–86, 187–95, 197
Aulén, Gustaf, 14

Bacon's Rebellion, 10
Baldwin, James, 163n78
baptism, as marker of Christian identity, 78, 83–85, 95
Barbie (film), 101
Barth, Karl
　on baptism, 84–85
　changes in positions relevant to this book, 53n62, 130n117
　on church as part of the world, 85–90
　on difference between Christ and church, 88
　on grace as God's freedom, 85, 89–90, 132–34, 177–79, 196–97
　on the lordless powers, 53–60
　on love of neighbor, 158–59, 199–200, 203–4
　plausibility of comparison with Foucault, 35–43, 61–62, 179–81
　reasons for pairing with Foucault in this book, 61–62
　on repentance as ethical disposition, 196
　on resistance to the powers, 142–43, 178–79, 196–97
　on revelation, 39, 130–34
　"secular parables of the Kingdom", 39n18, 89
Berkhof, Hendrikus, 14–15, 74–76, 78
Berlant, Lauren, 43n31, 151–53, 154n45, 171–72
Betz, Hans Dieter, 16n56
"blaming the victim." *See* complicity, as distinct from responsibility or blameworthiness
Blum, Peter C., 90n95
Blumhardt, Johann and Christophe, 14
Bonhoeffer, Dietrich, 61
Bonilla-Silva, Eduardo, 4
Breton, André, 34
Brown, Wendy, 6n16
Burton, Emanuelle, 186n70
Busch, Eberhard, 142n9, 158n61
Butler, Judith, 148n36

Caird, George Bradford, 15
Carr, Wesley, 107
Carrette, Jeremy, 91n96
cartography, as metaphor for theory, 129
Cavell, Stanley, 184–85
Césaire, Aimé, 164n82
Césaire, Suzanne, 164n81
Chen, Yin-An, 176n32, 182
Chicago, segregation in city planning of, 11
Chomsky, Noam, 100

INDEX

church
  ecclesial exceptionalism, 71–72, 96–98
  as opposed to powers of death, 19–20, 25–27, 30–31, 72, 77–83
  as visible or invisible, 85–88
Christ. *See* Jesus of Nazareth
Christus Victor theory of atonement on basis of powers' defeat, 14, 27, 77–78
climate change, responses to, 1–3
Collins Winn, Christian, 14n41
complicity
  assumed opposition to resistance, 31, 125, 139–40, 149–50, 152, 155–56, 161, 170–71
  definition, 5–6
  as distinct from responsibility or blameworthiness, 52–53, 63–66
  as prompting self-critique, 30, 52, 88, 105, 131–32, 134, 135–36, 179, 204
  as total in scope, 31–32, 62–68, 96–98, 136
Cone, James, 80n51
"Constantinianism," 78
Cooper-White, Pamela, 156n52
Cramer, David, 73n7
Cremonisi, Lara, 91n96
Crena, Lucila, 157n59
Cullman, Oscar, 15
cynicism, roots of, viii, 97–98, 136, 138, 151–53

Dargis, Manohla, 99–100
Davidson, Arnold, 173n20
Dawn, Marva, 78, 81n55
Deleuze, Gilles, 91n96
dominiation system. *See* Wink, Walter, on the "domination system"
Dreyfus, Hubert, 91n96

ecclesiology. *See* church
"ecclesial exceptionalism," 71–72, 77–83, 87–90, 96–98
epektasis, 67
eschatology, 79–81, 118–19, 133, 173
exteriority/exteriorities

  church as thought to dwell in, 19–20, 80–83
  definition, 5, 51–53
  human access to, 31n115, 62–63, 80–83, 96–98, 116–20, 127–29, 134–36
  intellectual form, 101–2, 119–20, 127–28, 134–36
  as an optimism, 151–56, 159
  voluntary form, 70–71, 78–83, 91, 95, 96–98
extremism, 154

Fiddes, Paul, 158n61
Fields, Sabrina, 129n115
Fisher, Marc, 92n102
Forbes, Chris, 16n56
Frankfurt, Harry, 183n62
Foucault, Michel
  against polemics, 38–39
  asymmetry of analysis with Christian theology, 37, 42
  on authority as distinct form of power, 49n47, 121, 128
  on care of the self, 155, 173–77, 187–95
  criticisms of normativity in, 144–49
  description of power and force, 46–49, 123–24
  on governmentality, 172–75
  on ironies or difficulties in resistance, 92–95, 124–5
  and Nietzsche, 35, 48n44, 159
  plausibility of comparison with Barth, 35–43, 61–62, 179–81
  on power and resistance as intertwined, 49–53
  on subject and agency as formed by power, 91–96, 126–27, 172–77
  on theory, normativity, and power, 38, 122–30
Fraser, Nancy, 147–48

gender
  attempt to contract into, 69–70, 83, 96
  creative performances of, 69–70, 167–70

INDEX

Gerwig, Greta, 101
Girard, René, 113
Goossen, Rachel Waltner, 73n7
Gorringe, Timothy, 158n61
grace, 60, 114–15, 132–34, 162–65, 201–3
Gramci, Antonio, 163n76
Gregory of Nyssa, 67
Guth, Karen V., 73n7
Gutiérrez, Gustavo, 138n1

Habermas, Jürgen, 146–47
Haddorff, David, 39n18
Hart, David Bentley, 36
Hartman, Saidiya, 167–70, 205
Hauerwas, Stanley, 35–36, 43
Hector, Kevin, 153n42, 157n56
Hendricks, Christina, 157n60
Hess, Cynthia, 93–94
heterotopias, 95–96
Hitler, Adolf, image in relation to structures, 19, 112
Hromádka Letter, 142–43
human agency. *See* agency, limits of
Hütter, Reinhard, 80

Jackson, Lauren Michele, 103
Jesus of Nazareth
    defeating the powers, 14, 77, 162, 201–3
    exposing the powers, 18, 77, 162, 201–3
    as model of Christian freedom, 162–64, 201–3
    as the one in which all things systematize, 74, 76
    as "royal man", 201–3
Johnson, Keith, 130n117
Jordan, Mark, 42, 96n112
Joseph, Miranda, 3n2
Joyce, Kathryn, 153n44

Kant, Immanuel, 182
Käsemann, Ernst, 16
Kierkegaard, Søren, 39, 132, 169n10
King, Martin Luther, Jr., legacy of, 93
Klein, Melanie, 154–55
Kois, Dan, 99–100

Kotsko, Adam, 7n17, 48n44, 106n21, 186n71

Lennie, Tyra, 184n64
Levi, Primo, 64–65
Lloyd, Vincent, 93
Lorenzini, Daniele, 125–26, 179n53
Lownes, Joseph, 153n44

Magritte, René, 34 n. 2
Mandela, Nelson, 50
Martens, Paul, 82n59
mass incarceration, 7–13
Mathews, Charles, 61n93, 185–6
McBride, Jennifer, 185–86
McCormack, Bruce, 130n117
McKenny, Gerald, 196n116, 204n157
Miller, Vincent, 35n3, 92n101
Milkman, Ruth, 94
Monroe, Marilyn, 18–19
moralism, 6n16
Muñoz, José Esteban, 150n37, 202n150
Munro, Kirstin, 1–3

narrative disparities between Barth and Foucault, 35
Nation, Mark Theissen, 82
Newheiser, David, 106n22, 144n16, 153n41
Niebuhr, Reinhold
    critique of Barth and Barthians, 140–44, 152
    as potential interlocutor in an argument of this kind, 61
noncomplicity. *See* complicity
Nussbaum, Martha, 148n36

Oberman, Heiko, 76n29
O'Farrell, Clare, 91n96

Packer, George, 153n44
Park, Joon-Sik, 82n61
Pitts, Jamie, 73n7, 74n12, 80n52, 136n132
Poisson, Jayme, 69–70

political spirituality, 66–68, 151–56, 165, 166–67, 170–71, 174–75, 180–81, 187–95, 204–6
political subjectivity, 2–3, 66–68, 174–75, 181–82, 187–95, 204–6
powers
  as alienated human capacities, 56–57, 163
  as coextenstive with human life, 62–63, 113, 135–36, 169
  as created and fallen, 18, 75–76, 114, 125, 162, 170n13
  "first-generation" understanding, 17
  as forms of the power of death, 21–24
  as heterogeneous or internally diverse, 58, 113, 162
  as ideologies, institutions, and images, 18–21, 57, 102, 112–13
  as object of Christian antagonism, 55
  as personal, spiritual beings, 32, 32n116, 41–42, 110–9
  "second-generation" understanding, see Stringfellow, William, Yoder, John Howard, Wink, Walter
  state of which as result of original sin, 56
  as structures of patterned regularity, 73–74
  "total complicity" v. "exteriority" accounts, 62–68, 96–98, 135–36, 137, 143–44, 149, 165, 205–6
  Twentieth century New Testament scholarship on, 13–17

possession, demonic, 14, 112–3, 122
Prather, Scott, 28n112, 54n63, 74n11
principalities and powers. See powers

quietism
  as bias toward inaction, 32, 136, 138–40, 140–4, 149, 160, 205–6
  as not authorized by limits of human agency, 60, 157–8

Rabinow, Paul, 91n96
race and racism
  church as embodied response to, 83
  problems with "colorblindness," 4, 9–10
  as reasserting itself within attempts to overcome it, 93, 103–5
  as structural "racial caste," 6–13, 105, 167–68
resistance
  assumed opposition to complicity, 31, 149, 151–53, 161, 170–71
  as call of conscience in response to the powers, 28, 160–61
  definition of, 28n111, 160–61
  as failure to attain exteriority, 63
  as occasioned by complicity, 176, 179
revelation
  in Barth (see Barth, Karl, on revelation)
  in Wink (see Wink, Walter, on revelation as liberatory)
Rose, Marika, 166n1
Rossi, Andrea, 44n34
Ruti, Mari, 162n73

Sartre, Jean-Paul, 144
Satan, figure of, 110–19
Schirato, Tony, 91n96
Schlier, Heinrich, 15–6
Schneider, Laurel, 156n51
Schwarz, Martin, 158n62
Scott, A. O., 99–100
Sedgwick, Eve Kosofsky, 150n37, 154–55
self-attentive asceticism
  comparison with major ethical theories, 181–87
  as offering a mode of resistance amid total complicity, 205–6
  as mode for the experience of repentance, 196–99
  as mutually illuminating with Barth's ethics, 195–96, 203–4
  as mutually illuminating with Foucault's ethics, 187

INDEX

self-criticism, 30, 52, 88, 105, 131–2, 134, 135–6, 179, 204
Sharlet, Jeff, 153n44
Shotwell, Alexis, 67
Sider, J. Alexander, 43n32
Simon, David, 74n13
Smith, Mychal Denzel, 93
Sonderegger, Katherine, 158n61
Spinoza, Baruch, 183
Standing, Guy, 94
Steinbeck, John, 138–39
Stevenson, Bryan, 10n32
Stewart-Kroeker, Sarah, 73n7
Stringfellow, William
  dynamics of urban poverty and suburbanization, 17–18
  on powers as power of death, 21–24, 162n74
  representing "second generation" discourse on the powers, 27
  on saints, 24–25
  and the "silent majority," 24
  views on the church, 19–20, 25–27, 30–31
structures
  as conditioning individual and community, 3–4
  definition or use in this book, 47n41, 73–74

Olúfẹ́mi, Táíwò, 65–66
Tanner, Kathryn, 162n70, 164n80, 178
Taylor, Charles, 145
Tonstad, Linn, 4n13
Toole, David, 35–36
total complicity. *See* complicity
Townes, Emilie, 162n71
Tran, Jonathan, 36–38
Tsing, Anna Lowenhaupt, 40–41

voluntary exteriorities. *See* exteriority, voluntary form

Wacquant, Loïc, 9
Walker, David, 13
War on Drugs in the United States, 8
Webster, John B., 177n37, 202n146
Wendland, Ernst, 16n56
West, Cornel, 93n103
whiteness and "whiteness studies," 104–5
Winant, Gabriel, 4n12
Wink, Walter
  on delusion as technique of powers, 111–3, 115–20
  on distorting effects of materialism, 107–9
  on the "domination system", 114–6
  on powers as demonic and not solely angelic or neutral, 107, 109–19
  on revelation as liberatory, 117–20, 127–8, 133, 134–5
  on Satan, 110–2
Wollen, Audrey, 19n64

Yoder, John Howard
  cases of abuse and relation to his thought, 72–73, 81n55, 82n58
  on Christ in relation to powers, 76–77
  on church as other to the world, 77–83, 89–90
  as positing a voluntary exteriority, 78–83, 89–90
  on structures, 73–74
  reading powers as structures of modern life, 74–76

Zamora, Daniel, 144n16

www.ingramcontent.com/pod-product-compliance
Lightning Source LLC
Chambersburg PA
CBHW022012220426
43663CB00007B/1053